To Irene.

The Journey

P.D   Lorde

May you encounter no JOY that I feel when writing this Book.

P.D Lorde

Copyright © 2012 P.D.LORDE

All rights reserved.

ISBN:-10: 1540753719
ISBN-13: 978-1540753717

DEDICATION

I dedicate this book to my beloved late mother, who taught me how to be me. Some days we have to stand in our moment and shine.

Also To my Daddy, my rock, best friend and confidant. Always. When you are no longer here to give me your wise counsel, I shall find the most prominent tree to talk to, as you will hear me through the rustling of the leaves. Mine lips to your ears only. For Eternity!

CONTENTS

	Acknowledgments	I
1	The Journey	Pg. 5
2	Jonathan	Pg. 15
3	I am Home	Pg. 23
4	Harold's Time	Pg. 47
5	Dr. Barrington Barnett	Pg. 82
6	Winnie's Awakening	Pg. 116
7	Phoebe's Surprise	Pg. 126
8	Confessions	Pg. 138
9	Maddie's Home	Pg. 144
10	Rock Bottom	Pg. 154

11	Revelations	Pg. 162
12	Barrington Barnett Junior	Pg. 191
13	The Blooming of Flowers	Pg. 198
14	Circumstances Define You	Pg. 226
15	Awakenings	Pg. 235
16	Butterflies	Pg. 259
17	Mr. Lover Man	Pg. 303
18	The Making of a man	Pg. 310
19	Fathers and Daughters	Pg. 330
20	Pressure Burst Pipes	Pg. 349
21	Farewell	Pg. 366

ACKNOWLEDGMENTS

Sitting in this moment I have to acknowledge God and the universe. I am a firm believer that *'nothing happens before its time.'* God has made winding path straight for me, and for that I am grateful. This project has been a decade in the making. I am consumed with emotion, yet I am joyous about the fact that this story 'Book One' is complete and successive tales have just begun.

Apart from my boys, nothing brings me more joy than writing. To my supporters in this life and the next who have made this book possible, I humbly thank you. I would like to acknowledge my late mother, Auntie Gloria, and my uncle Verly, you are the best story tellers on this planet. To the rest of my family, both the Moore's, the Lorde's and the Innes', thank you for the love, support and continued assistance. My adorable husband Richard, my sons Aaron, Richard Junior, and Joshua. *My boys for life.* My Swan Sisters, who are sisters to me in will and in spirit. We are the toughest Mudders on Constitutional Hill! I love you and thank you all. Adonica Simmons, Victoria Reynold Jones, and Beverly Allen. I would like to send out a special thank you to Melanie Newland Harse, who encouraged me to be my best self, and has contributed to me and this project 'getting over the line.'

To the best Editor this side of the galaxy. The amazing and wonderful Mrs. Silvia Borsan. Thank you for believing in this story and vision. You constantly stand in your truth and I feel that this will be the first of many collaborations. From Gold to Platinum baby! I am a firm believer that people come into your life for a reason, season or lifetime. I can do and be anything. We all can. All you have to do is dream and believe. Maya Angelou told me that there is no greater agony than bearing an untold story inside you. I am burden free fore I have released it.

P.D Lorde

Enjoy!

P.D Lorde

Book One

THE JOURNEY

Main Characters

Lucy & Vincent George (Married)

Angeline George (Daughter)

Edwina George (Granddaughter)

Dr Barrington Barnett & Phyllis Barnett (Married)

Barring Barnett Junior (Son)

Edwina Mallard & Harold Mallard (Married)

Jonathan Mallard (Son)

Phoebe Mallard (Daughter)

Maddie Mallard (Daughter)

Mr. and Mrs. Mack

Courtney Du Pille

Jackson Du Pille

Chapter One

The Journey

January 13th 2005 10 am

"Help meee!" Jonathan screamed down the corridor, his baritone voice ricocheting off the walls. The three Macmillan nurses on duty all looked up and, without pause, started to sprint towards his mother Edwina Mallard's room.

Nurse Alice Mckee was the Lead Macmillan Nurse for Edwina.

"Please, Alice," he sobbed uncontrollably. "Please," his voice caught between his tears choked him. "Alice, I am not ready! It's not her time yet." Jonathan could feel himself losing composure and was trying desperately to keep his emotions in check. *"How dare you! How bloody dare you! The last thing that mum needs is her sniveling middle aged son losing all composure. I am the mature dependable one, not this gushing river about to burst its banks. Get it together, Jon."*

Alice glanced at this man with complete empathy. He looked and smelt like he was in need of a long hot shower. He was unshaven, his clothes were disheveled, his beard over grown, and he was visibly exhausted; the poor love had been at his mother's side for the past 17 hours. It was an effort for him to keep his body upright. Every muscle was screaming for him to sleep, but he just couldn't. He was not going to leave his mummy. Alice could feel her heart swelling with emotion; she knew what this moment felt like. Despite this emotional machine gun discharging its ammunition into her chest, she pushed herself back to the here and now. She did what she was trained for. Alice got to work and started to review Edwina's vital signs. She looked up and noticed that Jonathan hadn't moved from his position. Alice walked towards him and gently ushered Jonathan out of the room. Every muscle clenched in his body; he was not leaving.

"Jon. Jon, look at me," slowly he took his eyes away from his mother, who lay helpless, gasping for any oxygen she could snatch from the room.

"Jon, you are going to have to give us a minute, we just need to assess your mum, and I will come out and let you know how she is doing." She held his gaze, squeezed his arm.

"Ok, Jon?" Alice made the point of speaking slowly and looking directly into his eyes, she patiently waited for an acknowledgement. Reluctantly, Jon nodded.

Unable to contain his grief, heavy prominent tears began falling uncontrollably from his large almond shaped brown eyes, his lips quivering, nose running, he threw his palms to his eyes, snapped his head back towards the ceiling and inhaled deeply.

"Ok," he began to cry again. *"Keep it together, Jon,"* he told himself.

Alice automatically started to stroke his forearms horizontally, "I will be back shortly, Jon, but it's time to call the family. Your mum is getting close, my love."

"How long, Alice?"

"Not long, Jon, not long at all. Call them in."

Slowly, Jon withdrew his hands from his face, and watched Alice close the door behind her. He marched through the corridor and down the stairs, once in the fresh air, he realised it was a beautiful sunny morning. He retrieved his mobile phone, looked up at the clear blue sky and dialed his sister Phoebe, she picked up on the first ring, which was unbelievable, as his sister was such a slob and usually either never had her phone, or was fumbling for it in one of her many oversized designer bags.

"Hello," she whispered. "What is it, Jon?" Phoebe's demeanor took him by surprise, his sister's voice, which was usually so confident and strong, was frightened and weak.

"Hi, Phoebes, it's time to call Maddie." He took many deep breaths before he could continue. His voice strained and cracking with sorrow, "She's close, Phoebes, she's real close."

"Where's dad?" Phoebe asked sharply.

"He's in the family room. I am going to wake him now."

"Ok, see you in 30 minutes. I will go to that Shelter, on Limes Street, and pick her up. I will be there soon. Hold on, brov. Love you."

Phoebe suddenly felt chilled to the bone. Goose bumps appeared all over her body. She slumped back on her bed, closed her eyes shut, and released one solitary tear from her left eye. This was the call that she was dreading. Not because her mum was dying. As upsetting and terrifying as it was, she had accepted that fact weeks ago. She could deal with that. She now had to face her elder sister, the ostracized one, the embarrassment. The Drunk!

"It's time," she allowed herself to say it out loud.

"What was that, Edwina? Did you say something?" Alice asked.

"I am dying, I feel it, my body is betraying me."

Alice looked down at Edwina and squeezed her hand. "We both knew that this day was coming," she said quietly.

THE JOURNEY

Edwina lay weak and helpless in her hospital bed. She looked out of her window and smiled at the crisp blue sky and winter sun. How she enjoyed those winter days. The radiating heat of the sun on her cheek warmed her face. *"I really love England, I will miss it,"* she told to herself. In particular Islington, London, where she'd settled with her husband Harold, nearly 48 years ago.

Her room was beautiful, and that made a difference to how she felt, it was significantly larger than the average hospital room, then again, she was in a hospice, the least it should be was comfortable. Her peach soft furnishings and perfumed crisp linen and lilac room plug in lingered in her nostrils, she was happy that her chamber did not smell of a clinical disinfected ward at a hospital, nor did it have the thick aroma of death. Without warning, Edwina's body reacted and thrashed against the familiar burning sensation and stab like pains, as it began to spread across her whole body; Dr. Alcock at Middlesex Hospital had informed her 25 days previously that her lung cancer had spread to her bones. She could not believe the news and took some time to process the information; she had begun to feel better up until that moment. How strange life can be!

"Today is my birthday, but this wretched disease does not care about that, it continues to wreak havoc with my body, in particular all my vital organs, everything feels slower."

"Arrrrrhhhhhh." *The pain is precise and vengeful. Perspiration is washing over my body again. Oh, that's hot. There it goes. Oh, no. I cannot take it. It's starting at the tip of my right toe and it's spreading, oh Lord, come soon, I cannot deal with this anymore, it's unbearable. Oh Lord, it's everywhere, spreading across my body like an uncontrollable bush fire.*

Alice was in the corner of the room washing her hands and saw Edwina writhing and moaning in her bed. This woman had the endurance of an ox, she thought. She rarely made a fuss when she was in pain. "Edwina, press the morphine pump, my love. I know it makes you sleepy, but it will take the pain away." Without hesitation, Edwina administered her pain relief.

-CLICK- -CLICK – CLICK –CLICK…

My morphine pump, my savior and new best friend, the relief you bring is like a fireman's, trained to extinguish a burning inferno. With the soothing of the fire comes the self-induced dreamlike hallucination. The burning is still here, but my mind is far away… I love morphine, I really do. The irony of it, after 69 years of a drug free existence, I truly wish that I had experimented with drugs in my lifetime. I smile to myself. I must be dying. After all the self-righteous talks I have given to my three children about the perils of drugs and addiction. If they could read my thoughts now!

I am not sure if it is the drugs or the cancer, but I sometimes hallucinate and it's heavenly, even sexual. I cannot tell anyone, I mean, I should be dying, not having drug induced orgasms. That's not right, is it? I will take these experiences to the grave. I did think of telling Alice, but she has bonded too well with Jonathan. The obvious fear is that she'll tell him, the last thing I need is that during my last moments of me leaving this world, I will be preoccupied by the thoughts that my own son thinks that I am having morphine induced pornographic experiences. As I am shaking my head at this thought, I see Alice eyeing me from the sink from the corner of my room. I smile wryly to reassure her that I am alright. She must think I am having some sort of breakdown.

I look over to the digital clock and I cannot believe that it is only 10.05 am. Why do I feel like the day has already passed? Because you have cancer dear, and every waking moment is filled with pain and discomfort, minutes pass like hours and hours like days, so shut up and deal with it.

THE JOURNEY

Oh gosh, it's happening again. "Embrace it, Edwina, come on, you can do it," I sternly tell myself. "Just think you may meet that lovely man whom you had much pleasure with last time you drifted off." *My body has lost its sense of gravity, slowly my head becomes adrift,* "Come on, don't be scared, this is what it will be like , being dead, passing over to the spirit world, being able to drift from one place to the next. It will be fine, all of this has to be worth something." *My shoulders and torso float towards the ceiling, that's it, my stomach is going to flip again, oh no, no, no, there goes the yogurt that I had this morning.*

"Edwina, love, is the morphine making you feel sick again?" Alice pressed a button for assistance.

At this point, I am on the ceiling, watching the activity in the room. I am just not sure if my spirit or my drug induced self is on the ceiling, but whatever it is, I feel exhilarated.

Maybe when I am dead I will understand why I feel so well. Not just my mind, but also my body. When I take the morphine, there is such much clarity. The energy that I feel is another story, I gave that sexy hot rod a run for his money the other day. Although, I cannot see myself, I feel myself and I feel that I look good, I mean really good. "I l-o-o-o-o-v-e-e-e-e-e m-o-r-p-h-i-n-e". *The pain and suffering is parked into a underground garage, just look at me. I am laughing, and nothing hurts. Death will not be the end, it cannot be. Well, I hope that it's not. Look at me, I am free of that body.*

"Jonathan, I am sorry," I blurt out.

"What was that, Edwina love?" Alice asks, leaning over the bed, whilst she starts to take my blood pressure.

"Tell Jon that I am sorry, I need to sleep, I am sooo tired," I whisper.

"That's the morphine, my love. Just rest, I will tell him that you asked for him."

I am floating, oh, I love the sensation it gives me. Whheeeeeee. Whoooaa. Oh look, that was New Year's 1979, now, that was messy. My body is horizontal, as I float backwards in time. This is such a surreal experience. I have never floated through time before, of course you haven't, you stupid woman, you were never dying before. I smile with myself. I loved the 70's, with that, I try to throw my spirit back to see some other years, but the vortex of pressure tunneling me through time restrains me. Wow, I am moving faster and faster each second. This is new; I have only experienced slow floating, time must be running out for me. The upshot is that I am out of the bed and moving, it feels magical. I open my eyes and there is a beautiful ocean beneath me. I turn to my left and see these plush green mountains, thick with vegetation and tropical foliage, it's magnificent and reminds me of Trinidad and Tobago. A blink of the eye, more mountains more oceans, the sun is now burning my face and chest. "Enjoy it, Edwina," I order myself. I release all the tension from my body and surrender to the vortex.

A few more blinks of the eye, oh good, we seem to be slowing down, the fresh sea air fills my lungs, the sun is no longer burning, but is warming my body. I feel myself glow, how I love to sun bathe. I close my eyes and throw my head back and stretch out my arms with grace and precision, directing my legs in the air, like I am a ballerina in Swan Lake. Wait we have stopped, the scent is very familiar. My body reacts to the scenery, before my head is able to engage itself. I feel my body tensing; I blink my eyes open violently. I am frozen. I try to vomit but there is nothing. I am no longer floating on my back, I am facing the ground and fall to my hands and knees heavily; there is someone in front of me. It cannot be. I raise my head and it is me. My six year old self standing in front of me.

THE JOURNEY

The year is 1941, how can this be? "No, No, No," I scream. "Am I to live my life again? What is this?"

I am back. Back to the land of my birth, Jamaica. The little girl giggles and starts running through the sugar cane fields, barefoot and care free, on the plantation that her grandmother owned. Wearing nothing other than her pink sleeveless summer dress, with white lacy trim, I watch her run through one aisle and came back towards me in the other. Still in shock, on all fours, I just watched the infant approaching me. Her energetic sprint slowed down to a cautious walk as she eyed me up and down suspiciously. The little girl stopped abruptly and squinted, wiped both her eyes with the back of her hands, and squarely focused on her adult self. Me. Free from disease, beautiful and in my prime.

"Why are you here? Is it my time to die?" the child asked.

Completely taken aback by this, I sharply inform her, "No, it's not."

I could see the annoyance in my tiny face and could not help the smile which crept across my face. That expression had not changed over the years, ask Harold and the children. I must say, my younger self was less impressed and angrily spat out the words, "Then why are you here?"

I giggled, I just could not help it, "I am not sure."

My younger self walked closer to me and sat down on the warm grass. She looked at me for some time, which was funny, as I was drinking in every element of my younger face. Staring at each other with the intensity of young lovers, my mini self slowly stretched out her hand and stroked my cheek, with the tenderness of a prize gardener tenderly stroking his petunias. This truly touched me. I have not been stroked with that level of gentleness for years. I forgot what it felt like. The girl was so focused on me, as if she was searching my face for a particular answer. Such concentration. Her tiny right hand touched her face, and with her left hand she held my right cheek. I dare not say a word; I just wanted to drink in this innocent me. It's been a long time since I have felt innocent. Pure. Neither of us said a word, yet a deep and meaningful conversation took place.

After quite a while she whispered, "It's not fair." Without warning, she threw her arms around me, her grip so tight that I could feel the bones crunching in my neck. I tried to pull away with no success. *Yikes, I am a strong little thing, aren't I?* I pull both her arms to adjust her pressure for fear of strangulation. I could feel her trembling, I am scared, I just held her close in the middle of the sugar cane field for what seemed an eternity. It's no use, I cannot keep it together, it's all too much being here. The silent tears started to roll down my cheeks uncontrollably, instantly being evaporating by the tropical sunshine.

"You look just like her," my younger self said.

"Who?" I quizzed.

"Mima," she replied, grinning from ear to ear.

It was as if a sledge hammer hit me in my chest. A switch turned on in my brain and a lifetime of memories flooded through me like a violent tsunami. I put my head in my hands, embarrassed by my emotional nakedness. It was here that I was happy, safe and loved. More important to me was that I was able to give love.

"Mima," I gasped. The air felt very thick, and I was having trouble breathing.

I close my eyes to regulate my breathing, the scent of lilac fills my nostrils. I was back in the hospital, fighting for oxygen; the pain was ravaging me like a mad angry dog. The memory of my grandmother has sent my body

THE JOURNEY

into some sort of shock. What is happening, am I dying? I am full of perspiration and can hear my six year old self screaming. Harold's large hands are over mine, and I can hear my Jonathan and Alice calling my name.

"Nooooooo," I moan with what little energy my body permits me to have, "not here, there is no pain in this place."

"What is that, mum?" Jonathan whispers.

I want to open my eyes but I can't. I just want to go back to 1941; I need to know why I went back. My six year old self is starting to disappear and get smaller, panicked, she screamed, "Touch the machine."

"What?" I say, barely able to breathe.

"Touch the machine, it will take it all away. QUICKLY!!!!"

CLICK CLICK CLICK

I scrunch up my face, praying that I have more time. Oxygen populates my lungs, and I open my eyes, I am back in the safety of the sugar cane fields.

"Hhmmmmmm, Huh, huh, huh Hhmmmmmm."

"That's better," I say, the silent tears flowing at their own pace. "I have not thought of Mima Lucy in so long. It has been a lifetime. It's as if I have blocked her out," I say casually, without thinking of its impact on the situation.

"I know," said the little girl, "she still loves you and she wants me to tell you that she is waiting for you."

"Waiting for me where?" I bark. I see my younger self wince, I recoil my temperament and gain a little composure. "Where is she?" I question quietly.

The little girl folded her arms and starred at me. "Edwina, she has been with you every day," she says annoyed and looks through the sugar cane to my grandmother's house.

Chapter Two

Jonathan

13th January 2005 12.32 pm

Jonathan has formed over the past four nights a bond with his mother's Macmillan nurse, Alice McKee. She was a delightful bubbly woman, who originated from Edinburgh Scotland. Coincidently, Jonathan, studied Geography at Edinburgh University. Within minutes of discussing Alice's hometown, it became apparent that they'd attended the same venues, for instance they'd both frequented the Bongo Club, one of the hippest clubs in Edinburgh. They both adored the Winter Wonderland held annually at Princess Street Garden. Each year and without fail, Jonathan made the effort to go back there with his partner, Jack. This was Alice's favorite place in the world for more sentimental reasons. Her father used to take her there as a child. Also, this was the place where Daniel had proposed to her. He'd passed away twelve years ago from a brain tumor. It was this life changing event that inspired her to care for the dying.

"Did you call your sisters, Jon?" Alice asked almost in a whisper, as she routinely checked Edwina's vital signs.

"Yes, thanks for asking," Jon replied without looking at her.

THE JOURNEY

"Are they on her way?" Alice inquired glancing at her watch.

"Any moment now."

"Ok, I will be doing my rounds. Just use the buzzer if you need anything." Alice replaced Edwina's chart and left the room. As the door was about to close, Jon heard her greet Phoebe in the corridor. Her shrill voice seemed to bounce of the corridor walls.

"Hi, Phoebe, I was just asking after you," she chirped.

"How is mum?" Phoebe's words reverberated like they had been dragged out of her mouth. She sounded different than her usual self.

"As well as could be expected at this time, love," again Alice's voice and tone resorted to a half whisper.

Highly strung and ready to explode, I could not contain my anger. "What time do you call this? Half an hour, you said?" *I am furious; I have been sat by my mum's side most of the morning, waiting for my sisters to make an appearance.*

Taken aback by my eruption, I see that Phoebe had to physically steady herself and pause for a few seconds before she replied. Already an emotional wreck, her eyes immediately sprung tears. She inhaled too deeply for her lungs and looked towards the ceiling, "Jon, I got here as fast as I could." She snapped.

"Where is Maddie?"

"That's why I'm late. I went everywhere I thought she'd be." Phoebe let out a huge sigh. "I left a message on all phones. I just did not know where else to look." With that her reassured voice broke.

"Can't you see that I am under it here?" my voice grew

louder with rage. "I ask you to do one thing. One thing, and you turn up empty handed! Did you get bored and go shopping instead?"

No sooner than those spiteful words came out of my mouth, I wanted to take them back. My sister looked like she'd been kicked in the face by that last comment. I need to get this under control. It's not her fault. That was a low blow even for me.

Calm down, Jon, stop taking this out on everyone else.

"WHAT!!!!" Phoebe was wide eyed and furious.

Oops, too late…

Phoebe threw her bag to the floor, she looked ready for war. "Just hold your horses, Saint Jude, I did what you asked. Maddie is out there with god knows who, doing god knows what. Open your eyes, Jon, I'm here where I'm supposed to be. Where I am bloody needed and you cannot be seriously tearing strips of *me* for that." Not realising she was now shouting at her brother, "ARE YOU JON?"

I lower my eyes, embarrassed by my cruel attack, she was right. I should not have taken out my frustrations on her. "All I am saying is…."

Alice flew into the room. "NOW, I don't know what this is about and I don't care, pipe down or get out." Alice looked at both of us with complete and utter disgust.

"May I remind you why you are both here?" with that, she glared at my mother in her bed. "Do I need to point out that your mother is *not* the only dying patient on this floor?" again that look. We both lower our heads, the embarrassment and guilt sting my face.

Alice tutted very loudly as she left the room.

THE JOURNEY

I reluctantly raise my head and look at my sister, her tears are already in free flow. She has backed herself up against the far wall and turned her head towards it, her shaking shoulders give her away. I feel even worse.

Phoebe turned around with multiple tear streaks down each eye, "Look, Jon, if you want to play Dempsey and Makepeace, be my guest, go find her. I just need to be here." She pointed adamantly towards the floor.

"Dempsey and Makepeace?" I stare at her, she registers my amusement, and we both fall about laughing.

"What so funny?" Harold enquired as he entered the room.

"Dad," I uncomfortably shift my body weight from one foot to the other. The temperature in the room went from a hot day in Sudan to the freezing conditions of the Antarctic, in a blink of the eye. Phoebe gave our father a stony stare.

"Coffee, Jon?" she asks icily.

"Errr, no thanks," I looked from Phoebe to my father to Phoebe again. *"Not today, Phoebes, please, not today,"* I pray.

Phoebe picked her bag to head towards the door, she is not going to blank him, not now. I watch in complete horror. That's when she stopped, as if she read my mind and turned around.

"Dad."

"Yes, Phoebe," I swear I thought Dad was about to breakdown.

"Coffee?"

"No, thank you, PP, I have just had some tea. Thank you for asking, that is."

Phoebe looked at the floor like an errant child, then rushed out the room.

"Well, at least she is talking to you, dad?" I said.

"You know as well as I do, son, that she did that for Edwina, not me." Harold sat down next to his wife and took the perfectly folded white starched handkerchief out of his right breast pocket of his navy blue blazer and dabbed his eyes. He took hold of my mother's hand and whispered to his wife, "You win, babes, you win," he started to chuckle and cry at the same time.

"What, dad?"

I looked at my father, searching his face for clues to this riddle. "We had a bet when we were sixteen years old, which one would die first".

"Really," I sound surprised. To think of my parents as young and invincible, that they would bet or even joke about death, seemed strange, especially in this moment.

"Your mother always said that she would go first, as she could not bear to be left behind," with that, dad threw his head back and closed his eyes.

"You'll be ok, dad."

"How do you know?" he snapped.

"Sorry," I sounded confused.

"How do you know that I will be alright?"

"I just meant…"

He cut me off, "Let's face it, my children do not care for me." With that, the neatly dressed old man rested his head in his hands.

He looked up and we lock stares. Suddenly, we both felt

THE JOURNEY

an unwelcome spectator at the doorway, we turn around and Phoebe was standing there, with a coffee cup in hand, "Whose fault is that, dad, eh? Eh?" she sniped loudly.

"Phoebe," I bark at her, wide eyed and ready to pounce on my sister if required. "Not now," I growled. She stares at me, then slowly lowered her eyes to our mother. My body language is unmistakably not playing with her. She senses this, she feels the warning and silently sat down, sulking at the other side of the bed.

"Where is Maddie? Anyone seen her?" Harold enquired.

"You noticed then, did you? That she's not here," Phoebe scolded.

"Phoebe, this is your last warning." I shot off my chair. Wide eyes, tense from the hair on my head to my toes, I had never slapped my sister yet, but today might be the beginning of many firsts.

"Really, Jon. *Warning?*" She could feel the anger swelling in her chest. "What you going to do? Beat me to a pulp?" she shot dad a scolding look.

Harold stood up and walked to the window, "Maybe you and I need to talk, PP."

"No, dad, I need to sit here and be with my mum. You need to stop calling me PP, you lost that right a long time ago."

Harold walked to his dying wife, kissed her head and walked towards the door.

"Where are *you* going?" Phoebe looked hurt and shocked all at the same time.

"I need some time alone," he answered crestfallen; he looked like he was going to cry.

"Oh, here we go. It's all about you, isn't it?" Phoebe started to laugh hysterically.

"Phoebe," I am shouting again. "For the love of God, put your differences aside and let's at least try and show a united front for mum." I look at my mother and feel my legs go weak, I fall back into the chair exhausted. "Please, Phoebe, for mum," I plead.

Nurse McKee charged into the room. "Right, I told you once, I am now telling you again, there will not be a third discussion. Shape up or get out! If you cannot respect your mother and all the other patients on this floor then you will be asked to leave. RESPECT THIS SITUATION! Maybe if you spent less time fighting amongst yourselves and more time focusing on your poor mum, she will be able to die in peace. Did you hear me? I said die in peace." With that, Nurse Mckee started to check Edwina's vital signs.

"Oh, Edwina," she looked at all three of us with unfiltered hatred. "It's alright." She lovingly stroked her head and reached over to the side table for a tissue.

"Mum. Alice, is she alright? What is it?" I plead with her.

"Jon," Alice said icily, she lowered her voice, but that did not regain the temperature in the room. "You were all so busy arguing with one another, you forgot why you were here. Look, she's been crying. She obviously can hear you."

You could have heard a pin drop. The realisation of what had occurred was overwhelming for all of us. This was a first for Alice. She wiped the tears dry from mother's eyes and cheeks. "Not another cross word, I mean it." The glare that she gave us reminded Jon of a lion protecting her cubs. He knew that she really meant business.

Hurt, embarrassed, and ashamed of our conduct, all we

THE JOURNEY

can do is nod our heads and search the floor for answers.

Disgusted by her behavior, Phoebe whispered, "She's right. Can we please just focus on mum, please?"

"No problem, love," dad walked around mum's bed and kissed me on my forehead. He muttered something silently and started to walk towards my sister. She sat frozen to her seat. Dad hesitated and slowly lowered himself. He put his hands in front of his chest to reassure Phoebe that it was going to be ok, and slowly planted a kiss on her forehead. She closed her eyes and cried silently. He tried to hug her, she shrugs him off.

"Please dad, don't," she whispered. He nodded, now visibly crying, he walked quickly around the bed and grabbed his wife's hand. Squeezing and rubbing it, terrified at what the future meant for him. Edwina was the glue, she kept them stuck together. Without her, where would his family be?

Chapter Three

I am Home

Lying on my back with eyes closed, my nostrils are delighted by the aromas and the sweetness of the sugar cane. I wonder how much time I have here. I shudder, reminiscing briefly of the hospital room. I inhale as deep as I can, I look to the sky. It's a miracle I am pain free. Wiping the tears from her eyes, I study my younger self who is crouched over me. We stare at one another for a short while.

"Oh, baby girl, I am so tired," I moan.

"We have to go," she whispers.

"Where Winnie?" I ask.

Winnie giggled loudly. "Only Mima calls me that," she informs me completely amused.

"I know" I whisper, "so Winnie it is," I smile.

Winnie's face became very serious, "We have to go."

"Why, where?"

"Home, Mima will be worried. We have to go, she doesn't like me out too late."

THE JOURNEY

It cannot be, this makes no sense. I follow this child through the cane field, even though wading through the field was making me exhausted, the long canes offered excellent protection from the sun's intensity. It was calm, cool and serine in there. The therapeutic howls of the slight breeze rustling through the cane is mesmerizing.

"Edwina."

"Yes, Winnie," my little self automatically giggled again. Clearly still amused by the nick name for her.

"Why did you forget us?" she asked, her face serious.

"What?"

"You said, back there that you had forgotten Mima? How did you forget?"

Embarrassed by my admission, "I am not sure how, but somehow I forgot her."

"Mima is hard to forget," Winnie said looking at the floor. Without warning, she threw her body to the floor with a thud, laced her fingers together and wrapped them behind her head. "What do you remember?" she asked excitingly.

"Not much." I lower my eyes from Winnie's intense stare. "Being back here I remembered how kind and loving Mima was. All I got was kisses and love here."

My mini me was smiling towards the sky. "Mima sings to me lots, and she make the best pineapple upside cake", we both giggled.

"What do you remember about Mima? You know, her dying..." I ask and immediately am met with sheer confusion.

"Grandma Mima is not dead," Winnie almost spat the words out at me.

"What?"

"Grandma Mima is still alive," Winnie was clearly cross at such an unforgiveable mistake.

"W-I-N-N-I-E, W-I-N-N-I-E. It's lunch time. Come and get washed up, P-L-E-A-S-E."

"Coming, Mima," Winnie shouted as loud as her miniature voice box would allow.

I stopped. I did not blink, breathe, move, or swallow. Eyes wide, my head spinning. I was back!

Back on the land of my fore parents and their fore parents. I was back with Mima, and the place where at six years old my world made sense. Tears sailed down my cheeks, I have an opportunity to see Mima, smell her, love her and have her love me again. My chest swells, goose bumps are all over me.

"Are you coming?" Winnie asked.

"Me," I whisper afraid she will see me through my haze.

"Yes," Winnie replied, most annoyed at her older self.

"Well, honey, I am nearly seventy, Mima will not recognise me. She may even think I am a wicked person that does horrible things to little children," I retort.

"What horrible things?" Winnie was truly intrigued.

"Well she may think that I am a child molester," I blurted out absently and innocently.

"What's one of those?" she asks innocently.

Stunned by her response. I could then have kicked myself. This was the 1940s, pedophiles were not part of the global landscape.

THE JOURNEY

"Never mind, sweetheart. Just forget I said anything. Mima will not be happy to see me," I say all very matter of fact.

"Is a mal – mal o-s-t-e r, like the man at the orphanage in town?" Winnie looked puzzled.

I choose to ignore her.

"Mima can't see you," Winnie whispered, as if divulging a very important secret.

I whisper back and smile at Winnie, "Really?" grateful that she had forgotten the child molester conversation.

"Only I can see and hear you, you're my friend," she smiles.

I just stood starring at Winnie, surprised by her revelation. After all, I had travelled back in time, so maybe I was dead. Or half dead? I still wasn't sure what this was.

"Hurry, Edwina, Mima will be cross if my lunch gets cold," with that Winnie ran like the wind. "Coming Mima, I'm coming."

"Alright, Winnie, it's on the table," Mima yelled. "Wash your hands."

"O – o – o –o K – a – a –a –y," she responded mid-flight through the cane fields.

For the first time in a long while, I could breathe. I mean, really breathe, inhaling and exhaling without pain, or any pressure on my chest. Just fresh fragrant air. I webbed my fingers and threw my body on the rich earth, then immediately crossed my legs, "Arhhh," I inhale, and it felt like an eternity since I stretched. Each muscle was relaxing, and the afternoon sun continued to warm my face and body. Fatigued and overwhelmed, an unwelcome heavy sleep is upon me. I close my eyes and reluctantly drift to sleep.

The breeze blowing on my face is cool and wakes me up, it must be after 5 o'clock. The sun is setting as the night insects awake. I brush the mosquito from the end of my nose. Once on my feet, I am blown away by the spectacular architecture and design of the plantation house. Encapsulated by the setting sun, it was a sight to behold. I suddenly felt proud that Mima and my Grandpa Vincent built this plantation house from nothing. I walk, heart in mouth to the house. My skin still radiating with warmth, tingling under the surface from the evening sun. I felt good, my body feels warm and nourished. "If this is death, then I welcome it," I mutter to myself. Walking towards the house, the sun continued to soak into me. I couldn't help but overhear the conversation which was taking place not more than five feet away from where I was walking. The cool evening breeze whistles through the sugar cane and creates loud whispers. I smile.

I sense I am not alone, I look behind me. Nothing. The intensity of feeling is stronger as I get closer to the house. "Oh no," I freeze, my dog, which Mima named "Daaag". It's my black and white border collie, she was my best friend as a little girl, but right now she is eyeing me suspiciously. I am the enemy and she was looking directly at me. I slowly walk towards the veranda. Daag is not taking any chances. Her beautiful black coat surrounds her ears, eyes and chubby cheeks. Her nose, throat, chest, and two front legs were white. I want to cry. I want to run and hug my dog, but I can't. I am a stranger, and she will not be petted by strangers. That much I remember. I cannot believe she has not barked her head off. She is just standing still staring at me, as I start to walk up the steps, Daag slowly steps backwards.

"Woof.. Woof woof woooooof"

"Daag, whose there?" Mima yells behind the door.

THE JOURNEY

"Woooooof Woof woof woof"

"Daag, what is going on over there?"

I am rooted to the spot, which is in the middle of the veranda, my heart starts pounding. I have nowhere to run as Mima would see me. *I am going to bloody wring Winnie's neck, invisible my eye.* Before I could do anything, Mima swung open the screen doors, shot gun underneath her left arm, lantern in the right.

"Daag, what is all this noise?" She swings the lantern and it nearly takes off my head.

"Mima, I can explain," I say panicked.

Mima, grabs my dog by its collar, as she was barking at me. She looks straight through me, "Daag, there no one here. You old fool."

"Woof Woof Wooof ..... Grrrrrrr..."

Daag untangles herself from Mima's grip and parades up and down the veranda like a soldier of war, her eyes not once deviating from my presence.

"Stop this foolishness." Irritated by Daag's outburst, she drags my dog curtly by her collar into the house. "Winnie needs peace. It will soon be bedtime." With that, she slams the doors shut.

Realization of my presence engulfs me. "She could not see me." I wait and wait then open the door; I walk through the main hall. My nostrils explode with the scent of citrus. It must be a Friday, it's cleaning and washing day. I smile at the polished hard wood floors, they are gleaming. I stand by the main reception room. Mima is sat with Winnie on her lap; they are both reading the bible.

"God Bless Lucy," I say.

"Shhhhhhhh," Winnie puts her hands to her lips.

"Winnie, why are you being so rude as to tell Mima to be quiet?" my grandmother says crossly, she was not impressed.

"No, Mima," Winnie shot me filthy look.

"Then why are you telling me to shush?" quite annoyed that the Book of Exodus was interrupted. Mima turned Winnie right around so that she could look at her insolent granddaughter square in the eye.

"Mima, my friend is back," Winnie mumbled positioning her head to the floor to avert her grandmother's annoyed glare.

Desperately trying not to laugh, "Winnie, you best warn your friend not to mess about as you, who I can see and hear, will have to pay the price with a spanking," Mima said curtly.

Winnie's eyes immediately sprang to tears; she lowered her head to the floor, "Yes, Mima." Mima picked Winnie up and took her to her room. Still annoyed with my outburst which got her scolded, Winnie stuck her tongue out at me, as she passed me in the doorway. I smile. I was a gutsy one.

I observed my grandmother's quiet demeanour as she encouraged Winnie to a tranquil state of sleep. Before she fell deep in to that restful place that all six year old's crave after a long and arduous day playing in the field, my grandmother spoke to her only grandchild, her companion, with fondness and love.

"Mima, can I, p-l-e-a-s-e, have one more coconut cake?" Winnie asked pleadingly already knowing the answer. "Please, Mima, please, please, please, please," she smiled.

THE JOURNEY

"Baby, you have just brushed your teeth," Mima sighed very loudly. "Ok, you can have one more but no more," she tried to contain her smile. "Go on to the kitchen and take one." My little face lit up like a bright flame. Winnie dashes to the kitchen, retrieved one cake from where they were cooling and shoved it whole in her mouth, she ran back to her room, her mouth, chin, and fingers engulfed in sugar and pieces of coconut. She flung her little arms around Mima's neck and whispered, "You are my best friend and I love you very, very, very much." She squeezed her grandmother and jumped in bed, "Night, night, Mima."

Mima blinked back the tears. "You are more like your mother than you know, my sweet darling. I love you too, very, very, very much." Lucy kissed her grand-daughter many times all over her face and neck, sat quietly by her side until she fell asleep.

Unable to contain my own emotion I leave the room. Although I am not visible, I had not quite worked out if Mima could hear me. I retreated to the kitchen and sat in Grandpa Vin's chair, which was situated by the east wall of their kitchen.

I do remember Mima telling me this was the very spot that Grandpa Vin would sit each evening and watch my grandmother cook. It was for a time, the place that my grandfather sat with my mother, when she was a child, until she fell asleep. As my mother grew older this was her favorite chair and she and my grandfather would jokingly squabble over that seat most evenings. Just the thought made me feel very joyous and exuberant regarding my family.

With Winnie sound asleep, I watched my beloved Mima enter her favorite room. In need of a warm beverage, she lit the stove and filled her kettle with water. Whilst she waited for her water to boil, she started to knead her rested dough as she was baking bread for the next day. Completely engrossed in her own thoughts, she began to talk to him.

"Vin, I know that you are there, I feel you," Mima looked around the kitchen.

I immediately jump out of the chair and look behind the door. "Grandad," I whisper looking underneath the kitchen table.

"I love you, Vin, and miss you more with each passing day. Mavis told Rene that Barrington was enquiring about me. Lord, I hope that he is still as ignorant as ever. If they know about Winnie, I will have to send her to school in America. Rene told me about a good school for coloured girls in Chicago. This year's harvest will be good. We have sold more cane than ever, so by the end of the harvest, I can afford it."

Mima looked straight through me. "I know you're proud of me, Vin, and I am proud of you, wherever you are. This was your dream." She smiles to herself then hums quietly a sad tune, that I had never heard before.

Watching Mima work and listening to her, made me miss her more than I ever remembered. This lapse in my memory is a wrong doing that I cannot shake or forgive. Drinking in every movement, I notice now, as I did as a child, how she struggled with her right arm. An accident, she had once explained, after relentless pressure from me.

Pride swells by belly when I look at this beautifully proportioned, petite, brown skinned woman. She was intensely powerful, articulate, and had the stamina and work ethic of ten experienced male plantation owners. Being female in a male dominated world is no simple task, let alone in the 1940s. On top of all that, she has a disability, but that did not stop her. My grandparents were respected in the village, there was always some farmer sending his son or daughter to help out at harvest time. They loved Mima and Grandpa Vincent, although

THE JOURNEY

he had been dead some years, I knew they loved him by the way they always spoke highly of him.

"Warrior Lucy," I say quietly. I cannot help it, I just stare at her, slowly I pluck the courage up to shadow her around her chores, looking at her face, pushing my nose into her neck and smelling her coconut infused hair oil.

I could have watched her all night, whilst she was cleaning her stove. Mima poured the washing crystals in a bucket, let them dissolve and went to work. I remember when she bought her AP Simmons Wilson Coal and Wood burning Stove. Mima had saved for half the year, and it arrived after being on order for three months from the United States of America. Although I did not know it at the time, this was quite a milestone. Only the affluent houses could afford such luxuries. Saying that, my grandmother's baking skills were legendary, so if anyone deserved a luxury stove from the United States in our village, it was Mima. We all benefited, and I mean everyone.

I reluctantly leave her in the kitchen and explore my old home. Walking into my grandmother's bedroom set all my hairs on edge. In here I am reintroduced to her personal scent. I stand in the middle of the room, close my eyes and inhale. I slowly open my eyes and turn three hundred and sixty degrees, and take in the sights that surround me. Mima's bedroom was like something out of an upmarket house and garden magazine. I look at the handmade blankets, with Hibiscus Sabdariffa flowers patiently hand stitched on them. Hibiscus was Mima's favourite flower, it grows naturally around the Red Sorrel trees on the plantation. The cross-stitched image in the center of the fabrics looked very professional. The white to pale yellow flowers with a dark red spot at the base of each petal was mirrored on the handmade curtains, accompanying fluffy cushions and blankets. I just did not remember my life being this prosperous as a small child, but later on, definitely; this house, my early home was exquisite.

Something was happening to me physically, I am starting to feel very tired, as I had earlier in the day. My eyelids are betraying me, my body's urgent request for sleep is as vital as oxygen. Quietly, I take off my shoes. I do not care that Mima cannot see me. Just in case this spell breaks, and she returns to her room to witness an old woman on her bed with shoes on, I am well aware, disability or no disability, I am going to get a beating! I fall into a deep sleep, it's peaceful and free from suffering.

What the hell is that noise, I open one eye. Merciful Jesus, I have not heard that sound in decades. I jump up and rush to the window. It's Buster, Mima's rooster. He was on time, that's for sure. He crowed every morning at 5.30 am and every evening at 6 pm.

I return to the bed that I lay peacefully in all night. Mima is laying on the other side, looking at me, I am unnerved, has my spell been broken, can she see me?

Her dark brown hair with a few unruly grey strands is draped across her forehead and delicately framing her face. Her piercing dark brown eyes were something to behold in the morning.

"Vin, is that you?" she whispers, "I feel something and I like to think it's you. Good morning, Vin, I love you. Help me today and give me strength to carry on. Lord knows I am tired." Mima stretched over and picked up my grandfather's picture on her side table, she kissed it repeatedly and stood up, opened the closet full of my grandfather's clothes. She leant in and pulled as many of the garments she required to her face. She stood there in his moment. As if reawakening from her sleep, she inhaled deeply, then went on to face her day. She turned around to pin up her hair, I noticed that there was a solitary tear rolling down her cheek. How I wanted and needed to comfort her and be comforted. Watching my beloved Mima in her grief, made me think of Harold. How will he cope, I pray that he can move on.

November 24th 1941

The sun was hiding through the clouds, it was the perfect afternoon, hot but not scorching. "The sun is manageable," as Mima would say. Winnie was playing a skipping game with her best friend Cora from the adjacent farm. Cora was aunty Rene's niece. All the farm staff had gone to the Morant Bay shipping docks to deliver the sugar cane and coffee beans to their supplier's handler from England and America.

Mima was in a happy mood. After today, the harvest was over. The smell of freshly grated ginger, interlocked with sugary coconut and caramel, trickled through the house out into the yard. Her mission that afternoon was to make fresh ginger beer and coconut cakes for the girls. Relaxing playful afternoons like these reminded Mima of her own delightful childhood with her best friend and sister Rene and beloved daughter Angeline. Listening to her granddaughter and her friend squeal with delight was heaven in a bottle. That's what Vin used to say when Angeline was a young child giggling and squealing with joy over nothing.

Enjoying the atmosphere, I lay like a lazy cat sunning its breast on the veranda when I saw the dust cloud approaching.

"Winnie, what's that?" I point at the road by the plantation.

"Mima, Mima, it's a motor car," Winnie and Cora squealed excitedly. It was the 1940s, only Doctor Barnett and other rich white families in the next parish owned cars.

Mima ran outside on the veranda, she took one look at the Master DeLux 1939 Chevy, recognition and fear crept into her face. "Winnie, inside," she barked.

"But *Mima*," Winnie tried to protest.

"I said inside," Mima screamed, Winnie instantly became scared.

"Cora, run home as fast as you can and tell your auntie that I have trouble. Quick, Cora. Move." Mima's voice hit an unbearable high pitch. Without hesitation, Cora sprinted through the cane fields. Mima ran into her house, heart pounding in her chest, she slammed and bolted the door. Once inside, she leaned on the door and tightly squinted her eyes shut for a few seconds. Once composed, she jolted back to the presence of her situation.

Grabbing Winnie's right arm, with immense strength she tipped her to an angle and dragged her helplessly like a rag doll up the stairs to her room. Her poor little feet barely touched those perfectly polished wooden floors.

"Winnie, darling," Mima's voice was shaking. "I need you to jump in the trunk at the end of your bed, once inside, cover yourself with the blanket." Desperately trying to sound normal, Lucy could not contain her cracking voice.

THE JOURNEY

"Mima, I'm scared," Winnie started to cry.

My grandmother was not wasting any time, she grabbed Winnie and shook her hard. Winnie's head snapped back and Mima knew she had her attention. "Baby," her voice broke again, "let's play hide and seek. Remember that game?"

Winnie nods and looks directly at me. She senses my fear. I stood by the wall, petrified and tearful. Although I cannot remember what occurred, I remember *this* feeling. I could hear the car engine roar as if the driver had flat footed the accelerator, the engine screaming louder and louder as it approached the house.

"Now go, hide, quickly. QUICKLY," Mima instructed, trying desperately to keep her voice even.

Winnie ran as fast as she could. She could tell that Mima was scared. She jumped in the trunk and covered herself.

Desperate to know who Mima was so scared off, I run to the window and immediately recognised the car. It was my father's. Mima is beside me and is frantic. She ran to the kitchen and returned with her shot gun. I can see that her hands are shaking.

"Quickly, Mima," I scream, forgetting that she could not hear me.

The brakes screech the car to a standstill, and we both hear the heavy clunk of the car door slamming. He is here, running towards the front door, and I could feel his rage.

"L----u-------c---------y," Daddy screams. "I will give you one opportunity to give me my daughter."

He bangs and bashes the door with such goliath strength it sounded like he was using a large stick to knock the door rather than his oversized fist.

"L----u---c----y...... did you think I would not find out? You *listen* to me."

"Nooooo, you listen to me, you son of a whore," Mima spat the words out with such venom, as she cut off my father. "Leave my property, or I swear to God, I will finish what my Vincent started."

I awake from my paralysis, "Oh, my God, Mima. Son of a "Whore"?" I had never heard Mima speak that way to anyone; Daddy was not the only one in rage. She was furious. This was not a side that I had seen to my grandmother. She was always kind and loving, not a personality trait I could label my father with.

Daddy bashes the door with his fists, the heavy oak door sounded like it would give in his attack. "You old bitch, give me my daughter now! She belongs to me, you hear. You have five minutes."

Mima ran to Winnie's room and opened the chest. "Listen, Sweetie, Mima is going to start counting, and when I get to five hundred, I want you to come out."

"Ok," with that, my grandmother raised me up and kissed me so hard on the lips and hugged me like it was the last time we would ever embrace. She covered me up with the blanket to my chest and made sure my head was adequately supported. "See you soon, Winnie, alright, baby love?"

"Ok, Mima, see you soon." Winnie lets rip one of her delectable smiles, parading all her teeth, including her wobbly bottom tooth.

"If we don't see each other after today, I will be with you always, you hear?"

Winnie nods, terrified of what Mima was trying to explain

THE JOURNEY

to her.

Mima ran into the drawing room.

Daddy bangs the door again, this time it sounded louder than the previous assault. "Three minutes, Lucy."

I start to shout, "Mima run. Mima, please take Winnie and go." The feeling in my chest is tighter than before.

Oblivious to my pleas, Mima ran to the window, smashed the glass, and pushed the shot gun through the hole created. Every tendon and muscle around her right shoulder was screaming, she raised the riffle as high as she could with her left arm, and took aim. "Today I am going to finish you," she muttered.

Barrington heard the smash of broken glass and turned around. He was confronted with the barrel of a shot gun, and instinctively he threw himself to the left of the veranda behind the big oak chair. Within that split second he saw a bright yellow flash, and was pushed backwards, cracking his head on the hard wood. Momentarily dazed, he lay seething on the floor. "Stupid old bitch missed." Grateful that she no longer possessed a competent aim, he jumped up. Something was wrong. Feeling weak in the legs and slightly giddy, he looked down and saw warm red liquid running down his waist. *What! She did shoot me.* Panicked, he stood up and examined himself; there were two bullet holes to his abdomen and at least six on his right waist and thigh.

"Think, Barrington. Think," adrenalin racing around his body like a prized fighter. *"The car, get to the car, assess your wounds, get your revolver and go kill that told hag."* He tried to run to his car, however, his right leg buckled underneath him. "Arrgghhhhhhhh." He steadied himself and locked his knee and ran awkwardly back to his vehicle, praying that Lucy would not finish him off.

This is not happening. It cannot be happening. Although

I have watched these events unfold before me, it seems so very unreal. The frustrating truth is that I am just a bystander to my life, and I'm totally ineffectual as to how my path will develop.

"Why?" I scream out of pure frustration. I look out of the window at my wounded father and I view my beautiful Mima.

"This is the last time I will see you," I cry. "Lord, why did you do this to me?" I run to Mima and franticly dance and wave my hands in front of her, she felt me once, so she can feel my presence again.

"Mima, Run," I scream. Every turn, every move I am screaming at her, "Pllleeaaassse, Mima, run. He is going to kill you. Please," I sob, "just go." Defeated and weak, I fall to the floor on all fours.

Mima, for the first time during my visit, looks old and tired. She is breathing heavily, and I am not sure whether it's the adrenalin or exhaustion. She checks the barrel of her shotgun and wipes her brow. As she watches my father in the car, she prays loudly and franticly. "Lord, stand with me today against this devil. If this is where my journey ends, then, Lord, guide and protect my granddaughter, I beg you."

Barrington sat in the passenger side of his car and was ripping the bottom of his shirt into strips. Half-naked, he bound his thighs, and was relieved that all bullets holes appear to be flesh wounds. Shaking his head in disbelief, he could not accept that Lucy George shot him. He had underestimated her husband once, and that nearly cost him his life. Today, he'd miscalculated the ease with which he could take his daughter, he was not about to make a third mistake with Lucy. He opened his glove compartment and pulled out a black velvet purse. Inside was a lavishly gold engraved Colt 45 single action army revolver, a departing present from his creole lover Margerita Salido. How he wished he was there, wrapped in her loins, rather than here, about to do what he thought he would have to.

Loading the gun, he appreciated the craftsmanship of his revolver. Barrington drew a long breath, looked to the house, kissed his crucifix, rubbed his abdomen, opened the car door and stormed to the house, shooting directly at the exposed shotgun.

In her drawing room, peering out of the broken glass window, Lucy felt nothing but pure hatred for Barrington and his mother. It was hard enough being a good Christian and accepting that she and the Barnett family were inhabitants of the same earth, let alone country and district. That vile sick dog and his mother had caused her so much pain, so much suffering, but most of all, what she would never forgive was that they had murdered her husband. And her only daughter Angelina was dead to her because of him, he was pure evil.

In one move, he was out of the car, shooting at her. The first bullet kissed the left side of her head; her left ear was ringing from the sensation. Lucy threw herself to the floor to avoid contact from his assault. She took the impact of her full body weight on her right shoulder. She felt and heard something pop and tear within her. The pain ripped through her body like the unrelenting machete attack. Her body tensed, then thrashed around in the floor, while she screamed out loud inwardly. Tears ran from her eyes, she knew that if she had any chance of survival, she had to get to her feet. Her chest heaving, she let out a cry from deep within her throat.

Through the crippling pain, Lucy stood up and took aim and cocked the shotgun into her shoulder, this time her left arm buckled under the strain. "Steady," she told herself. "Finish him. Do not get weak now," she winced at the pain that ripped through her collarbone and down her right side. Fresh tears sprang to her eyes. "This is for you, Vincent," with that, she pulled the trigger; the flash of light momentarily blinded her. Within seconds, she realized that she missed, damn. Their eyes lock, he was ready for war, and now he was running with his injured leg to the house. Barrington was heading to the rear of the property. "Old woman, you forgot to lock the side door." Cursing her forgetfulness and disabled by the pain in her shoulder and right side, Lucy ran as fast as she could, when she arrived to the side door in the kitchen, it was too late. Barrington was running up the steps. Shot and injured, he was still quicker than she was.

She attempted to raise the shot gun again, this time her right arm failed her, "Noooooooooo," she screamed in sheer frustration. She looked at the counter towards her knives, she attempted to grab the long sharp kitchen knife. She was not fast enough.

Daddy was running straight for Mima, I jump in front of him to try and head him off, "Mima, runnnnnn," I screamed. Daddy passed straight through me. I jump in front of him again, filled with terror, " Daddy, please. It's me. STOP."

Mima attempted to raise the shotgun one last time, the muscles around her shoulder and collar bone resisted the action and failed her. Panicked, she put her finger on trigger, it was too late, Barrington was running through the door, gun aimed. Mima saw the flash of light, and then she heard *CRACK*. The force of the revolver catapulted her limp body from the floor and violently pushed her against her stove, she winced, as the immediate pain in her chest far outweighed the pain in her shoulder.

"Nooooo, daddy, nooooooooooooooooooooooo," I scream. I am on bended knees. Head in hands, eyes screwed shut. "No, daddy," I breakdown, unable to control any emotions that I have left.

Breathing heavily, Mima tried to gain her breath and sit up. It was fruitless. Her left lung is filling with blood, and she knows that she is slowly drowning. This is it.

THE JOURNEY

"Lay down, Mima" I tell her, trying to cradle my grandma in what I know are her last moments. "Please, don't move," I say to her through my sobbing.

My beloved Mima is looking at me through her glassy eyes. She is responsive as if she can hear me. She knew she was dying, tears in her eyes, she starts to mutter a prayer.

"Yea through I walk through the shadow of death, I.....," her breathing is labored. "I know you're here, Vin, I feel you. Forgive me for failing you. I just could not protect her."

"Where is my daughter?" daddy growls over her. His gun is pointed to her head.

"No, daddy," I scream. I try to push him, but it's no use, I just fly through him. "Leave her alone."

"Go to hell," Mima is amused by this situation as she giggles.

Barrington leant over and dragged Mima to her feet. He pushed her to the wall and shoved his face in hers. "Where is she?"

With sheer defiance, Mima just looks my father square in the eye, she smiles the broadest smile I have seen.

Daddy could not contain his anger; he punches Mima hard in the stomach, twice. She falls to the floor, "arrrrrrggggh". She coughs and splutters blood violently, as she tries to negotiate air through her blood filled lungs.

I feel as if I am suffocating, the air has been sucked out of my lungs, this beautiful kitchen has become my furnace, sweat is pouring from me, my skin feels like it is on fire. I know what is coming. My throat is dry, I cannot speak. Rooted to the spot, I attempt to cover my eyes through open fingers. I watch the man known to me as my daddy conduct himself without mercy or compassion. It's hard to believe that I am a product of this animal. Daddy grabs the lapel of Mima's shirt and drags her blood-soaked body to her feet like a ragdoll. She has lost the use of her limbs, but still holds the fire in her eyes. Her deadweight body is too heavy for him; he throws her to the floor like foul smelling rubbish.

His wounds start to affect his breathing, he is panting loudly and breathlessly says, "Where is she?" with his usual gruff tone.

Blood is voluntarily trickling out of her mouth, Mima spits out her words with lingering hatred. "You may be Winnie's daddy, but who is yours?"

"What?" daddy's screams his eyes wild with fear.

Mima is sat with her back against the wall, her head tilted to the ceiling as she is gasping for oxygen. Her blood soaked teeth and mouth are smiling through the pain. She steadies herself and looks daddy straight in his eyes and pronounces each word slowly, "Winnie is not the only bastard in this house."

"Shut your filthy mouth!!" I saw the vein in daddy's head emerging from its hiding place, his eyes wide and ready to pop out of their sockets from the strain.

Although he was always adamant with himself about his southern bloodline, he knew deep down that she was right. He never quite felt connected to his father. This could explain why. Incensed by the revelation, the moment completely overwhelmed him. Flashbacks of memories flooded to the forefront of his mind. The painful rejection of his father's dismissive attitude towards him. Never feeling that he could make his father proud. His father's obvious absence at all major events in his life to date: his first nativity play, piano recitals, football games, to name a few. She was right, and she

THE JOURNEY

knew that he knew that what she was telling him was the truth, but she was gloating at him, reveling in his pain.

Unable to contain the volcanic eruption within him, he felt his conscious spirit leave his body, it was as if his soul was ashamed to be a part of what he was about to do. Without the feelings of emotion and responsibility, Barrington raised his pistol to Mima's head. My beautiful grandmother looked into my father's eyes, not with anger or fear, but with acceptance. She closed her eyes with a huge smile on her face and said, "Vin, I am coming home."

-CRACK- -CRACK- -CRACK –CRACK – CRACK-

My father shot Mima in the head twice. He stared at her for a few seconds, raised his pistol and shot my beloved Mima a further three times randomly around her body. A bullet lodged in her elbow, knee and groin. Momentarily stunned by his madness, he looked at the dead old woman's corpse for what seemed like an eternity. Finally, as if his spirit had returned to him, he inspected the room and was repulsed by himself. He ran out of the back door, the contents of his stomach refused to remain in it after his behavior. Once outside, he promptly vomited in the perfectly manicured herb bushes in the yard.

Memories of my father's irrational, violent and unreasonable behavior started to flood my memory. Through my own tears, I saw her standing still like a statue staring at Mima. What the hell do you say to a child who witnesses this? I immediately run towards Winnie and attempt to cuddle her. It's no use, she is transfixed by Mima's corpse, and she looks at me with wide eyes and whispers, "What happened to Mima?"

"Don't look, Winnie. Winnie, look at me," I beg.

"What happened to Mima?" she asked quietly.

Neither of us noticed that daddy was standing in the doorway. "Mima had an accident, sweetheart. You are coming to live with me," he told her without emotion or consideration to his estranged daughter, who has never met him.

Winnie ran to Lucy and threw herself on her blood soaked corpse. "Mima," Winnie shook her grandmother. "Mima, wake up," she shook her as hard as she could. "Mima, wake up," she screamed.

"Mima, Mima, please wake up," Winnie cried. She looked at me, "Mima won't wake up, Edwina, why won't she wake up?"

"Come on, little girl, daddy has to go," my father had his irritated stance on.

"Daddy? My daddy and mummy are dead," Winnie spat the words out with venom through her cracked voice, the emotion of grief not quite realised in her tiny self.

Barrington looked up and starred at Winnie. "What did you say?" he asked quietly.

"Winnie," I scream. "Winnie, say nothing." Winnie looks at me confused.

"You're not my daddy. My daddy is dead, just like my grandpa Vincent," she shouted through the tears. She was angry at him and he could tell.

I look on, realising that my younger self's ill-considered comment will cost her dearly. "Winnie, I know you're upset, PLLLEEEAASSSSE listen to me, say nothing, he is a dangerous man and HE IS YOUR DADDY," I scream. "Be quiet, please Winnie." As the little girl turned to look at me, she was met with a hard unprovoked punch to middle of her face. Winnie fell off her grandmother on to the kitchen floor with a thud. Bouncing across the floor in the other direction was her

THE JOURNEY

wobbly tooth, with a friend to accompany it.

"Daddy," I cry. "Daddy, no."

Winnie lay flat on her back, legs apart, both hands holding her nose and mouth. She did not utter a word or make a sound; she just held her face which was bleeding heavily through her fingers. That one punch was all it took to strike fear into this young vulnerable human being. He leant over her and dragged her by her hair to her feet. Winnie yelped in such a high pitch tone it had Daag barking. "I am your daddy, do you hear?" he asked through gritted teeth.

"Say yes, Winnie," I yell at her, feeling completely helpless. "Please, say yes. If you can't speak, nod."

My little self was in no mood to toy with this animal, she nodded. He picked her up and threw her over his shoulder and moved towards the car. Daag started to growl and bark viciously. He jumped up and sunk his teeth in Barrington's backside, she swung round forcing his flesh to depart his body, he yelped, cocked the gun and shot Daag in the head.

Once in the back of the car, I consoled my younger self. "Winnie, lay your head back and pinch your nose like this," I showed her how to control the bleed.

Confused and shell shocked, she carefully lays her head back, squeezed her nose, and tried to push the tears from her eyes, by squinting tightly every few seconds. I sat next to her holding her thigh and rubbing the bump in the centre of my nose, sixty three years later paralysed by the realisation of how it became so. I am filled with such grief; I look at my little self and start to cry for her. For me! I hold her thigh tighter; she looks at me, I smile through the tears. I cannot even tell her that everything is going to be ok. I know that it's not. Physically battered and emotionally crushed, I see myself for the first time. I am petrified. Covered from head to toe in my grandmother's and my own blood, wearing my favorite yellow dress, that is no longer yellow, but a muddy brown, I ask myself how the hell I made it. No wonder I blocked this out. No wonder I became who I am.

Chapter 4

Harold's Time

13th January 2005 18.42 pm

The mood and atmosphere in Edwina Mallard's room had changed from a volcanic eruption earlier, to sorrowful and quiet reflection. Harold had not moved from his wife's side, he couldn't, watching his wife's life slip away was more than his spirit could bear. The last two and a half weeks had been emotional. In fact, it was sheer hell. When Doctor Alcock delivered the news, it was me that crumbled like a sand castle. Edwina, even now, especially when she needed me to be her rock ended up comforting me. She was the backbone out of the two of us, and always put me first, especially at times when I had deserved to be last on her list. Maybe Phoebe is right, it's all about me, always has been.

Harold inhaled deeply. Jon and Phoebe looked up.

"You ok dad?" Phoebe asked.

"I'm fine love," he looked pained. *Don't lie, not now, just tell them how you're feeling.* I took off my glasses and look directly at my children. "Actually, I'm not. I still can't believe that this is happening. Since Doctor Alcock gave us the diagnosis, I've been numb. At first, I told myself that it's the wrong results. Not my Eddie. Not now, we just reconnected." Harold wiped a tear from his eye. "Then I was angry. Angry at god, with the doctors and with your mother."

"How typical for you. It had to be her fault, didn't it?" Phoebe snapped.

"Just shut up girl, you're so angry that you don't even listen to what is being said," I barked. *I could not help it, she was starting to rile me with her rude and inappropriate behavior.*

Jon looked at Phoebe with a childish smirk, "Good for you, dad." He muttered.

"I admit it," I sniffed, "I blamed your mother. I *was* angry. After her breast cancer fifteen years ago, she should have been more insistent with her GP about her health. She had a cough, a persistent one, and would not do anything about it. She was in denial, and I allowed her to be comfortable there. When I dragged her to the doctor's, she played it down. I should have insisted that she keep going back. Your mother just blew me off, like I was having one of my moans. I was furious really."

Phoebe tutted very loudly.

"With myself Phoebe," I say sarcastically.

"What dad?" Jon looked at me confused.

Harold's voice broke, tears streaming down his face, "With myself, are you deaf? I was angry with me for not being able to make her go and take care of herself." Harold started to cry.

"Dad, no one blames you," Jon said quietly.

"I blame me Jon. I blame me. I have bargained with God and every one of Jesus's disciples, nothing." I threw my hands in the air. They both chuckled quietly, as they know that I was very resistant to religion. "She'd gotten worse. Even after all that prayer, your mother is still dying. Then it hit me. I will be a widower very soon and I cannot cope with that prospect. We have known each other since we were fifteen years old. Do you know, this morning, when showering, I cried like a baby. I'm not ashamed to admit it. You know why? I used the last of your mother's shower gel, and knew," my voice breaks again, "and knew that I would not be replacing it. My beautiful wife will never shower again in our bathroom. We will not have dinner together at the table. I will not make her omelettes for breakfast. There will be no one to shout at me when I ruin the whites in the washing machine. She will not kiss me goodnight or rub my back when it aches. You may not believe me when I say this, but it's true. I loved your mother, truly, madly, deeply loved her, and am still in love with her, and will always love her. She was, is, my best friend, my warrior, the mother of my children, my biggest fan. My lover. She made me feel like a man, even when I did not act like one." Harold could not contain his emotion. He let the tears flow freely, and through the emotion and the pain, he lay back in his chair, looked lovingly at his wife and muttered, "You can go, my love. I will be ok."

THE JOURNEY

Not wanting to infringe any further on her father's transparent intimate thoughts, Phoebe thought that she would go for a comfort break.

"Jon, dad, I'm going to the loo and to stretch my legs," Phoebe whispered.

"Good idea Hun. I will do the same, I need to call Jack and give him an update, it's been a while," Jon said quietly. He was still reeling from his father's recent disclosure. His mother's terminal condition had promoted a more revealing and communicative side to his father. He loved it, but wished he'd found his voice twenty years ago. His whole existence might have been different.

"Kids, take your time. If anything happens, I will call you. There's an Italian down the road, go eat. I'm here. Jon, if I am honest, you look like you need a break." Harold smiled.

"You sure?" Phoebe asked concerned.

"I'm sure."

"Thanks, dad. We won't be long, one hour tops," Jon reassured his dad.

"Take your time. It will be nice to have her to myself for a bit. Oh, can someone bring me a coffee on the way back?"

"Sure," Jon replied.

Once the children had left, I stood up and kissed my wife on the lips. She was starting to develop a grey tint to her skin. Whatever that was, I knew it was not good. I stretch my legs, walked over to the sink in the corner of the room and washed my hands and face. I smile to my wife through the mirror. "Look, I know that you will cuss me if I don't keep myself looking presentable. You know what you're like. "*Harold, you must always maintain a certain standard when you go out,*" I mimicked her in a high pitched voice. I so want to laugh, but couldn't. The urge to cry is strong but I wouldn't. "You're not dead yet Eddie. I will have plenty of time to cry and mourn when you're dead."

"When you're dead," the words stick in my throat. Edwina was full of such energy, to see her like this was an abomination to her spirit. "You love me, our children, and music, so if Eddie is not the life of the party anymore," I wipe my eyes, "I will be the life of the party for Eddie." Her favourite song of all time was "My boy lollipop", by the Jamaican teenager Millie Small. This was released in 1964, which was the year that Jonathan was born; laughing to myself I recall how she danced to this tune, even when heavily pregnant. The harmonica solo started to play in my head, it was too late. Something happened to me in that hospice and I started shaking my legs like I was in his mid-twenties again.

Da um dum dum dum

My boy Lollipop

Da dum dum dum dum
You make my heart go giddy up

Da dum dum dum dum
You are as sweet as candy

Da dum dum dum dum
You're my sugar dandy

Whoa oh, my boy Lollipop
Never ever leave me
Because it would grieve me
My heart told me so

Edwina opened her eyes and fixed them on me. My heart leapt and whilst dancing I put both palms across

THE JOURNEY

his chest and continued to sing to his wife.

> I love you, I love you, I love you so
> But I don't want you to know
> I need you, I need you, I need you so
> And I'll never let you go
> My boy Lollipop.
>
> Da dum dum dum dum

It has been a long time since I have sung to my wife. It felt good and for the first time in a long while I felt young again. Sharing this moment with her was precious and priceless. She was happy that I was here. We held on to this moment, and with utter reluctance she closed her eyes, with the smile on her face.

The hairs on his neck stood up to attention, someone was watching us. I swung around to the door and there was Jack, that homosexual person that had corrupted my only son. The moment, our moment was over.

"Umm. Errrrr Good evening, Mr. Mallard. I came to see Eddie and to check on Jon. I didn't mean to intrude," completely embarrassed by his arrival, Jack's cheeks went crimson.

"Well you did, and he's not here," I snapped.

Jack's eyes shot to the floor. He knew that I could not stand his presence near me.

"How is she?" Jack whispered looking at Edwina, desperately trying to manoeuvre himself out of this awkward situation.

"She's dying. We're not sure how close, but we're close, if that makes sense," I whispered back. I started to feel ashamed momentarily about the way I had treated Jack.

"Take a seat, she'd be happy that you came," I pointed

to the chair. "Sit."

Not wanting to cause any further distress, Jack followed the order and sat down. He smiled at Harold and picked up a magazine.

"How are you, Mr. Mallard?" Jack enquired.

"Why do you *still* call me Mr. Mallard?"

"Because, with you, I cannot presume that I can call you Harold," Jack said as a matter of fact.

"Please call me Harold. I may not approve of what you and my son do, but that does not mean you can't call me Harold."

Jack was staring at me as if confused. He started to nod his head. "Ok," he said. "Thank you Harold." I saw a smile creep across his face.

"How long have you been together?" Jack asked.

"Over 50 years," I responded. "Why?"

"Oh, I knew it was a long time, but could not remember if it was fifty or sixty years," Jack responded.

"And you?" I asked looking squarely into the eyes of the man who was having sex with my *only* son.

"I'm sorry," Jack look confused.

"How long have you been in a .... a... you know ... thing with Jon?" I asked frustrated that he was pretending to not understand me.

"Thing?" Jack snarled doing the inverted commas sign with his hands. "By 'Thing' do you mean a relationship?"

"To you it's a relationship, to me it's a 'thing'," I repeated his sign.

"It will be twenty two years next month," Jack said sarcastically.

"Really, that long," I say back with the same amount of sarcasm.

"Harold, don't you think that it's time for you to accept the situation?" Jack asked quietly.

I cannot believe this impertinent homosexual. Who does he think he is? He is lucky my wife is in that bed or else I would let him have it.

"Accept the situation. *Accept* the situation," Harold whispered loudly, looking at his wife, who he could have sworn was smiling. "Jack, I do not like what you do. Full Stop. I cannot understand why you do what you do, and I will not apologize nor accept you, or the way that I feel about you."

"And what exactly do you feel about me," Jack was clearly annoyed.

"I feel disgust. There, I said it. It's nasty. You and your homosexuality."

"I just do not understand that thought process" he said.

"What is so ambiguous it is my belief that you gays, you batty men, queers, you to me are all dirty. That is just how I feel and there is nothing more to be said." I could not help it. I turned by body away from him and pushed my lips in to my nose and scrunched it up as if I smelt something foul.

"On the contrary, Harold, you have said enough. Something wrong with your face?" Jack asked in his overtly polite British accent. He started to unnerve me.

"Yes. When I think of the acts that you perform on my son, I cannot stomach it. Eddie always said that my face is the window to my soul, and she is right. I cannot pretend. I find it so ... so ... repugnant."

"Harold, why have you not considered the acts that you son's does to me? He is just as willing a participant."

"*I cannot believe you said that,*" Harold thought, wide eyed, hurt, angered, and stunned. He looked at his wife, then back to Jack. A horrific memory which occurred over twenty years ago sprang to mind.

"Harold, look, I'm am so very sorry, I did not mean to upset you."

"Yes, you did," I snarled. "May I remind you that I have never witnessed my son doing anything to you." He starred at Jack so intensely, feeling the heat of his gaze, Jack threw his eyes to the floor.

Jack did not want to anger me, as he had previously been on the receiving end of my rage, which left him in hospital. "Ok, maybe a little. It's just that you have never engaged with me in any way."

"After the way you have just spoken to me, is there any wonder?"

"I'm sorry," Jack mumbled quietly, with humbled eyes.

"Didn't your family teach you any manners? Clearly you have no respect for your elders," I stare him down.

"Harold, err, um ... I'm sorry ... I love your son very much. The fact that we have been together for over twenty years, does that not count for anything?" Jack pleaded.

"It does, I suppose. But I don't have to like it. Jack, I am entitled to my own opinion."

"As I am entitled to mine."

THE JOURNEY

"Meaning?" I snap.

"Meaning that when you came to England, you experienced severe racial abuse. We, that is Jon and I, have to deal with that same prejudice and discrimination all the time, just because we are a couple. We are more similar than you think."

This homosexual must be smoking weed in his spare time. "We are not similar, and it's not the same. I *cannot* help being black."

"But I can help being gay? That is so ignorant."

"Ignorant? No, it's not ignorant. It's a fact. You have a choice with whom you sleep. I am black, no choice, end of story." Harold was very dismissive.

"Unbelievable," Jack threw his hands up in the air.

The silence was deafening. "When did you know?" I ask with obvious annoyance.

"What? Know what, that I liked men?" Jack asked astonished. This was the most dialogue that he had with Harold in twenty years, and the most direct that he'd had with anyone about his sexuality.

"Of course, that's what I mean, when?" I snapped.

"I think I was 4 or 5 years old."

"Were you abused?"

"I beg your pardon? Was Jonathan abused?" Jack retorted angrily.

"I've asked him, and he keeps saying no. What are you so indignant about? According to you less than five minutes ago, I was the ignorant one. Now I am asking questions about you, and you're acting as if I am offending you. Is this what your relationship is like with my son?"

"What?" Jack felt defensive.

"Contradictory. Abrasive. Look at the situation that we are in," he pointed to his wife. "You do not appear to have any real compassion for your surroundings. You are an angry man, aren't you, Jack?" With that, Harold took the time to observe this young man.

That was like a sledge hammer to the head, "Err, no." Jack thought about my words and observations.

"I love him, Harold. That may be hard for you to hear, but I do. He is the love of my life, and I do want to spend the rest of my life with him," Jack pleaded.

"What exactly do you love about my son?"

"I'm sorry? I don't understand," Jack asked.

"Yes, you do. What do you love about him? He is the love of your life, after all." Harold turned his whole body so that he could review Jack's complete response.

"Well, he's, err, funny. Umm, errr a really good cook. He's smart. We have a great time together, he's generous." Jack continued to talk about my son, but I surprisingly zoned out.

Poor, poor Jonathan, this man was not the person for him. I'm not convinced that he is as genuine as he makes out. Eddie always said he was a snake in the grass and, having spoken to him, maybe she is right. I just wish that I could go back in time, had I spoken to him twenty, fifteen years ago, I would have told Jonathan to find another man.

"Jack. Jack, stop. Let me make myself clear to you. If you hurt my son, you will experience more of your fair share of drama from me," I said.

THE JOURNEY

Stunned, Jack's jaw dropped, "What did you say?" he asked quietly.

"You heard me," I wasn't in the mood to joke and was looking deep into Jack's soul. I did not like what I am seeing.

"It's a bit late to start doing the concerned father routine, don't you think?"

I leaned over the bed, "Keep your voice down. It may be late in your eyes, but as long as I draw breath in my body, Jonathan Mallard is still my son. My wife always knew there was something suspect about you. Now I know too. Hurt him, in any way, and I will hurt you. Now, if you don't mind, I would like to spend some time with my wife. Alone."

Jack looked at me opened mouth. "Right then. That's it. Tell Jon I popped in."

Jonathan walked through the door as Jack stood up. "Hello, love," he looked at Jack and his dad. This was a surprise. There was clear tension, "Everything alright?"

"Just fine," I said. "Jack and I have been having a lovely chat son. He was telling me how much he loves you."

"Really!" Jon asked, practically floored by this information.

"Really," Jack said dryly.

"I'm going to go," Jack said. I took the time to truly observe this man with my son and saw that his body language was abrasive and bullish.

"No, stay," Jon begged. He gently tugged Jack's elbow, but he shrugged it off. He turned his whole body round towards me and puffed up his chest like a penguin.

"No," he drooled in an over exaggerated camp way

purely for my benefit I am sure. He threw me a filthy look, "I must, this is a family time, and I have taken up too much of that time already."

Jack kissed Jon, then threw me another filthy look. "Walk me to the door, babes."

"Bitch, I can tell he's the woman," Harold thought to himself, then chuckled aloud at his own joke.

Jonathan looked at his father, "Dad, you ok?"

"Yes, son," I replied quietly. "Erm, where's PP?"

"Getting your coffee, she will be up shortly," I nodded. "Take your time, don't rush back." As he was out of earshot, I looked at my wife, my thoughts were filled with worrying prospects for his son.

"Oh, Eddie," I stroke her cheek with my forefinger. "What did I do all those years ago? Had I killed him, Jonathan would never have forgiven me, but right now I wish I had. Something has made me uneasy about that man. I just cannot put my finger on it." My heart felt heavy and all I could do was sigh.

Eddie's eyes opened again. I could tell that she wanted to say something, I leaned in closer, she whispered angrily, "You should have killed him."

I jerk back, "What, Eddie?" I gently nudge her as she had closed her eyes. *Woman, you cannot fall off somewhere now without explaining this to me. Why should I have killed him? My heart is racing as I am starting to feel sick. My spirit never liked that homosexual toff, and now I detested him. If Eddie, my precious loving wife who loves all things, including beetles, is telling me this, it is with good reason.*

"Eddie," I gently prod her. Nothing.

THE JOURNEY

"Eddie," I squeeze her hand.

Damn it, woman, wake up. My mind is racing, and as I am staring at my wife, who has frustrated the hell out of me, dying of cancer or not, I need answers. I close my eyes and am confronted with a memory that I have been trying to erase from my memory banks for twenty two years.

23rd December 1983, 07.35 am

"Harold, I am so happy that Jonathan is coming home. I will give him a piece of my mind regarding how long he is coming home for. Four days, what kind of vacation time is that?"

"What for?" I scolded my wife.

"What for?" She moans sarcastically at me, "Are you serious Mr. Mallard?" Eddie eyeballed me so hard, I averted my gaze. She knew that I knew all too well why she was annoyed with our son.

"Eddie, give the young fella a break. He is in his first term at university, and he is finding his feet."

"Doing what? Term finished last week. What could he be doing?"

We both looked at each other smiled.

"Studying," I chuckle." Now leave my only son alone, after all, without practice, how can we expect grandchildren?" I walked over to Eddie and cuddled her, she felt good and smelt even better. I planted a wet kiss firmly on her luscious lips.

"Hmmmm, Mr. Mallard, that feels nice, now what was that for?" my wife asked in a flirtatious manner that made me tingle in places that reminded me why I have three children.

"Nothing baby, but give him a break, he most probably has a young woman stashed away somewhere."

"Oh Lord, that reminds me. Harold, he asked to bring a friend home for the holidays. That's ok, isn't it?"

"Of course," I chuckle. "See, that explains it, he has a special friend who he is spending time with. Relax, woman. I bet she is pretty."

23 December 1983 2.46 pm

"He said lunchtime," Eddie moaned at me whilst we ate the lovely prepared rice and peas, curried chicken, and fresh salad that my wife has spent all morning preparing.

"Eddie, I know he's acting selfish, but there will be a credible explanation, you'll see."

Phoebe bounds in, "Hi, Mum."

"Hello Love, where have you been?" Eddie asks.

"Woolworths," she throws up five bags filled with Christmas goodies. "It's madness on the high street, but I am done, done, done," her voice echoes like an opera singer.

"Anything for me, PP?" I grab a bag, like a school boy giggling and run across the room with it.

"Dad," Phoebe squeals, "you'll ruin the surprise," and grabs the bag back. "I am going upstairs and, yes, I will be wrapping presents, so, please, keep Inspector Mallard downstairs mum."

"No problem," Eddie says smiling.

As Phoebe opened the dining room door she squealed again, this time twelve octaves higher than last time, "Jonathan."

THE JOURNEY

I jump out of my chair. Tears momentarily spring to my eyes, I am so proud of him; he was the first Mallard to ever to make it to University.

"Alright, PP, let my son go so that we can have a go," I snap. My daughter looked at me disapprovingly, but I couldn't help it, I had missed him. I embrace my son, the only way a father can. I bear hug him close, kiss his ear. He feels thin and smells the same. Old spice aftershave fused together with coconut oil, and I sniff a couple of times then push Jonathan away, "You smoking now?" I asked accusingly.

"Err, well, yes, sir. I am just trying something new."

I look at my son, he looks different. His hair is longer; his face is, well, sort of smoother. His clothes were grungier. I shrug off the feeling. He's a student. This is how they are; they look like peasants, smoke too much, and drink even more.

"Oh well, make sure it's a short lived habit. Anything else you're trying that you want to tell me about?"

"Like what?" Jonathan chimed in with an exasperated expression on his face.

"Like drugs, you know the ones I am talking about: marijuana, heroin, and the new one, cocaine."

"Dad! I'm at uni, and I like to smoke a few fags with my beer, ok? Don't start. I've been back all for five minutes."

"Alright, so where's this girl that your bringing home?" my eyes excitedly walk around him.

"Girl?"

"Yes, your friend," I ask frustrated of his innocence.

"Oh, you mean Jack."

"What, is that short for Jackie?" I see his blank expression. "Jacqueline," I ask obviously confused.

"No sir, it's short for Jack," a young white posh man in his early twenties appeared from behind my son. He looked like a student, but a lot more stylish. His long blond hair has every strand strategically placed and scooped off his brow. He had piercing grey blue eyes, square jaw, and a dimple in his chin. He reminded me of a young Kirk Douglas. He looked like one of those male models in Phoebe's 'Jackie magazine'. Perfectly manicured. Too perfect.

"Oh, hello," I was visibly surprised, which embarrassed me. "I just presumed Jon was bringing home a girl."

"Well, I hope that you are not too disappointed," Jack asked awkwardly.

I feel awkward as to my open disappointment.

"Hello Jack," my wife stretched out her hand. "I am Edwina, but everyone calls me Eddie."

Jack shook Eddie's hand, then gently raised it to his lips and kissed the back of her hand very gently, whilst maintaining eye contact.

"You are definitely charming," Eddie said "Harold stick with him, you might learn something," my wife joked. *"Flash git,"* I thought to myself. I look at Jack for a few seconds longer than is necessary, and he feels my stare.

"Mr. Mallard, is it ok that I am here?" he looked concerned. *"Come on, Harold, behave. This is your son's friend,"* I tell myself and shrug off my uneasy feeling.

"Yes son, of course, any friend of Jon's is a friend of mine." I stretch out my hand, and both men glance at

THE JOURNEY

one another, Jack shakes my hand firmly.

"It's a pleasure to finally meet you. Jon talks very highly of you." I blush. It makes me proud that my son speaks of me to his new posh uni friends.

"Ok, Harold," Eddie started to direct the situation, she looks at Jonathan and holds his square shoulders. "You must be starving lads, come and eat. Jon, get the plates off the side and tuck in."

Jon did what he was instructed. Jack was served a healthy helping of the rice and peas and curry chicken.

"Mrs. Mallard, this is absolutely gorgeous. Is that coconut in the rice and beans?"

"Please call me Eddie, and yes it is coconut. We call this dish Rice and Peas."

"It's lovely, Eddie," Jack said, licking his lips.

"So, Jon, how come Jack is not going home to his people for Christmas?" I enquire.

Jon turned to me, "His folks are in the Caribbean. His parents have a villa in West Moreland Barbados, they holiday every year there."

"Lovely," Eddie chimes in, eyebrows raised clearly impressed. "Why didn't you go?" my wife asks suspiciously. "I mean, Islington compared to Barbados, no contest."

"I had an assignment that's due in the New Year. I just wanted a head start Eddie. When I am in Bados, I just don't do anything but sunbathe," Jack responded shyly.

"I have never been to Barbados, but I hear that it's beautiful. What are you studying Jack?"

"Yes, it is, and Law and Philosophy," he announced

proudly.

"Do you like it?" I chimed in.

"I love it, sir," Jack smiled.

I drink in the atmosphere and embrace this feeling that I have. My family. It's just perfect. I look at my son filled with pride. Both Maddie and Phoebe are on top form, completely embarrassing their brother for his love of clubbing and brit pop bands Wham and the Pet Shop Boys. I don't get it myself, but he's young. This is his time. I have to say I am taken aback by Jack, he is a nice fella; clearly well to do, but very down to earth. He even has a healthy appreciation of cricket, which makes him every West Indian's best friend. I see my son, my daughters and wife all smiling at me. I know what they are thinking, and it's true, I am making an effort. I want to. This is my son's friend from university; he must think a lot of him to bring him home. Also, Jack will be the type of people he will be mixing with in the future, so I need to put aside my class prejudice and get over myself. This is for my boy.

4.06 am

I wake at the same time every night. It's so frustrating, but after twenty three years, it's irritatingly reassuring. I turn and kiss Eddie, still sound asleep like an angel. I swear this woman could sleep through a hurricane.

"Hmmmmmm Huh Huh Hmmmmmmmm," I blink myself awake.

"Hmmmmmmm Huh Huh Hmmmmmmm..."

My heart is pounding. There it is again.

"Ummh..."

I sit up. I hear a thud, then another. Lord, we are being

burgled. This cannot be happening, whoever the poor deluded thief is, he will get a beat down of major proportions.

I jump out of bed and pick up the hockey stick that lives behind the door. "Ummh." That's a muffled sound. Mercy the girls. I panic.

"Eddie. Eddie, wake up."

"Hmmmmm," she is still asleep. I shake her violently awake.

"Wake up, love, we're being burgled." My wife jumps out of bed disorientated.

"Stay here," I order, "and call the police," I start to feel sick, as it sounds like some pervert is taking advantage of our daughters, both of them. I run out to the landing. Nothing. I wait, looking around. Both girls doors are closed. I put my ear next to Phoebe's door. Nothing. All I can hear is my own heartbeat. I slowly open the door, she is sound asleep. A wave of relief sweeps over me. I then creep next door and open Maddie's door, she too is asleep.

The thudding sound reappears. I am less panicked, my girls are safe. I open Jon's door, as I could do with reinforcements. His bed is empty. "Maybe the boys went clubbing," I think to myself. I take the slow approach down the stairs. My heart is racing, but I have the advantage. I know where every creaky floorboard is. I take my time, as the element of surprise is going to help me break some bones.

I hear whispers in my living room. I burst in, the sight before me weakens my core. I must be in shock, as I cannot move. My stomach falls to the bottom of my ankles, and my mouth starts to water like I am going to be sick. I open my eyes as wide as they could stretch, as I need to see the full picture, my mind must be playing tricks on me. The TV is on, and in front of *my* TV, on *my* rug, is my son and Jack naked. Jack is lying on top of my son, and moving his hips in a motion that only a man should move on top of a woman when naked.

"Mr. Mallard " Jack shrieks fear in his eyes. "We were, we were just"

"I know what you were doing," I scold. I stare at my son, who's face is buried in his hands, he is on all fours and his backside is still in the air.

"My son, look at me," I say coldly. I could not camouflage the rage within me. Jon's face was still firmly in his hands. "I said looooook at meee!!!" I scream at him.

Jon turns his head, tears swell and burst their banks and roll down my face. I cannot help it, I kick him hard in the side of his arse that is still in the air. Both men look scared, my son especially, as he knows how unpredictable I can be.

"You let this batty man fuck you?" I scream at the top of my lungs. Jon looked to the floor, ashamed. I could feel the bile and rage in my stomach rising. "Batty Boy, answer me!" I start to shout at the top of my voice, "You let this batty man fuck you? Hmmm hmmm? You bring this abomination to God and man in *my* house?" I bellowed.

Jon's face was streaked with tears and snot. He was shaking, I did not know whether it was from cold or fear, but, he was visibly shaking. He nodded and lowered his head.

That admission was the welcome mat my bile needed. It rose without warning and lurched out of my mouth onto the Christmas tree and presents. I kneel to try and focus the vomit. That's when Eddie walked in. She did not speak for a few seconds, she absorbed my shame. She whispered to Jon, "Jon, what is going on here?" Jon

THE JOURNEY

lowered his head.

"You are not a.. a... homosexual, are you?" she said, her voice cracking. She moved slowly towards me and knelt on the floor and put her arm around my shoulder.

"Why?" Eddie snapped.

"Mum, I am just discovering who I am," Jon croaked.

"Discovering who you are?! Discovering who you are! You're my son, and you are *not* gay." Eddie shouted at him and shook her head vigorously. Her eyes were screwed tight, as if to try and push the image out of her head. "No, not you."

"Mum," Jon tried to interject quietly.

Eddie's voice changed, she was furious. "Why would you disrespect us like this? Jonathan? Jonathan, I have just asked you a question. You bring this nasty, ungodly act to my home. You introduce your lover to us, as if he is your friend and do this. Look at your father. Look at him. Is this what you wanted?" Eddie screamed.

"Eddie," Jack pleaded, he looked worried about his situation. He was red in the face, I wasn't sure whether that was from embarrassment, or that was his flushed just got fucked face.

"Shut your filthy mouth," I screamed at him. I cannot listen to his lies anymore.

"Dad? Mum? What's going on?" Phoebe asked, as she bounced through the door like a carefree teenager who has just been expectantly woken up. Maddie was behind her. Both girls, once they entered the room just fell silent. There was no giggles or jibes. Just shock.

"Jon, why are you both naked?" Maddie whispered eerily.

"Because he's gay," Phoebe informed the room. With that, she walked out the room, "Come on, Maddie, I think mum and dad need to have a chat with Jonathan," she shouted disapprovingly, as she stomped up the stairs.

I could see Jack putting on his clothes in such a rush, he nearly fell over getting his jeans on. I just sat in shock, looking at my only son. It was as if my life had ended, I was having flash backs to when he was a young boy, his teenage years, all our father and son chats. Jonathan Mallard likes women. I know this, he told me so. No, this is not him. He is being influenced by that posh twat. I am sure of it. I bet he went to some private school and was buggered to kingdom come, and he meets my fine young black buck of a boy and convinces him that he's gay.

"Mr. Mallard, Mr. Mallard, err, sir," I hear that filthy homosexual voice pulling me back to this disgusting scene. My body erupts with heat, as if I had a litre of hot pepper sauce poured all over me.

"Mr. Mallard," he walks over to me and puts his hand on my shoulder. Oops, too late something snapped inside my head.

"Take your hands off me, batty man." I scream. I am trying to control the rage, but he is now in my face.

"If I could just explain," Jack said pleadingly.

"Explain? Explain what? That you were raping my son in my living room?" I screamed.

"Dad ... no, I'm ..." Jonathan tried to intervene.

I push my hand in the air so hard, I am sure he felt a breeze on his face. "Noooooo son, please, do not say it. Please." I beg him.

"Look, Mr. Mallard, this is not the way that Jon wanted

THE JOURNEY

you to find out, but it's better out in the open. Earlier, we were all friends, we are still the same people, aren't we?"

I grabbed him by the shirt and threw him into the Christmas tree. Christmas balls, tinsel, and lights were strewn across the living room floor.

"Harold," Eddie screams, "please, Harold don't. I know that you have been provoked, but, please, Harold," Eddie was crying. "Please..." she whispered.

"Jonathan, get your friend out of my house," Eddie screamed at her son.

Jonathan cautiously walked towards his lover, without taking his eyes of his father. He gently pulled Jack off the flattened tree. He walked towards the door and came back, "Dad, I am so sorry," he sobbed.

I couldn't say anything. Tears were streaming down my face uncontrollably.

"Dad, it's not"

"What?"

"It's not nasty, it's natural." Jon tried to reason with me.

"Then why is the government informing the whole fucking country that 'batty man has spread the capital' letters? Why is it that if you are a batty man, you will contract AIDS, and they are showing tombstones everywhere? Hmmm? Why?" I stare at them both, disgusted with their presence.

"It's not true, dad, let me explain," Jon tried to reason with me.

"Have you lost your fucking mind Jon? You must be taking cocaine to backside, it is *not natural*. A man poking his penis into another man's arsehole is not a natural act. If it was, God would not be punishing you all.

How can you get satisfaction from that? Hmmm? Hmmmm? The Bible says it's abhorrent. If we lived in another country, you two dirty batty man would be dead for" I point at the floor violently, "for this."

"Dad." My son looks crestfallen.

"Don't dad me. You have that battyman disease? HIV? AIDS? Do you have it?"

"No dad," Jon whispered, his head hung low, and his eyes are firmly looking at the floor.

"We really care..." Jack piped up.

"*Shut up, SHUT UP! I did not raise no batty man!!!!*" I bellowed. I could see my wife wincing in the corner of my eye. Jon physically stepped back.

"Well, actually Mr. Mallard, you did," Jack said, with his arrogant posh accent, stepping forward and looping his fingers in my sons.

That arrogant selfish prick. This is my home. In it I am King, he is in *my* castle, and he dares provoke and push me like I am nothing. I grab Jon with both hands by his afro and pull him as hard as I could from Jack. I straighten him up and slap him across the face so hard, his body tumbles into a half summersault, before he lands on the floor.

Jack charges towards me, everything slows down, I hear Eddie scream, "Nooooo, Harold!!!" the living room door swings open, Maddie and Phoebe run towards me, it's too late, I push through them and connect with Jack. I pick him up mid movement and throw him to the ground, I am kneeling in his chest, my hands are wrapped around his cock sucking throat, I close my eyes and have my first flashback in years, his penis is entering my sons anal passage, I squeeze as hard as I can. I feel the bones in his neck crunch, I start to retreat into that place,

THE JOURNEY

it's getting dark and the volume in the room is getting quieter and quieter.

My wife hits me in the face with her fists, she is franticly screaming at me to let him go. I cannot hear her, but I know what she is saying. I look at the batty man rapist under my hands and see his lips are turning blue. Good. I'm going to choke the life out of you. The cheek of him. I did not raise a batty man. I am a man. My son is a man.

Something cold and hard strikes me in the back of my head. Pain cripples the right side of my head, and I lose the feelings in my arms. I topple over like a bag of heavy rocks. Dazed and momentarily confused, I lay on the floor. I see Maddie with her mother's Dutch pot in hand. *"I cannot believe she hit me with that,"* I say to myself before I black out.

I must have been out a few moments. I wake up to find Eddie over me with a cold cloth on my head. She looks terrified. I turn and see Jack in the corner. He is sat up drinking water, holding his throat and staring at me wild eyed. I see the fear in his eyes when he realises I am awake. I try to move but the room starts to spin, and I realise that my legs do not appear to be working as well as they should be.

Phoebe and Maddie are sat behind me, when they see my eyes open.

"Alright dad?" Phoebe asks, I nod.

"You should have killed him dad," Maddie whispers and winks at me before she plants a huge kiss on my head.

Eddie bends down and kisses me, "You old fool," she whispers. Tears of relief grace her cheeks. "I thought you were going to kill him."

"Get them out of here Eddie. Please. Get them out," I moan, I roll to the opposite end of the room, so that I do not have to look at my son. My head is banging, and my face is started to swell from the pounding that Eddie gave it a few minutes earlier.

I weep like a child, uncontrollable. I am inconsolable. My heart and spirit are broken. My son is gone.

THE JOURNEY

13th January 2005 21.44 pm

As the day languishes into night, my thoughts take hold of me. I am struck between two valleys. This first is that I want Eddie to stay like this for as long as possible. At least she will be alive, maybe not well, but with me. The thought of facing the rest of my life alone was not part of the deal. My second valley, is where and I feel ashamed to admit this, I want her to die. Quickly, pain free and with dignity. Seeing her like this makes me sick to my stomach. This suffering happens to other people. Not us. Not Eddie. I am not sure why I think that she is immune from the evils of the world and disease, but I do. History tells me different, somehow this was never our story. My wife was as strong as an ox, healthy and energetic. Only a few weeks ago she was so full of life. Today, this sick, decrepit old woman is alien to me. I start to question my own mortality. My failings as a man, her man, and the father to our children. All in all, we made it through some pretty rough years. To be more accurate, she made it. She had to dig deep, I did not make it easy for her, but she stuck by me. The Lord only knows why, but she did.

She is so peaceful now, her honey tone has a slight ashy tint to it. She's leaving me, I feel it, and now I can see it. My Eddie looks as she did as a young woman, whilst asleep. Free from all the pain and suffering any other human wouldn't be able to endure. I look at her lovely white nightgown and straighten her collar for her. I want to cry but can't. I need to holla and scream out, like my life depended on it. The lump in my throat is larger than any rock I could carry, and my sorrow, heavier than a clunky old chest on my back. I stand over my wife, my Eddie, and cup her face in my hands, as gently as I can, her eyes reluctantly open, she looks at me confused, then she smiles. I smile back.

"I should have behaved better than I did, and for that, darling, I am sorry. I disparaged you, when I should have loved you without fear of regret. I attacked you, when I should have celebrated you, and just for the record, I did love you. Through my own failings, I loved you, and over the years, I have learned to adore you. I know I was never ... him. I tried, and I hope that you are not sitting here now with regrets. If you are, it's ok, I just want to say that I am sorry for not living up to your expectation of what and who I can be. I acknowledge daily that I was not good enough for you. We both know this. When I finally learnt how to be a man, your man, and do better, I did. That's what I hope that you take with you. I loved you enough to change."

Eddie's eyes smiled at me, "It's alright, baby, you did ok, and I was happy," she croaked. Eddie looked straight through me, "I need you to promise me something."

"Anything, darling."

"I need you to move on, meet someone else and find happiness quickly. It's hard being alone, and you will find it excruciating," she said weakly. "Find love and be happy, Harold. You deserve it." She inhaled deeply and fell asleep.

Still hunched over, I cup her face tighter than before, my tears run down my face and wet hers.

"Oh, how I love you." My chest feels tight. I feel nothing but regret. How I wished I can turn the clock back. It's fruitless having these thoughts, I know this. They change nothing. I still wish things were different. I sit back and close my eyes, my heart breaking and my soul glum. I am so exhausted, that as I close them, they burn. My body relaxes and I fall quickly into a deep sleep.

I wake to abruptly alarmed that there are people in the room. I bolt upright, attempting to regain my visual focus, my eyes are blurry from the interrupted respite. The

THE JOURNEY

room is in darkness, the monitors and low lamps are the only source of light. She is sat there holding her hand, stroking her forearm. Angela McDermott was the closet figure to a mother that Edwina had. They had been firm friends for over fifty years. We were the only two black families that lived on our street, ours and Angela's was the other. She was petite, do not let her size fool you, she was like a warrior, I felt for poor Niall, he was dragged around by his eyelids most days. Her small frame was muscular, she was always jogging, and until her 70th birthday she ran the marathon every year. Proceeds went to some orphanage in Jamaica. She moved to Islington with her Irish husband, Niall, in 1955, she had a son, Phillip, who was in his fifties now, living in New Zealand. They are family. Angela was stone faced, she has visibly lost weight.

"Angela, what are you doing here?" I whisper, concerned for my elderly friend.

"I just couldn't stay at home not doing anything. I wanted to be here. I didn't like the thought of her being all alone. I just can't think of anything else right now," she whispered.

"She has me," I say, more curtly than I mean.

"You know what I mean," she tells me, exasperated by my childishness.

"Look," I stare at my shoes, embarrassed by my behavior. "I am exhausted. The kids are in the family room, and I want them to sleep, especially Jon, he is dead on his feet. Are you ok to sit with her?"

She looks at me as if I am crazy, "Of course. Go."

I walk through the door, as I turn to close it, I see Angela bending over and stroking Edwina's face. "My precious child, how are you?" she is holding it together, kissing Eddie on the forehead, cheek, lips and left hand, which was free of needles and tubes, she sat down next to her and put her cheek to Eddie's hand and held it there. She turns to look at me. I close the door, as I can sense that I am intruding.

I walk through the corridor. The night staff nod at me. I go down the stairs, out of the main doors, the crisp January night recoups my spirit, and I am now awake. I decide to walk around the gardens. I recall the last time I was out this late, it was when Angela tore me a new backside for being an arse to Eddie.

31st December 1983 6.24 pm

"Harold, I think you need to sleep, Hun. You have not had a decent night sleep since … Jon came home," Eddie tells me in her quiet voice.

"I'm fine. It's a new year and a new start. I need to look ahead. I cannot be stuck in 1983 forever. I want to forget it and the year that he was born."

"Stop it," she snapped.

"What?"

"You heard me. You talk such gibberish when you are drunk. He's gay Harold, not the Yorkshire ripper," she barked at me, clearly annoyed at my stance.

"It's just as bad, Eddie," I shout. "And in my house, on my bloody carpet."

"Is that what this is about? Would you be happy that he is gay and had sex outside your house? Would that please you? So you would prefer that he was not being gay in here, with you, under the same roof," she laughed at me.

"I would prefer that he was never born. He is dead to me," I yell at her.

THE JOURNEY

"I'm not like you, I just can't cut him off like that. He's my son, I love him, I miss him. I have to help him, maybe he is just confused"

"You think? I don't want you conversing with him. I forbid it. Not in my house."

My wife, who was dressing for her party, suddenly stopped. She looked at me with her steely eyes. "You do not have the authority to forbid anything," she instructed me slowly and precisely. "You do not own me. I am not your property. You do not dictate to me, Harold. Understand?" Her quiet, yet very serious voice was back.

"Understand?! Who the hell are you talking to?" I was furious.

"You. He's my son," she screamed at me.

"Not anymore," I shout, as soon as the words leave my mouth, I realize they sound stupid.

"I will not lose him," Eddie tells me quietly, as if she is afraid we are being listened to.

"This is my house," I shout. "I should be able to comfortable in my own home."

Her quiet voice returned. "Actually, Harold, it's not your house. It's mine. My grandfather brought this for *me*. He is *my* son, and if I choose to see him, I will, in my house. You do not own me. I will not be dictated to. I will not be ordered. If you don't like it, *you* leave." With that, she walked to our en-suite

"What?" I say, stupefied by her response. I cannot believe that she is siding with the gays.

"You heard me. You leave. I will not have you treating me like your chattel." She is shouting now. I can tell how this will end.

"You're taking his side?"

"It's not about sides," she yells again. "I am not going to lose my son, you may want to throw him away, but I cannot do it. He's my flesh and blood."

"So what am I?"

"You're Harold." She realised what she said. The hurt written all over my face is immediately readable. "Harold, look, I'm sorry, I didn't mean that," she touches my arm. I punch her hand away hard, a little too hard as she falls into the bed frame.

"Argghh," she moans. "What are you doing?" She spins around, and she's in front of me.

"Woman, get out of my way," I snarl.

"No," she says defiantly. Her eyes were wide, and she was angry and ready to give me some of my own medicine.

"What is going on?" Angela yells at both of us.

"What are you doing here?" I ask embarrassed and annoyed that my neighbor is in my house *again*, and at a time when I need my privacy the most.

"Maddie came and got me," she says, she looks at Eddie rubbing her wrist. "You ok?" She shoots me a death glare.

"No, no, Ange, I am fine," Eddie tried to reassure her.

Angela Mc Dermott looks at me. "Leave," she said quietly. I could see that her usual 'happy go lucky' disposition has left the room, what was left unnerved me.

"What?" I asked.

THE JOURNEY

"Don't let me ask you again. You're upset, she is upset. Leave."

I look at Eddie who is sat in her bed. "Eddie I didn't mean to," I stop myself, as I don't want Angela to get the wrong idea. I look at her, it's too late, she thinks I am a prized shit, and now I feel like one.

"You never do, that's the bloody problem. Ange is right. Go," Eddie screams at me.

I storm out, the girls are downstairs in the kitchen with uncle Niall. He looks at me, "Get your coat mate, you and I are going to the pub."

"One sec," Angela shouts from the top of the stairs. Niall slowly closes his eyes. "Harold, can I speak with you outside for a quick min?" Angela asks sweetly. She was smiling the whole time, that was for the children's benefit. I knew this was not going well. I followed her to the cloakroom situated by the front door.

"Inside, please," she says nicely.

"Look, Angela, I am not sure what this is but"

"Not sure?! Are you sure about that?"

I was about to say something, and raised my hands.

"Shut up," she interrupted my thoughts.

I look at her completely stunned. "What is with you today?"

"With me?! With meeee?! You're the one hitting on your wife."

"I never hit her. It was more of a reflex reaction," I try to explain.

"Do you hear how that sounds?" she yells. "She is your

wife. Treat her like your wife and not some scratch you picked up from the gully. You are screwing your marriage up."

"What do you know about it?" I mumble, as my neighbor chastises me.

"More than you, by the look of it. Stop being this man who over reacts, becomes a bully and a pig. That's not you," she looks at me with concern.

My ego becomes bigger than my rational mind, "I don't need to listen to this." I turn to leave the room. As I grab the handle to open the door, I see a flash in the corner of my right eye. Angela grabs my right arm and pulls me back into the room. I look at her, it's inconceivable that this little woman has the strength of ten men.

"Sit down," she barks.

"If you listen to nothing else, hear me now. Take care of her. Love your family, you just never know when it's going to be gone. She is a rare and precious jewel your wife, so if you hurt her, I will hurt you, Harold. Man up!" she shouts. "This is your only warning."

I try to placate my self-esteem, but it's too late, he rears his ugly head again and tells me that I have had enough of this. My ego, who has no manners, pushes Ange very hard out of the way.

The extraordinary event which occurred after my shove was quite frankly unexpected. What I can only describe next is that Ange was really Bruce Lee's former instructing Kung Fu master. All I remember is that I got to the door handle and attempted to walk out. Bruce Lee's instructor grabs my shirt collar and wrenches me backwards, as I am hurtling back to the floor, she karate chops me in the side of the head with her petite, yet lead like forearm. I am not kidding, the force of that crack makes my bloody head snap back. Not only do I go crashing towards the floor, as I have lost all sensation in my legs. I try and regain all sense of self, but it's no good. As I careen to the floor, I feel her bony knee, with its steel like interior crash into my ribs hard. I hear a crunch, then feel the burning sensation immediately in my left side. I fly, and I mean literally fly backwards and land with a heavy thud on the door. I am winded really bloody badly. I look at this 5 ft. bony Bruce Lee impersonator, and slide down the door, as I negotiate air into my lungs I slump to my knees. My ego who has left the building enables my sensible mind to reconvene as I hold up my hands in surrender.

Angela kneels down in front of me, I am breathing very hard and am sweating, everywhere. Even my balls are sweating. She eyeballs me for a few seconds.

"Harold, I love her. She is so very dear to me and I will do anything to protect her. Now," she says quietly, "get it together. After our little chat, I think we understand one another now. Sweetheart, If you are foolish enough to put your common little hands on me again, I am not going to leave you with the use of your legs. Understand?"

I nod repeatedly. She opened the door, even with my body weight behind it, and stepped over me. Niall was waiting outside the closet. His hands were behind his back, he looked at me crumpled on the floor then to his wife.

"Night, dear," he leans in to kiss her. He looks at me, "It's going to be a long night, darling."

Niall watches me trying to console myself. My left hand is holding my head, and my right hand is clutching my ribs.

"Harold, I think you going to need more than a beer, mate," he says in his thick Irish accent, he cannot help it, he laughs hard. "She kicked your arse mate, and by the looks of you, she did it well."

Chapter 5

Doctor Barrington Barnett

November 24th 1941

My life on days like these is just perfect, the sun is embedded deep into the blue sky, bouldering its heat like a functioning furnace. It's lazy afternoons like these that fill me with excessive joy. It reminds me of home. How I yearn for my southern roots, my people, my mother, father, and older brother Mason, most of all I miss my Black Mammy Viola. Can you believe that she is still alive. She is 76 years old, and I never miss a birthday. She taught me everything I know about life.

If I could turn back time, I would still be in Madison County Mississippi. I look out onto the plantation and see all the field workers picking coffee. The grief of losing my family stills cuts deep. I was young, impulsive, and stupid. Even though I go back, it's not the same. The feeling of loss is a funny thing. The deprivation of one's family, and all that they hold dear, changes a person. That loss shrinks you to become insignificant. It makes you consider the "What ifs?" in life, which is always a dangerous road to travel. It turns a loving man into a hateful one, an honest man into a criminal. A kind man into a mean son of a bitch. When you are in depravity, what little you have you hold on to it, even when it sickens you to the pit of your stomach.

"Hmmmmm," I roll backwards in my rocking chair with my pipe attached to my mouth. I am going to enjoy the haze of the sunshine and good old fashioned Louisiana tobacco. I take the deepest breath that my lungs could muster, the fragrant scent of my plantation, the sweet perfumed smell of the ripe mango, bulging from the fragile bulbs that keeps it in place, transforms the aroma of my yard.

I smile to myself. I may be lonely and alone, but look at all this. I have achieved it all.

I hear the clicking of her heels on the highly polished wooden veranda. My wife, Phyllis, glides around this place giving instructions to the yard boy, about tidying something or the other. I quietly contemplate, as I have on many occasions before, that my wife is sure one beautiful specimen of a woman. Born and raised in New Orleans, a product of two worlds, that is her Spanish father and a mulatto mother. In the United States of America she is described as a "Quadroon". To my white southern family she is a 'nigger". Her pale olive skin and thick black wavy hair to her waist made her a vision to behold, when we first met over twenty seven years ago and now. There is a saying "Beauty is only skin deep," and the longer I am with her, the more I believe this saying. I gave up my distinguished southern family and prestigious life for this woman. I was far too inexperienced to realise it, but I have surrendered to the fact that the worst day of my life was the 24th July 1915, it was this day that I married Phyllis DuBois.

What I know now as a middle aged man is that my wife, as stunning and beautiful as she is, is the most deceitful, manipulative, lying, two faced, cheating whore I have ever had the misfortune of gracing my presence with. I despise the way she walks, talks and even breathes. The very oxygen that I breathe is wasted in her wretched soul. If I could find a way to kill her without this sin staining my soul for all eternity, then, so help me God, I would do it in an instance.

I chuckle to myself, as I would be left with that bastard, which the whole village and districts knows is not my son. My mother always knew that she was no good. "It's nigga blood you can't trust son," she said in her silky southern Madison County of Mississippi drool.

I hear the Chevy screaming up the drive, Barrington, my spoilt jacket, is hitting the horn like a drunken fool.

"Barrington!" I hear Phyllis shriek.

"What now woman," I shout back, jolted out of my own thoughts. "I swear, if he's drunk again, I will take that car away from him."

I mutter under my breath, "Spoilt selfish SOB." I make my way to the south of the veranda reluctantly. I better go and see what he has done this time.

As I get to the veranda, I see Phyllis running to the stalled Chevy. The thought of my wife running makes me smile. The field hands run over to the car and stop dead. Something is wrong. Why are they stopping, is he dead? *If only the Lord would grant me that one wish. I smile to myself, insisting that I behave.* Why won't they help him? Phyllis is dumb struck by something. She appears dazed by the contents of the car, as I get closer I see that he is not alone, but can't quite make out what or who it is.

"What have you done? What have you done?" Phyllis screams.

THE JOURNEY

A knot the size of Alabama starts to form in my gut. I start to sprint and say a prayer, whatever it is, I know is not good as my usually placid field hands are getting het up.

"Miss Phyllis," one of the field hands punches the air. He repeatedly points to the back of the car accusingly. "That's Miss Lucy's granddaughter, why is the little girl bleeding?"

Another field hand pushes his head in the car, "You hurt Winnie?"

As news spread amongst the field hands, Phyllis sensed anger starting to rise, "Where is Miss Lucy, they start to shout?"

Phyllis calmly walked to the passenger side and pulled Barrington with all her might out of the driver seat, she needed to get him to the house quickly.

The same insistent field hand pushed his way through the crowd in the car, he tenderly rubbed Winnie's knee, she recognised Rex from church, "Where's Mama, baby?"

Lucy let go her face and blood sprouted out of her nose like a fountain. Startled, Rex jumped back, hitting his head on the back of the passenger chair.

"Baby love," he wailed, pushing his hand in her face. As the blood seeped through his fingers, he felt himself weaken with emotion.

Winnie looked at her limp father's body in the passenger seat. "He did it. He did it. He did it," she screwed her eyes shut as if remembering a horrible memory. She pushed Rex away and held her nose, she leaned her head back to stem the flow of her blood with little success.

Transfixed on the young child in the rear view mirror, Phyllis put the car into drive. She looked at her son and wondered, *"Am I to blame for all of this?"* *Blinking back the tears she wished that she had kept quiet about Winnie. Oh, Barrington, what have you done this time?*

I cannot see my wife as there is a lot of people crowding the car. Phyllis is driving towards me, momentarily annoyed, I stop my sprint towards them and run back to the house, my field hands are in hot pursuit. *Whatever has happened, this is not good. My wife's haste to get out of the car motions me to my professional demeanor.* I look in the car and see a blood soaked Barrington Junior. I run to the car as she stopped in front of the house. "What happened?" I enquire curtly. For a split second I am concerned for him.

"Not sure," Phyllis said quickly, I look in the back of the car, and my heart sank, it cannot be. In the back, whimpering and terrified, is Lucy and Vincent's granddaughter covered in blood. My pulse quickens, and the heat within my body is rising out of control. I look at Phyllis with cold steely eyes and she immediately throws her eyes to the floor. "If you have had anything to do with this, I will deal with you, so help me, you will holler for mercy."

Phyllis steps back, eyes averted everywhere, anywhere, but mine. I have my answer.

I forget Barrington and immediately open the back door. "Hello, Sweetie. My name is Doctor Barnett, and I am going to help you," I stretch out my hand, but this poor child is petrified.

"Come on, darling. It's ok. You're safe." I glance over to Barrington, who has lost a lot of blood, I don't care about him, he is not my concern right now. This little girl, by the looks of it, had been to the gates of hell, and once again that boy is responsible for another human being's suffering. Rex is sat with her, arms around her. He looks

THE JOURNEY

at me like I am the enemy.

"Rex get out the car, I've got this," I say, trying not to break down.

My loyal field hand of over twenty some years looks at me with an expression I have never seen before. It's hate.

"Rex," I raise my voice. "She needs attention, so get out the car or move along." He holds Winnie's hand and pats it gently, eyes transfixed on Barrington, he opens the car door and steps out.

Winnie is in shock, and unsure who to trust, she just stares at me, willing me to be kind to her. Her nose is broken, I can tell that without even getting close, her eyes are closing, she must be in agony. I am astounded that she is not making a sound.

"Winnie, darlin', do your legs hurt," I enquire.

She shook her head no.

"Your arms, back, tummy?"

Again Winnie shook her head no.

"Ok. Just you head, right?"

A slow nod yes, cautiously eyeing up this stranger. I take my time and lean in slowly, I gently pull her close to me, and I carefully pick her up. I carry this broken little girl into my house. I see and feel the crowd forming around me.

"Winnie, Winnie, Doc, Sir, is she ok? Why is she bleeding like that? Where is Lucy?"

She sinks her pure body in mine, and I carry her and cradle her at the same time. I head straight for my study and lay her on my patient bed. As I turn to look at her, my heart leaps out of my chest. She looked like my wife. She is beautiful now and will grow up to be a real treat. I walk at pace to my medicine cabinet behind the bed and pick up a huge pair of scissors. Her little girl's eyes grew round like saucers. She just stares at me.

"It's ok, darlin', I am going to cut your dress off. I need to see if anything is broken when I examine you. Is that ok?"

Again, she just looked at me like I was an ogre. Winnie held her nose together like her life depended on it. I stroke her blood soaked cheek and remove strands of hair, which disobediently lay across her face. "Does it hurt to talk? Blink once for yes and twice for no? Ok?"

With that, Winnie blinked once.

"Is your nose where all the pain is?"

Winnie blinked twice.

I wipe her face with a damp cloth and notice that her eye was swollen, and her perfectly pert princess shaped lips were split down the middle. "Your mouth, does that hurt as well?" I asked gently touching her mouth. I thread my fingers in her mouth under her bottom lip and pull it down, the raw gum flesh freshly disturbed, was bloody for all to see. I clench my jaws to assist my facial expression, I could not help it, I was finding it hard to control myself.

Winnie blinked once.

As I cut off her dress and see her brushed body I go cold. I put the thickest towel I could find to cover her, then I find another and wrap her in it. She is just a child. I notice that she is trembling beneath my touch, and it wasn't cold in the slightest, she was terrified and in shock.

THE JOURNEY

What has he done to you? I start to think dreadful things, that even I do not believe is possible, but we are talking about Barrington. I am yearning to hug her and reassure this young child, but thought better of it. Carefully, I release one limb at a time and gently wiped her clean.

I leave her face until last as I know she will scream from the pain. She looks me dead straight in the eyes. I say nothing to her, she blinks once and reluctantly lets go of her nose. The gushing, warm, red stream keeps flowing, with more force than before. I pushed my forefingers on the bone, she whimpers, tears stream out of her eyes, she does not move or squirm, she stays still and continues to look at me.

"Oh Darlin', I know it hurts, but I am gonna make it ok. I am gonna make your nose better," I hold her delicate nose between my fingers and pushed the cracked bones together as hard he could. Her bones crunched beneath me. Not a sound from this little girl. Astonishing! She just screwed her eyes shut and started to shake. She was in pain and would not or could not make a sound, I wasn't sure which. I could feel my indignation hemorrhage out of me. *Keep cool, son. Keep cool, he will keep, they will keep.* I head once again to the medicine counter, took out a needle and prepared it, and I gave that poor child a generous shot of morphine.

With her face all cleaned up and her right eye closed, her left eye was straining for sight. She needed to see me. I wanted to cry for her. She was just a small defenseless child. I give her the shot, to her thigh, again nothing. My voice cracks, "This will take the pain away, sweetie. Can you hear me?" she nods and whimpers.

The door flung open and Mackie, my son's minder and confidant, stood there with his wife in tow.

Mackie knew he needed to tread carefully, "Sir, is Winnie alright?"

"It's Miss Winnie, and who wants to know?" I wash my hands in my basin without looking at Mackie. I cannot face his glare or his pity.

Both Mackie and his wife took another hesitant step together, looked at one another, "We do," they both said in unison.

"Dr Barnett?" Miss Mack asked quietly. "Please sir."

"So you know her?"

"Yeeeeees," she wailed.

Mackie looked at me hard. "Sir, there are many angry people congregating at the house sir. The field hands, they think Winnie is dead, please, can I tell them something?"

"You tell them to mind their own business?" I say quietly.

"Sir," Mrs Mack chimed in. "Lucy and Vincent are our business. Do not forget that Vincent was born and raised on this plantation. Lucy and Winnie are a part of his legacy. If we tell them that, there will be trouble tonight and not just for you."

I look at the floor, the truth is that I was too embarrassed to speak to the crowd or even look at them. I dry my hands and walk to Mackie, I look him in the eye, he sees that I am cut up, he feels my shame. "Ok, I will be out soon."

"Sir," Mackie pressed forward. "Is Winnie ok?"

"She has a broken nose, and she has lost a couple of teeth," I mumble. "I have given her some morphine for the pain".

Crest fallen and visibly disgusted, Mackie squeezed his wife's hand.

THE JOURNEY

"And Lucy?" he says, with a force in his voice and renewed strength, that not even I have heard before.

"Lucy? What about her?" I ask indignantly.

"Sir, is it true what they are saying outside?"

"What are they saying?" I ask, but not wanting to know the answer.

"Rex's son ran to the plantation, she's dead. Barrington murdered Lucy," Mackie said, as much as he trying to control his grief, he couldn't and started to openly cry.

I looked at Mackie and walk less than an inch away from his face. "Repeat that Mackie," I whisper, all the blood drained from my face.

"They are saying that Barrington murdered Lucy," Mrs Mack chimed in, holding her husband's shoulders, trying to keep him upright.

Tears ricochet off my face, I stand there in disbelief, the room started to move. I looked at this broken child in my house, she nods her head as if confirming the truth.

The door swung open and before me was my wife, impatient and annoyed at the delay I was taking to give her son, my bastard, medical attention.

"Are you coming anytime soon to tend to his wounds?" she scolded. She looks at me and can see from my face that I know. "I'll … I'll come back," she tried to retreat.

"Is she dead Phyllis?" I bark at her. My tone is different, it steely and filled with hate.

"Who?" Phyllis asked, knowing full well who I was referring to.

I walk sturdily towards my wife, with every intention to knock her head off her shoulders, Mackie steps in front of me and restrains me. "Do not test me, Phyllis?" She takes a step back and realises that the rules of engagement have changed.

"Yes, I believe there was an altercation, and she shot him, and he responded," Phyllis added quickly, but refusing to match my gaze. The silence between us is deafening.

I push past Mackie and grabbed her like a common tramp and threw her to the chair. Her perfect bun roused to the top of her head toppled like a pack of cards. "If I find that you had a hand in this," I point violently at Winnie, "I will *break* your neck."

Phyllis was paralysed by her husband aggression towards her. She stood up, fixed her hair and asked, "Will you tend to your son? He needs your help," she quietly pleaded.

"He is no son of mine," I scream loud enough that the whole plantation house stood still. "Mrs. Mack, stay with the child, find her some clothes and feed her some soup in an hour. She may throw it up, but persist every hour until I say stop. Is that clear?"

"Yes, Sir, Doctor Barnett." Mrs. Mack was still in shock by my violent display to his wife. I knew all too well that my wife was a rose with many thorns, pretty but vindictive, and she could strike out at anyone at any time. This was a side that she had never seen of the me, and I could read her thoughts that she would not want to be on the receiving end of this side of me again.

"Mackie," I shouted.

Mackie was still starring at Phyllis, bewildered by what he had just seen. "Mackie!" I scolded.

"Yes, sir."

THE JOURNEY

"Get the car, we will go to the plantation now."

"What about Barrington?" Phyllis objected.

"That son of a bitch can bleed to death if what they say is true," with that, I stormed out the room. She followed me trying to protest, listening to her footsteps clip clopping behind me in a hurry. As I he got to the door, I turned back and leant into her. I could not help it, something snapped inside of me, I carefully, but forcefully placed my right hand around her throat. "If I hear that you have uttered a word to upset that little girl, or harm a hair on her head in any way, I will beat you like the wild dog that you are, do you understand me?"

Phyllis flushed scarlet, and nodded her head immediately. Mrs. Mack could not stop starring. Once Phyllis left the room, Mrs. Mack jumped in the air, and clapped her hands, "Thank you Jesus, he has a spine!"

As Mackie and I approached the veranda, there were over 60 workers and members of the community standing at the front of the main house.

"What did the young master do to Miss Lucy, Sir?" Rex asked visibly upset and angry. Rex and Vincent had grown up on the plantations; Rex was Vincent's best man at his wedding and was still very close to Lucy and Winnie. Such was his commitment to his friend's memory, that he and his other field workers would often go to Miss Lucy's plantation after church and tend to any matter that was outstanding. Miss Lucy would always cook up a storm, she was a real gem.

"Rex, I don't know for sure, I have just been told that there is a possibility that she has been killed. I don't know the details, but I am very sorry for your loss if this is the case."

"Sorry for our loss," somebody else chimed in, I could not identify who.

"Man, shove it up your backside. This is just wicked. Wicked, I say. They won't arrest him. Why? He and his murderous, rapist, drunken son is above the law. We don't matter. We are not white enough to matter," the man shouted angrily. Many voices agreed with him.

"What about Winnie's loss?" Rex shouted. "It's bad enough that Vincent is dead, and the child's mother is gone. So what, you decided to allow your son to finish Lucy off as well?"

"There is not a day that goes by that I do not regret what happened to Vincent. Today, I don't know what today is about. I'm sorry, it's been an upsetting day for us all. I am sure that you understand, I need to get to the bottom of things."

Mackie pulled up to the house and the motor was running. Doctor Barnett slowly walked through his angry mob and got in.

"You know where, Mackie. And quickly," he said, his voice shaking.

Mackie drove like a mad man, Lucy and Vincent had been like family to his people. In the big storm in 1929, most of the village had sheltered in the big house. No-one, and I mean no one was left to weather that storm alone. It had taken Mackie's family nearly three months to get back on their feet and rebuild their homes. It was not a problem. Lucy and Vincent had welcomed them, fed everyone and made sure all the children had clothes and shoes. They were good people, God fearing, kind hearted, and blessed. They had not deserved what had happened to them. None of them.

"You're quiet," I say to Mackie.

"There is nothing for me to sing about, if what they say is true. Lucy was ... is ... she is a good woman. I am praying that Winnie got it wrong, and Barrington just wounded her," Mackie whispered.

As they approached the driveway, Mackie's fears were indeed confirmed. Rene, Lucy's best friend and adopted sister from childhood, and her mother were being consoled by Mavis, the elder sister. Everyone was crying. It was dusk, the moon was shining brightly in the sky, and it seemed eclipsed around a million shiny stars. Through the cane fields, shadows of mourners emerged, head bowed, walking towards the plantation. I recognised some of the figures, many of them worked for me. They were good people and had lost a great friend and pillar of the community.

The realisation of what had occurred hit me.

"Oh Mackie, my heart is heavy," I wipe the tears from my face and reluctantly drag myself out of the car. Walking towards the veranda, I felt the weight of the world on my shoulders. Not only was I ashamed to the core and deeply sorry for Rene's loss, but I also felt somehow responsible.

I glimpse Rene and quickly look at the floor. I can deal with anyone tonight, but not her. She was the love of my life. Over the years, she had regained my faith in women, and I cherished her with all my heart, how can I reach out and tell her that I am sorry.

She watches me get out of the car. Her big, beautiful eyes were swelled deep with water. If I could just hold her and tell her that it's all going to be ok. This time, I cannot, I dare not. I am going to have to face her sometime, it might as well be now.

She jumps off her chair and is walking briskly towards me, I know she is going to slap me.

The love of my life screams at me and slaps and punches me over and over again. I just need to stand here. Of course she blames me, they all do. As far as they are all concerned, my family has ruined Winnie's life and they are right.

"Why, Barry? Whhhhhhhyyyyyyyyyyyyyyy???", she wailed. "Look at what you have done! You must be very proud."

She goes on with her assault on me, "Where is she? With that witch, where is she?" she screams at me.

I stand there motionless, willing her to continue battering me. I need to feel, as I am numb. Giant tears roll down my face, like two crooked streams, leaving streak marks where the orange dust had settled.

"Rene," I plead quietly, trying to reason with her.

"Where is my niece?" she screamed, grabbing my lapels and shaking me hard. I just stand there and avert my gaze. Once again, the floor and my eyes meet. I cannot provide words of comfort.

"Please, Rene," I gently unhook her fingers from my lapels. I look deep into her eyes, I whisper, "I am so very sorry for your loss," I pull her close, and she collapses in my arms. "Oh, my darling, I am so very sorry. Believe me, I did not know he had found out. I would have killed him myself if I knew this would have happened. Darling, believe me."

Mavis prized Rene off me, I gave her a look that said: "Thank you".

The house was how I remembered it. That smell, oh, it took me back to happier times, Vincent, Lucy, Rene, and me. That smell of citrus hangs in the air and radiates the downstairs. This aroma is hitting all the right senses. I strolled slowly through the hallway, that's when I see her feet sticking out over a white sheet that someone had covered her with.

THE JOURNEY

Intoxicated by the moment, I am starting to feel like I am losing control. My body temperature has soared. This is not happening I try to convince myself, it's a very bad dream. I close my eyes shut, trying to deny the corpse in front of me. It's no use, I open my eyes in the hope that this is a mistake. Lucy is still there.

Gently treading on her floor, I walk towards my friend, and I slowly kneel by her. I hold her hand and mutter a prayer. I pull back the sheet, knowing it's going to be bad.

"I just cannot believe it," I say out loud. I am bewildered by the trail of destruction Barrington had created again. More tears make my crooked stream, oh my, there are six bullets holes here. Two in her head and four in the body.

My body starts to shake, I cannot contain this wave within me. I weep openly on my friend's corpse, repeating the words: "I am so sorry. Please forgive me, I am sorry."

The bustling room is now silent. I feel very aware that there is no movement around me. All eyes are on me. I attempt to gain my composure, as I know that I am very vulnerable in this situation and emotions are running high.

Rene stood at the door. Her eyes were venomous, I have never seen her like this before. "Sorry does not undo all of this though, does it?" she spat the words out at me.

My inner spirit tells me that I need to leave. I stand up, only to be met by a right hook to the nose. I am momentarily stunned. I look at my assailant, it's Rene. I shrink back, she punched me square in the face. I look at Rene, my love, she does not mean to hurt me, her heart has been ripped out of her chest, this is her grief. I did not move, she lunges towards me for a second time.

I will not defend myself, I just stand there numb, she rips at my face wild with mania, both of her hands in the claw like clasp. She dragged every nail she had deep in my flesh, I will not move, I cannot move. I am paralyzed, this is not happening to me.

Mackie pulled Rene off me with such force, she crashes into the wall. He pushed me hard to get out of myself, I look at him, not realizing that my face is bleeding. Both of us swiftly retreat through the back door.

"You ok, Doc?" Mackie asked with genuine concern, as we jump in the car and drive off at pace.

"Stop at the undertaker's office on the way home," is all I can muster to say.

Mackie nods at me. I look out the window. My heart broken, feeling the weight of my grief, I pray for Lucy and her soul. Trying without success to contain his own emotions, Mackie is sporadically wiping the tears from his eyes.

"You seemed very familiar with the house," Mackie enquired, breaking the solitude of my grief.

I was breathing deeply while wiping the blood from my face and trying to regulate my heartbeat, looking into nothingness out of the window. "I used to go there after my rounds, back in the good old days, after the hurricane. Many of my patients were there, especially the injured ones. Vincent and Lucy made me feel very welcome. We used to eat bun and cheese in the kitchen, with hot freshly made chocolate tea."

Mackie smiled, "Boy, Miss Lucy could bake and made the sweetest tea."

My crooked streams began to run rapidly in quick succession. "This is not the life I wanted for me or my son. This is not how people live. This is not how civilised people behave."

"Amen to that," Mackie said. After a long pause, "We, Mrs. Mack and I, will be moving on soon."

"Because of this?" I knew the answer to the question, but needed to ask it.

"Yes, sir," Mackie was aggrieved that I had to ask. The irritation rang out of his tone.

"We may not have much, but we have pride, loyalty, and love. As much as I love Barrington, I am not proud of who he is and what he represents. I cannot watch him treat my friends and family like they are nothing. Like we mean nothing. Vincent is dead because your son took something sacred from his child," Mackie was looking at me, dead in the eye.

"Mackie, please believe me when I tell you that I need you."

"Sir, I cannot control Barrington and I.."

"Not for Barrington. For that little girl. She is going to need protection in that house. Please, if not for me, for Lucy and Vincent."

Mackie screeched the car to a halt, and stared at his employer. The silence was deafening.

"For Lucy and Vincent. If your son crosses the line with me or my wife, I will bust his back wide open, so help me God. If that means that my actions will cause problems between you and I, so be it. I will not end up like Vincent, Sir. One of us will die, and, on Vincent's and Lucy's memory, it will not be me."

"I understand," I say quietly.

"I am grateful that you do, Sir, as this right here," he points to his puffed up chest, "is no joke business."

Mackie drove to the undertakers and waited what seemed like an eternity. The arrangements were made and I was physically tired, emotionally tired, and battered. I dragged my body back to the car. Rene really did rip my face to pieces, my wounds were still weeping.

"Mackie."

"Yes, Sir."

"Take me to the nearest rum bar, please."

"That is not a good idea. There will be many friends of Lucy and Vincent out tonight doing the same thing, drowning their sorrows and dealing with their loss. I cannot guarantee your safety."

I look at Mackie for a while, my eyes filled with tears, and I whispered reluctantly, "home *then?*

■■

Phyllis was waiting for me on the veranda when I returned home. She had changed and was in her white satin night dress and matching dressing gown, her hair tucked behind her ears, flowing down past her shoulders, she was a vision of beauty even now.

"Will you be alright, Sir", Mackie asked, looking towards the veranda.

THE JOURNEY

"I will, thank you for your concern." With that, I reluctantly opened the car door and made my way to the house.

"Where have you been?" Phyllis scolded me. *I cannot deal with this wretched woman. Just keep walking Barry, I ordered himself.*

Phyllis was not one for rejection on any level. I could see that she was agitated and saw through the corner of my eye that she followed me through the door. She grabbed my arm and spun me around with such force, I nearly lost my balance.

"I said where were you?" she screamed at the top of her voice, a few members of the kitchen staff popped their head through the door.

"Do not touch me," I yelled back, and, without thinking, I pushed her off me. I just could not bear her touching me. She looked startled. To avoid a confrontation, I walked up the stairs. Mindful of my wife's presence following me, I was desperate for a bath and glass of brandy.

Once inside my bedroom, I started to remove my jacket. *I will be sure to have these clothes burned. I do not want anything to remind me of this day.*

"Barrington," her tone had softened, realizing that she would get nowhere speaking to me in that previous fashion. "Your son needs medical attention, the district nurse and I have done what we can, but we are not doctors," she pleaded.

Barrington stared blankly at his wife. "Please, Barrington," she held her head to the floor, "He's hurt, and he needs you. He needs his father."

"Then maybe you should send him a telegram," I snarled. *How dare she try and use 'he needs his father line on me?' It's such bad taste.*

"You have raised him as your own son, Barrington," Phyllis cried.

"Well darling', that sure as hell does not make him mine, does it!"

"He needs you. I know he's a little out control, but he needs you. Please," she could not contain herself, which was unusual for her. She sat down and started to cry. This was momentous for Phyllis, as she never showed emotion. Ever.

"Stop that sniveling. He is injured because of his own blinded aggression and stupidities. I only wish...."

"What?" Phyllis snapped. "What?" she screamed.

"That it was him in the mortuary and not Lucy. That poor woman has endured enough torment at the hands of this family. At the hands of him," I yell. In need of long awaited drink, I walk across the room to pour myself a brandy at the bar. When I turn around, I am rooted to the spot; my wife is on her knees.

"Ok, you want me to beg. I am begging, please help him." Phyllis read the look of contempt and disgust on my face.

"Get up," I say quietly. I strode towards the door, doctor's case in hand. The quicker I tend to his wounds, the quicker I can get to my bed and sleep. Walking towards the east wing of his house, to where Barrington Junior resides, I saw Donna, one of my chamber maid. "Fix me a hot bath as soon as possible."

"Yes, Dr Barnett, Sir."

The thought of offering that animal medical attention repulses me. 'I despise him and his mean and violent rages,' I muttered under my breath. Phyllis pushed past me and opened the door. Barrington lay on the bed, he

THE JOURNEY

was pale, and his skin was visibly clammy. The district nurse was sat next to him with a worried expression on her face.

"How long has he been like this?" I asked.

"An hour, maybe two, at most," the nurse whispered, he could barely hear her.

I stand over Barrington and see the young broken frightened child a few doors away. Then I flashback to Lucy's corpse. I squeeze my eyes shut. Within a few seconds of seeing him on the bed, helpless, frightened, and drained of life, I went into professional mode. I washed my hands in the bowl of fresh water by the bed and immediately set about checking Barrington's wounds. The remaining and offending bullet was lodged deep in his abdomen.

A page turns in my head, something sweeps over me. I cannot describe it. I step away from the bed, slowly observing for the first time the man whom I had raised from birth. I am wondering 'Who are you? Why has evil penetrated your soul?'

"I knew it," Phyllis shrieked. "He dying, isn't he?"

I slowly focus on my wife, for a split second I actually felt sorry for her. "It is unfortunate for me that I have to tell you that the injuries that he has sustained are not life threatening. This bullet did not hit the large vessel in the abdomen, that is, the aorta, so he will be fine. We just have to remove it. I was just stood here wondering what my options were."

It took a few seconds for the news to digest and for Phyllis to realize that her son would survive.

"Muuuuuummmmmm," Barrington groaned.

"Yes, my darling, I am here."

"It hurts, mummmm, please get him to help me," he said, looking at me. "Daaaaaaaddddd," his breathing was labored and slow, "I *am* sorry."

"It's not me you should be apologising to. How about your daughter or Lucy?" I screamed.

Barrington was startled by my unpredictability. "*Please*, dad, I can explain."

"Barrington, I have just come from the plantation house. You shot that old woman six times. What exactly are you going to explain?"

Phyllis was visibly taken aback by her husband's revelation.

"She shot after me. I just wanted my daughter. I did not mean to… Then she started saying that … and I lost my temper, I couldn't help it."

"What did she say?" Phyllis enquired.

"She said… She said that you were a whore," looking at his mother, "and that I am a bastard, just like Edwina." Barrington looked hurt and helpless.

Phyllis and I exchanged looks.

"What?" Barrington asked. "What was that look?"

I ignore the question and proceed to my bag, which was situated adjacent to the bed, on the bedroom table.

"Nothing darling," Phyllis tried to sound convincing.

"Liar," Barrington groaned. "I know when you are lying."

"We are just worried about your injuries, that's all."

"Ahhhh, found you," I had retrieved my scalpel and long prongs. He turned around, and Barrington looked visibly scared. "This is going to hurt, so I am going to call a few men to hold you down."

I walked out the door and down the stairs. I opened the front door, there was a few guys still hanging around, not knowing where to go.

"I need two strong men to hold down the good master, while I take out his bullets. After today's events, I promise he will suffer like the son of a bitch deserves to. Who's in?"

Five men immediately jumped up, I allow the first three in my home. I smile as I walk up the stairs.

"Mum, was she telling the truth?" he whined.

"Of course not, darling," Phyllis smiled. "Lucy was an old, bitter, twisted woman, and, at that moment, I am sure she would have said anything to cause trouble." Barrington nodded and smiled at his mother. She always knew how to make him feel better.

Phyllis felt the hairs on her neck stand on edge, she turned around, and I was glaring at her. She could tell by my face that I heard her pathetic excuse. I strode over with haste, my three new pals stand behind me, looking apprehensive.

"Hold him down tight," I instruct them.

"What's going on, Barrington?" Phyllis tried to hide the panic in her voice.

"I am going to remove the bullet, go and get the lamp, so that I have more light." With that, I rewashed my hands and started the process of sterilizing the equipment. As I head towards my patient, he looks at me uneasy. I raise his night shirt and retrieved my scalpel, and smile at him.

"Wait, aren't you not going to put him to sleep first?"

Phyllis asked me with panic in her voice.

"Hold him tight," I shout at my off duty field hands. Barrington looks at me petrified.

"Mum. Dad. No, please, give me something."

"Tell me, Barrington, what did you give Lucy before you shot her six times, or your daughter before you broke her nose and rearranged her face. Hmmmm, Hmmmm?" *I am not sure what has come over me, but I cannot stop myself. I lean into my so called sons face, grab both his ears hard and pull his head towards me, tearing the delicate skin around them*

"Arrrhhhhh. Dad, I'm sorry. Please, I am begging you, give me something," he cries. With disgust written all over me I throw his head hard on the table. My new pals look uneasy.

I picked up my scalpel and expertly opened the wound, in an attempt to expose the bullet. Barrington screamed so loud, the whole house heard him.

"Barrington, please give him some gas, I will run and fetch it," Phyllis pleaded.

"If you move, I will leave this bullet in him and will stand by and watch his wound being infected, with the hope that he will die painfully and slowly."

"Daaaaad." Barrington looked shocked and hurt, "Please, I'm your son."

I looked him square in the eyes. "Well, Barrington, here's the kicker boy. You have my name, but you don't have my blood. You murdered Lucy for telling the truth." Barrington's eyes grew wide with surprise.

"Hold him down hard," I yell. My newly acquired friends smiled at me whilst obeying my instruction. Barrington

THE JOURNEY

tried to wriggle free, but it was no good. I proceeded to shove my 9 inch surgical prongs deep into his abdomen and retrieved the lodged bullet. One field hand looked like he was going to vomit.

"Take deep breaths my boy, the feeling soon passes." I reassure him kindly. As instructed, he coaxes as much air into his nostrils, slowly, still gripping Barrington like his life depended on it. His chilling screams brought the plantation house to a standstill. Unsure of the horrors that were taking place, all maids in service held their breaths.

"There, you will live to destroy another life," I said, as I stitched up his wound. He had passed out from the pain. Once finished, I rinsed my hands thoroughly and walked out.

Once the field hands had released him, they left immediately, they had seen enough. Phyllis on the other hand, tried to console her son, as he came round after fainting during the procedure.

"Let me go," Barrington said faintly, as he was still trying to regulate his breathing. "Lucy was right, you are a whore," he spat the words out to his mother.

Crushed by her son's comments, Phyllis tried to explain. "Get out now," he continued, still wincing in pain. He had a look in his eyes that she had not seen before, it was hatred.

Desperate for some rest, I locked my bedroom door

behind me. My emotions still raw, I need to contemplate today's events and start to grieve in my own space. I take my time undressing myself, not by design, the life within my limbs diminishing by each waking second. I throw my blood soaked clothes on the floor. I look at them and immediately wipe a stray tear from my eye. I cautiously settle myself in the hot bath that Donna had prepared.

Arrrrrrrhhhhhhhhh, just how I like it, I thought. I look in the water, and the atrocity of today's crimes disintegrate within my bath, turning my clear water to a shade of pink. Repulsed by the memory, I take the wash cloth and brush, soap them both up and scrub every inch of my body. Within minutes, I am finished. I did not entertain my usual routine of having a soak and getting the hot water topped up. I wanted to leave that bath water as quickly as I got myself clean. I step out naked, towel free, another first. I walk over to my bureau and mini bar and pour myself a large glass of brandy.

Glass in hand, pajamas bottoms on, I sit on my blue velvet chaise lounge chair. My mother had it especially made for me a decade ago. This was the closest thing to home I owned, and I needed to be sat on it, right now. This chair was strategically placed under my patio window by my mother.

"Oh, Barry, what lovely sunsets you have here?" she drooled. My patio doors were open, the moon was full and seemed closer than I had ever noticed before. The feeling of loneliness overwhelmed me. It was too much to bear. The one person on this whole island that loves me for me, whom I adore and love with my everything, now hates me. I feel just as alone and scared as Winnie does downstairs. Oh, how I wish that I was still under the guidance and protection of my parents. 'How I wish I was there now,' I tell myself out loud. I continue to observe the bright yellow moon, I smile to myself. My face stings in the night air. I delicately touch my wounds and they are seeping a little. Too tired to tend to myself, with fatigue washing over me, I drift off into a deep sleep.

"Barrington! Barrington! Open this door now," Phyllis shrieked, she sounded different as if she was slurring her words. "Barrington, open this door or I swear I will. Just open the door."

Conscious that Edwina may be woken up by this madness, I reluctantly open the door. She was clearly drunk.

"I was wondering when we were going to have a little chat about things," I say dryly. My limbs were screaming for rest, but with everything that I had, I threw my ten foot hand crafted mahogany door open, "Come in, Mrs. Barnett, and join me in a brandy," I say sarcastically.

Phyllis stomped into the room, her silk nightdress clung to her firm body. She looked as if she had been crying. Her hair was slightly disheveled, her red eyes swollen and her cheeks flushed, I could not help myself. "My, my, don't you look like you're in a state of despair, darlin'."

"Shut your mouth," she spits the words out to me. "How could you do that to your own child?"

"We have had this conversation before, and I will not repeat it again," I try to slam the door shut on this topic.

"He's a boy, and you have destroyed him," Phyllis whined.

"Correction my dear, he is a man with the temperament and the conscience of a wild animal. You know as well as I, if he was a local black man, he would be swinging by his neck right now."

"He's just a little excitable, that's all," she tried to defend him weakly.

"Wake up woman. You have created a monster. He is a murderer, rapist and a God forsaken human being. People fear him, he is wretched, wicked, and vile, and he came from your loins. He is *not* my son."

"He is this way because he craves a father's love, your love."

"Do not try and shift the responsibility of his deviant behavior on me. He is the spurn of the devil, and has been that way from the moment that bastard was conceived. He is his father's child. Admit it Phyllis."

Barrington's comments were very sobering, and Phyllis could not contain her anger, her husband had hurt her son, so now she would hurt him.

"I opened my legs to his father because you were not man enough to do the job. I was so desperate for a real feeling, that I would have slept with a field boy first, than open myself up to you again. You are not a man, you're a limp fish." She glared at me with real venom. Her words caught me completely off guard, and I was annoyed that my facial expression betrayed me. This was weakness, and she would go for my jugular, now that she drew first blood.

"Get out of my room, you despicable whore," I snapped. "Lucy had you figured out. Is that why you ordered her murder. I yell at her.

"I may be a whore, at least mines have a use," with that, she grabbed her vagina in a vulgar way. She walked to her husband and grabbed his penis. "This worthless piece of flesh has no use to woman or beast, and in case you are wondering, your beast is your dirty field hand, Rene." She laughed at me. I stare at her, not knowing what to say. I felt humiliated all over again. "I am glad that you are not his real father, he would be

THE JOURNEY

spineless and weak just like you. She cleared her throat and nose, inhaled deeply to the back of her throat and spat all of her green and yellow phlegm into my face. It landed on my nose and chin and ran down my face like gunk.

I blink, and blink, and just stare at this pig of a human being. *'Nooooooo, she did not just do that,' I scream in my head.* The heat rose from my toes. By the time it got half way up my body, I felt my body language and face change. I grab her dressing gown and wipe my face, not once taking my eyes of her. Like a rupturing volcano, the rage within me building up for the last 26 years could not be contained. *How dare she defile and humiliate you this way, I hear the an angry voice in my head shout at me.* My whole household would have heard her, as well as the fields hands as my veranda doors are wide open. I grab both shoulders and throw her with all my might to the floor. She quickly tried to recover but is winded, she had never witnessed the sheer strength of me before. I kept the beast at bay, no more. Watching her trying to recover, made me smile. I marched to the door and locked it. I felt my jaws clenching, my tired limbs had renewed strength. My eyes wide open and my back is straight, she saw me for the first time in her life, and knew she was in trouble.

Phyllis ran to the door behind me. "Open the door," she said weakly, the fear in her voice coming through.

I could not help myself, her time has come. I raised my right fist and punched her hard in the face, she fell backwards into the chaise lounge chair and bounced to the floor, her lip was split and her nose and upper lip immediately started to swell.

"Barrington please, I did not" she screamed.

I grabbed her by the hair before she could finish her sentence and slapped her as hard as I could across her face. She cowered and curled her body up in a ball on the ground. "Noooooooo. Please,"

I feel exhilarated, adrenalin takes over me, as she lay on the floor, I raise my right knee and stamp on her ribs as hard as I could. We both hear her ribs crack, she jolts up, and her body reacted and threw her on her back.

Towering over my wife I feel reborn, "You're nothing. Say it. Say it," she lay curled up on the floor, gasping for breath. "Say it."

I bent down over her, she crawled to the opposite corner of the room, I slowly followed her and grabbed her by her hair, then I slowly drag her to her feet, Phyllis yelps like a dog and looked at the floor, she was shaking, her lip was bleeding, the right side of her cheek was starting to swell, and her ribs were on fire. She is going to pay for everything, and I mean everything. I have lost everything because of her. I took my index finger and lifted her chin, so that she had to look me into my eyes, "Say it," I whisper.

"I am..." she starts to cry, "nothing." I let her go, and she fell to the floor on all fours. I poured myself a large brandy. I feel joyful and happy to be alive. Who would have thought that beating my wife like this would make me feel so good about myself. I smiled at her, she is watching me with suspicion. "You know something Mrs. Barnett I have allowed you to rule this roost for too long. You are my wife, which means you are my property. I should have treated you as such long ago. Your whorish ways has caused me much embarrassment, and I took it like a gentleman. Well, no more." I down my brandy in two gulps and threw the heavy tumbler on the floor. The thick glass connecting the wooden floor made a heavy clunking sound, but it did not break. Phyllis jumped out of her skin. "I forgive you," I tell her.

"What?" she whispers wiping the blood that is trickling down her chin from her split lip.

THE JOURNEY

"I forgive you. For cheating on me, for bearing me a bastard child, humiliating me tonight," now I am smirking at her. Phyllis felt uneasy.

"Barrington, I am sorry. I just want to go to bed, please let me out," she begged.

"Let you out?! No, no, no, no, no, nooooooooo. Phyllis, you have neglected me for far too long," I walk straight up to her and take her by the hand. I pick up my soiled bath towel that was draped over the metal bath, I moistened the corner with my dirty stale bath water and wiped the blood from her face.

"What are you doing?" she asked.

"Cleaning you up and getting you ready," I replied.

She looked at him confused. "It's ok, I can do that when I get to my room," she said nervously.

"You are my wife, so tonight you will lay with me. I desire it." I say it like I am ordering candy. I laugh, then grab her hand and push it on my penis "Let's see if you can find a use for me again," I stare directly at my wife.

Her eyes sprang with tears, "Barrington, no, please, I beg you."

"You are my wife, now get undressed."

She ran to the door, "Please, Barrington," Phyllis screamed. I walked slowly to the door, I couldn't believe how aroused I was. Taking the power back in this relationship is making me feel like a confident man again. I am the King of this plantation once more.

"It's ok, Phyllis. Darlin', look at me. It's going to be alright." She momentarily relaxes. I hold her hand and look at the bed. My arousal is solid and erect, I push myself onto my wife, her back is by the door, she feels him, looks deep in my eyes, and recognizes that I mean business. He was going to punish her. She had taken *her* rage too far. I lovingly kissed her on the lips, I wanted this moment to be pleasant, and she bit me. She was bombarded with a slap to the face, and a punch to the stomach. She lost her breath and was doubled up in pain. I am going to teach her who the boss really is. I picked her up and threw her on my extra-large queen size bed.

"Barrington, nooooo," she shrieked.

I grab the top of her nightdress and ripped it down the middle. "You will fuck me whore. I want the same fuck you gave his father."

She fought hard to no use, she kicked me in the stomach, but it did not perturb me. The adrenalin was racing around my body. I did not feel pain. Not now. Not after Rene hates me. It's all her fault. I ripped open the remainder of her nightdress. Phyllis desperately tried to roll over, in one move I turned her back. My erection was not hearing her, it was resistant to her pleas and cries.

"Please, Barrington... No. Not like this."

Ignoring her, I pull down my pajamas bottoms and I forcibly parted her legs, I opened them so far that I heard her hips crack. She winced with pain and tried to push her legs up, but my weight was too strong for her. *Who is weak now?* In one move, I have placed my body on her, she could not move, and he was inside her.

"No, Barrington ... Nooooooooooooooo. Please stop. Stop. Nooooo," she screamed at the top of her lungs. She started to fight me.

"Enough," I slap her harder than before. She is silenced, she stops fighting, I grab both arms and forced them over her head. All of my upper body weight is on her arms. She is powerless, and I love it. His thrusts were hard, deep and angry. I want to hurt her. I need to hurt her like she has hurt me. I was treating her like she was nothing but a gully whore.

With each grunt I made, she would yelp in pain, begging me to stop. The more she cried and screamed, the more toughened my erection became. She started to relax her legs, as the pain in resisting me was tearing her apart.

I grabbed her hair and pulled her neck to one side, I licked her skin and smiled. The smell of my brandy soaked breath repulsed her. I didn't care. I kissed her, she did not dare refuse me, but she did not respond.

Her slow surrender aroused me more. I pulled her buttocks to the edge of my bed and splayed her legs apart and continued with my aggressive relentless attack from the floor. I no longer needed to hold her hands; instead I just held her hips, ensuring that I had her in the right position to drive myself deep into her. It pleasured me to see her cry in pain. I was not going to have mercy on her until I was done.

As the time came for me to climax, I withdrew my beast, climbed on top of my wife and ejaculated in her face, she squirmed and turned her head to the side. "Whore, I did not give you permission to turn your head." I grabbed both cheeks and forced her mouth open and directed to remainder of my juice down her throat. To shake off the last of my ejaculation, I slapped my penis in her face a couple of times. I look at her and smiled, I climbed off her and immediately sit in my bath; I washed myself quickly and stepped out. Phyllis lay crumpled on my bed. She was silent; she just lay in the foetal position, hugging herself. Guilt free and victorious, I pound my chest. I let out a cry like Jonny Weissmuller in Tarzan. I am king.

"I have really enjoyed our chat tonight Phyllis, maybe you should retire to your own room, hmmmm?"

She nodded; she dare not look at me. She slowly got up and winced with each movement, her ribs and stomach were sore, her head was pounding, her lip split, and her left eye closing. As she tried to put weight on her feet, her vagina and pelvic area ached. They were under attack and on fire.

Like a gentlemen, I aided her off the bed and gave her my dressing gown. She looked at me, and we lock stares.

"Wait here," I walked to my bureau and picked up my wallet and opened it. Fully robed, she walked silently to the door, which I open. As she walked through it, I pressed a piece of paper in her hand, it was one Jamaican dollar. "Thank you for your services Mrs. Barnett."

Multiple tears rolled down her cheeks, Phyllis just stared at her hand, I knew that she wanted to say something to me, but thought better of it. Head bowed, she limped out of my room.

"Night, darling," I half sung and spoke the words to her. I shut and locked the door behind me.

As she walked to the north wing of her house, maids were scurrying away. They clearly had listened to her brutal rape. She did not look up, she just needed to get to the safety of her room. As she opened her door, her chamber maid of twenty three years, Donna, was waiting for her, her own face soaked in tears. She had her Mistress Phyllis bath waiting for her, with piping hot water and Epsom salts in it, the room was filled with steam and aroma. Donna immediately helped her lady to the bath. She tried not to show her disgust at her Lady's bruises, but her face betrayed her. She slowly peeled off her night gown and saw the blood running down her inner thighs. She helped her Mistress sit down in the bath and slowly tried to wash away the evening. Miss Phyllis did not say a word to Donna, she just lay in her

THE JOURNEY

bath silently crying, clutching her one dollar note.

Chapter 6

Winnie's awakening

It has been four days since I witnessed my father kill my grandmother, and I am weak, emotionally, spiritually, physically, and psychologically. The brain is a wonderful and complex organism. I consider at length how impressive mine is, as it deleted until now, all these horrific memories, which has enabled me to live a relatively normal life.

Staying strong for Winnie is my priority, although, she is not speaking to me. I know that she can still hear and see me. It's heart breaking to watch my younger self so frightened and vulnerable. Something died within her that day. The spark from her spirit is gone. She is no longer innocent, just damaged. I lay next to her and kiss her head and tell her that she is beautiful. All she can do is cry silently and whimper.

Mr. and Mrs. Mack have lovingly protected this child. It breaks my heart that I have not remembered any of this. For the past four nights, Mrs. Mack has slept on the lounge chair in her room. She has tended to Winnie's every need and has refused entry to her father and grandmother at the request of Dr. Barnett.

It was late afternoon, and Mrs. Mack had bought in chicken soup for Winnie's lunch. She set it up by the table. She looked at this beautiful little girl, and pity washed over her. She was crestfallen to see Lucy's and Vincent's beautiful young granddaughter battered and bruised like this. Both of her eyes were puffy and swollen, her light skin illustrated the bruise in magnificent technicolor, illuminating the black, blues, purples, and pinks under both swollen eyes, her lips were both inflated, and where the skin had been split, it became dry and sore. Mrs. Mack rubbed Vaseline on it almost hourly to give this little soul some ease. Her nose was tender and her neck inflamed. She did not know what happened to her, but she had a very good idea.

"Baby girl, today you are going to sit at the table and eat your lunch," Mrs. Mack said, trying to sound cheerful and happy.

She delicately picked up Winnie, and placed her at her seat. Winnie's body automatically hunched over and leaned away from Mrs. Mack, it was her upright foetal position. Slowly, she fed her, and for the first time, Winnie allowed her to do so without resistance.

Winnie looked at me, "This is as good as Mima's," she said. She attempted a smile but remembered that her face and lip was sore.

I purposely said nothing. I just smiled, as I did not want to alert Mrs. Mack to my presence.

"That's wonderful, Winnie," Mrs. Mack said smiling. Both Winnie and I looked at each other and smiled weakly.

"Can I get you something else sugar?" Mrs. Mack asked sweetly.

"Some chocolate cake please, and chocolate tea," she whispered.

Mrs. Mack said, "I won't be long," and ran out of the room.

THE JOURNEY

Once she had left, I looked at Winnie. "Honey, how are you? How does your face feel?"

"It still hurts." She looked at the floor. "Is he really my father, Edwina?"

"Yes, Winnie, he is."

"Then why did he kill my Mima?" she whinnied, fresh tears sprang to her eyes, and she whispered, " Did I do something bad?"

"No, Winnie, daddy is just a bad person who is always very angry." I got on my knees, so we were both at eye level. "Listen to me, darling, you are going to have to be careful. I mean it. Do not speak unless spoken to. Always, and I mean always, be nice to him and never ever give him back chat." I look into her terrified, tear soaked eyes.

"Edwina," she whispered, "can I come and live with you, I don't want to stay here. I'll be a good girl I promise."

My heart broke, "Aww, honey, I can't take you."

Tears streamed down her face. "Please, please, take me with you. He is going to hurt me," with that, she started to sob.

I cup my hands around her cheeks, "Listen to me, my sweet darling, you are at the beginning of your little life, and I am at the end. I am going to join Mima very soon and"

"Take me with you, Edwina. Please, take me with you, as I miss Mima and want to see her."

I firmly hold her shoulders and look at my younger self in the eye. "You have to live the middle part of your life and the enjoy it with people that love you. I am going to sit down on a nice chair and talk to Mima in heaven, and you can't come yet."

"Why not?" she pleaded.

"It's not your time."

"Why not, I want to be with Mima."

"It's not your time, you have to stay here. Mrs. Mack and Mackie, they are nice, aren't they?"

Winnie nods.

"They will look after you, and Dr Barnett, he is a good man, he will take care of you. Ok?" Winnie was silent for a long time. "Edwina, can you please do me a favour?"

"What is that?"

"Tell Mima that I miss her, and that I love her," she whispers.

"I promise sweetness, it will be my first conversation with her."

The door opened, both Winnie and Edwina were looking for Mrs. Mack, but knew by the sound of the shoes on the wooden floor. Those footsteps were too heavy for Mrs. Mack slight frame.

It was my father, he looked pale but well, for a man who had been peppered by a shot gun. They shared the same light caramel complexion and the same colour hazel eyes. His face was pretty, rather than handsome, and his dimples in his cheeks tippled every time he smiled or pulled a serious face. His straight hair made it hard to decipher if he had any black in him, but his nose and lips were the only features that were not European in nature. He wore a white short sleeve shirt and blue khaki trousers. His shoes black patent leather, shinier than any shoes Winnie had ever seen.

THE JOURNEY

"Hello Edwina," he said and walked awkwardly towards the bed.

Winnie searched my face, she was frozen.

"It's ok, Winnie," I said. "Say 'Hello, daddy'."

"Edwina, can you not hear me?" He had strolled around the bed.

"Hello dad- dad-dy," Winnie whispered.

Barrington sat at the edge of the bed, Winnie did not notice that he had a package in his hand.

"Daddy has bought you a present," he tells her, and he puts the gift next to him on the bed. He stretched out his hands to pull Winnie close, and she screamed and jumped back. She split her lip again in the process, and it started to bleed.

"It's ok, its ok, I am not going to hurt you." Barrington was surprised and hurt by his daughter's reaction.

Winnie had thrown her back by the headboard and screamed at the top of her voice, everything was throbbing, she could not take any more, "Mrs. Mack, Mrs. Mack!" Every time Barrington tried to get close, Winnie broke out in her petrified scream. It was blood curdling.

Mrs. Mack and Phyllis raced into the room.

Barrington stood up to attention. "I did not do anything to her mother, I swear," Barrington said anxiously. "I swear," he stood back and held up his hands. He could see that his daughter was sweating and had urinated all over herself and on the bed.

"What are you doing here," Mrs. Mack scolded.

"She *is* my daughter," Barrington shouted. "I came to

give her a dress."

"For what?" Mrs. Mack screamed at Barrington, forgetting herself. "Is the dress your apology for killing her grandmother and breaking her nose?" she spat the words out.

Barrington walked towards Mrs. Mack and slapped her so hard across the face, she fell to the floor. He straddled her and slowly undid his belt, Mrs. Mack eyes grew large with fright. She backed her way to the wall. "What are you going to do?"

"Teach you some manners." He lurched forward, and his mother jumped in between the both of them.

Phyllis held her sons chest with all her might. "Barrington, enough, enough, stop! You do not want any more trouble. Please. This is *Mackie's wife!!*" Phyllis pleaded. He heard her, and reluctantly, he stopped and gave Mrs. Mack a blood curdling stare and stormed out of the room. Both Winnie and Mrs. Mack knew that from this moment onwards she was not safe. They had unfinished business to take care of.

Mrs. Mack was breathing heavy by the wall, trembling at the prospect of her first ever beating or worse. Once Barrington was out of the room, Phyllis turned to Mrs. Mack and walked towards her slowly. She was an inch away from her face, "I will only save you once. If you conduct yourself in that way again to the young master, I will take care of you, all by myself." She turned and walked to the door painfully slow, as she approached the door, she turned around, "Clean up that little runt, as I can smell her piss from here."

Phyllis shut the door, and Winnie let out a wail. "Edwina, please take me home, take me to Mima," she screamed hysterically.

Mrs. Mack took Winnie and held her close. "It will be ok,

THE JOURNEY

baby girl, I will not leave you. It will be ok."

Hearing my grandmother's voice again makes the pit of my stomach churn. Memories of my Grandma Phyllis are filtering their way through to me, and I feel nauseous. What kind of people are they? I screw my eyes shut as I already know the answer. My father's blood line is sinful, dishonorable, villainous, and malevolent. No wonder I forgot this part of my life. I look at Winnie with dread. I know, I know what is coming, and there is nothing I can do to stop this. I look at my younger self with despondency and despair. She too is staring at me, as if reading my thoughts, she lays her head on Mrs. Mack shoulder looks me deep into my soul and whispers, "save me". My heart breaks. Mrs. Mack quite naturally presumes she is speaking to her and smothers her own grief. She pulls Winnie away from her and smiles. "I promise I will, baby girl, on Mimas memory, I will."

I feel my body fading, fatigue consumes me. I sit underneath the window and fall into a much needed deep sleep.

P.D Lorde

"Edwina, wake up... Edwina, is that you?" I feel small slight hands rocking me. I slowly open my eyes, and I am somehow on Winnie's bed. Dawn is breaking, the air is fresh, and I smell Ackee and Saltfish, and the smoky scent of the roast breadfruit being prepared for breakfast. I open my eyes, and my younger self is looking at me. She is different, I jump up.

"Winnie, what's happened?" I ask.

"Nothing has happened," she says curtly, she crinkles her lips. She is angry with me.

I look at her, "Why do you look so different?"

My younger self looks down at herself, "Do I?"

I momentarily blink, her bruises have all gone, her hair is longer, freckles are on her nose, it cannot be, she is older. "Winnie, how old are you?"

"Ten," she says, hitting me hard with her words, like a blunt instrument. I stand up and look at her again, distrustful of her own admission. Skeptically, I scan the room and notice the changes. First, there is no Mrs. Mack, second, the room is softer, more girlie. I have

THE JOURNEY

violet drapes and bedding to match. I remember this room now. I walk to my window and pull the curtains back, the plantation is coming to life. The enormity of my wealth is visible, my bedroom is huge. I have my own balcony, as I look out, I see a small table with two chairs. My dresser is white, with a large mirror. In all four corners of the room, there are large chandeliers for the candles. Opposite my bed, towards the door, is a small white bureau and chair, where I complete my studies, as I swing round, I see Winnie staring at me, looking less than pleased.

"Where have you been?" she shouts. She is wearing a white blouse and a purple skirt, she is at school, she looks so cute.

"Winnie, I don't know. The last thing I remember, I went to sleep, and now you're ten. Ten? I don't understand myself. How have you been?"

"You know how I have been, as I am you," Winnie glares at me. "Remember?"

"Winnie, I know that you are mad, but I just can't explain it, as I don't know myself. I am dying, so I do not know how much time I have," I plead.

"You should be dead. You're no use to me here, are you? I mean, I thought that you would stay with me, but you're just like the rest."

"What does that mean?"

She looked at me sadly, "You'll just leave me, and I will be here all alone, with them."

"Darling, I am so sorry, I am not in control of anything anymore. Time has just fast forwarded, and I am now here."

"Soooo you're not with Mima," she smirks at me. It's

unnerving. I am very cynical and have become quite spiteful.

"Not yet, darling," I pause momentarily, this is quite a quantum leap.

I look at my miniature self, "How have you been?"

Winnie shrugs her shoulders and walks to her queen size four poster bed. She lies on her resting place, and I accompany her. I lay on the next pillow, and we face each other like lovers. I feel on tender hooks, anxious to hear her news, but already feeling the dread sweeping over me, preparing myself for whatever comes next.

"You know how I am, you are me, and I am in hell," she tells me.

"No. Noooo. Nooooooo," my body starts betraying me. I feel myself drifting. Winnie sits up, she looks horrified that I am leaving again. I am crying, *noooooooooooooo, not now, she needs me.* I awake to my family all looking at me and Alice wiping my tears. When will this torture end? I want it to end, and now.

-CLICK CLICK CLICK

THE JOURNEY

Chapter 7

Phoebe's surprise

January 13th 2005 4.39 pm

"You ok, dad?" I bounced into mum's room with the coffee, the break had regenerated my spirit in a small way, and I felt upbeat, even though I was already in mourning.

"I am doing ok, and mum has not changed, so I suppose we are alright." With that, he smiled.

"You seem different, dad," I asked, eyeing up my father.

"Phoebe, I have been different for a while now, but you would have not noticed me or that fact," dad said, looking at mum.

"What's that supposed to mean," I snapped. *All he ever wants with me is some sort of conflict. What more does he want? I bought him coffee, that is a real big step for me. What does he want from me?*

"Exactly what I said," Harold exhaled. "You are so angry with everyone, that even the simplest pleasures pass you by."

"Why is that? You made me who I am, dad, and you know it," I scowled at him.

Harold stood up, he was going to walk away, and then recognised the "typical" look in his daughter's face. He slowly sat down and held his wife's hand. Smiling at something that he chose not to share with me, he looked at me, and his expression and emotion changed.

"When you were born, I was the first set of eyes that you saw. Even though it was not PC for men to be with their wives when they gave birth back then, I insisted on being in the delivery room to Matron's complete and utter dissatisfaction. When you came out, you were this screaming banshee, defiant, even angry. You were my activist, did you know that is what I called you for a day, but your mother was having none of it."

"Yes, dad," *he had told me this stupid story a million times, and I am still not interested.* I didn't mean to sound exasperated, but I did.

"Yes, I called you 'Annie Activist', but that didn't sound right, so ended up with PP, that was short for my 'Punchy Protester'. As I held you, you doubled both fists and punched the air. You may not believe me, but I loved you the moment our eyes met, and I promised you then that I would protect you from all harm. It was my job as a father to ensure that you always felt safe." Harold had a proud grin on his face.

"But you didn't, did you?" I snarled.

"I ensured that my children wanted for nothing." Harold looked hurt by the suggestion.

"Love is not buying me dresses, it's listening to me. Like

you said, dad, it was about keeping me safe. I did not feel safe around you, especially after that Christmas. It was as if you blamed us all. We didn't know who was coming home, what mood you were in, and which one of us would receive a slap, punch, or kick. I remember, dad, I remember. I remember when you broke Jon's arm, when he was 8."

"That was an accident, you stupid, malicious child." Dad was indignant.

"I remember when you slapped Maddie so hard, her nose bled for three hours. She was ten. I remember you ripping my nose ring out of my nose and using my head like a ball with the radiator. I remember you, and who you are, and what you did to us. Do you wonder why I hate men? Why I am angry all the time? Why I can't be with a man more than a few weeks? I have real intimacy issues, why Jonathan is with a man? And yes, it's to spite you. Why Maddie is an alcoholic? Do you not wonder?"

"It is not all down to me. You have to take responsibility for the life that you choose to lead," dad snapped. "I cannot be held responsible for all your wrong turns. You are all adults, and yes, we make mistakes, but we cannot be responsible to anyone else apart from ourselves."

"Have you taken responsibility for the lives that you have impacted upon?" I barked.

"Don't you have any happy memories?" he asked, with his tear soaked eyes.

"Yeah, I do, but I just don't think they're enough happy ones, you know," I tell dad quietly

"I hear you," dad said openly crying. "I hear you."

There was a knock at the door, which forced us back to

the present moment.

We both straightened up in our chairs. Dad looks at me and I wipe the tears from my eyes and give him the nod. "Come in," said Dad with complete authority.

Completely taken aback, Dad could not believe his eyes. "Thank you Jesus," he said.

Is it really you? The last time I saw Maddie was six years ago, and she looked terrible then. This woman looked well, she looked like my sister, sober, clean, and well presented.

"Maddie," I squealed, "Look at you, you look great."

Sheepish and nervous, Maddie stepped into the room. "Hi Dad, where is Jonathan?" Maddie always called our brother by his full name. She looked around the room. She did not acknowledge me at all. Her hair was full and her soft curls nestled perfectly on her shoulders. She was dressed head to toe in designer clothes, courtesy of Karen Millen. She had on a navy blue stylish fitted jumper, black leather skirt, high heeled ankle boots and a bold as brass Karen Millen royal red coat. My sister looked on fire!

"He's with Jack, he will be back soon," Dad got up and hugged his daughter. He kissed her hair and whispered, "Welcome *home*, honey, welcome home. You look fantastic. Are you" dad hesitated, "well?" He peered deep in her eyes for the answer. Maddie matched his gaze and nodded with deep affection for our dad.

I couldn't help it, I was hit with a pang of jealousy, that I just could not explain. My father had not embraced me like that, ever.

"Where have you been? We've been trying to get hold of you for days," I enquired.

THE JOURNEY

"Dad, I have been in rehab for the last 90 days, and I only received my personal possessions back this morning. I rushed over here, thinking I was too late," Maddie whispered.

"Why didn't you call," Phoebe snapped.

"Well, that did not take long," Maddie looked directly through me.

"What?"

"For the bitch in you to come out," Maddie's words sliced through me like a samurai sword.

"I just meant..." I clumsily tried to explain.

"I know exactly what you meant. I did not call because I knew that you all had to see me to believe that I am sober, which, I have been for 163 days now. I feel great, energised, scared, and vulnerable, but I am here." Looking at her mother in the bed, Maddie started to tear up, "Dad, how long have we got?"

"Not sure, but it's not long," I said, still no acknowledgement, she was just stayed transfixed on mum. *Maybe it's the emotion of the day. We will catch up later, I am sure of it.*

Maddie pulled up a chair, sat next to her dad and held his hand, "Oh dad, for the record, I did not drink because of you, I drank because I was unable to deal with the heartbreak of ... well, I am a recovering alcoholic and have an addiction. You were not my trigger, never have been." With that statement, Maddie threw me a filthy look.

Suddenly feeling hot, I stood up, it's like that, is it, sister dearest? "I'm going for some fresh air, guys, give you two some space."

"You do that my love," Maddie said sarcastically and pulled her chair closer and put her arms around our father's shoulders.

"Oh Maddie," Dad rested his head on her shoulder, "I am so glad that you're back. I need you. I need my girl, I can't shoulder this alone."

Stomping down the corridor, I could not reconcile my emotions. *Just what did dad mean, "I can't shoulder this alone"? He's not alone, granted, he is not my biggest fan, but I'm here aren't I? I'm even talking to him. I even bought him a coffee. How typical is this? Betty Ford walks in and all is right with the world.* I continue to stomp towards the stairs, and before I knew it, I was outside. I decided to sit in the grassy verge on the bench. I just needed air. I exhale slowly and deliberately, as if I am practicing yoga. My thoughts are all over the place. I need to center myself and gather my thoughts. Life was easier when Maddie was drunk. Sad but true. The truth is, when Maddie is sober, she is on her game and brilliant. Me on the other hand, am not brilliant. She is beautiful, funny, and very intelligent. Me, not so cute, well, maybe a little, not funny, and mildly intelligent. It's all an act, one that I do so well, and Maddie knows it. She was always her authentic self, even when she was drunk, she was real. Me, I am just the fake.

I search my bag for my packet of emergency cigarettes. I just need some nicotine. I get it, it's not PC, now that I am at a hospice, but I need something to get me through the night. I light my cigarette and am about to suck this cancer stick dry when I hear Jack and Jon. I look up, and across the small grass verge, was the car park. They could not see me, as there were thick bushes separating the verge from the car park.

"What have you been telling him?" Jack yells.

"Nothing love, I promise," Jon says, desperately trying to appease his irate lover.

THE JOURNEY

"Then why did he lay into me? Threaten me?" Jack screamed, inching closer to my brother in a manner that starts to really bothers me.

"What?" Jon was stunned.

"Jack, look, darling, I promise I have not said a word. Dad is losing his wife, he is all over the place. Believe me."

Said a word about what? What is going on, and why is Jon acting so passive?

Jack pushed my brother violently on his car, and clasped his jaws with one hand, so tightly, that Jon lips were pushed out, and it appeared he was unable to move them. Jack was saying something to Jon in his ear. His face changed, it was really menacing. I could not hear, but Jon, he looked terrified.

What the hell was happening? I started to feel sick. No, not Jack, he was so nice. I start to think back at all the snidely remarks he has made over the years. I just put it down to his warped sense of humor. My brother was different around him, I thought it was just nerves, you know, being with his family and his gay lover. Then it hit me. My brother was on edge not because of my family, but his nasty, abusive boyfriend.

Jack pulled Jon off the car and threw him to the floor like he was dirt, he jumped in his red sports Audi car and drove off, leaving my brother on the ground.

Once Jack was firmly out of site, I ran through the bushes and scraped my arms and back, even though I had a thick polo neck on, it was no protection to the frost bitten hard branches, but I did not care. "Jon. Jon, are you ok?" I started helping my brother up. He could sense my anger and concern.

Smiling through his pained expression, "Yeah, I'm fine."

He swiftly wiped a tear from his eye and tried to regain composure.

Jonathan looked devastated. I was not sure whether he was upset that I had witnessed his attack, or by the fact that he had just been attacked in a freaking car park. "Phoebe, please don't say a word, it was just a petty argument."

"Well, it looked like a domestic, and not the first one that you've had," I yell accusingly.

"Phoebe," Jon tried to keep his voice low to placate me, "this is just a dispute between two people that love one another, he loves me you know that, this is just stressful for him."

"Love," *I cannot believe what I am hearing*. "What is stressful for him?" I grabbed my brother broad shoulders and tried to shake them with no luck. "For him?" I repeated the question sounding incredulous. "He is not the one whose mother is dying of cancer, how this can be difficult for him I don't know. No wonder Mum couldn't stand him."

"Really?" Jon said genuinely surprised. " Look Phoebes, he's a bit jealous and possessive and likes to be in control, and for once in our relationship, he's not, as I have to be here."

"Jon, you are with your mother who is *dying*. Where else would you be?"

"He just needs reassurance," Jon protested.

"Reassurance of what? Will my foot planted firmly in his backside do it? He needs a right hook hun, maybe two." I try to sound calm and compassionate, but it's not working. "How long, Jon?" I was not in the mood for him to fob me off.

THE JOURNEY

"What?" he tries to play innocent and deflect the question.

"What? Do not play with me. How long has Jack been knocking you around?" *I had raised my voice, but could not help it. I am furious, how could he allow himself to be treated like that.*

Jon looked around the car park to scan who was in ear shot. "Phoebe, you are such a comedian?" and tried to laugh off my suggestion.

"Listen to me, I saw what I saw. You can try and blow me off, but I saw Jack hit you," I hiss furious that my brother, who could most probably take on most Fijian rugby players, is getting beaten and battered by his Spike Milligan look alike boyfriend. If Jon wanted, he could snap his spine like a fish bone.

Jon looked at me, "Don't look at me like this."

"Like what," I snapped.

"Like that. Like that," he points to my face and starts to silently cry. Trying to maintain what little dignity he had left, he looks far away into the sky. "Like I am weak and a pathetic victim. Like I am useless."

I ran to my brother and hugged him, he sobbed for what seemed like an eternity, and in between hiccups, he mumbled, "I'm sorry."

"For what?" I ask.

"For being weak, for allowing him to do this to me. I deserve this," he mumbled with his head down.

I grabbed Jonathan's face, "No John, you don't, and deep down you know that."

Islington High Street has always been my most favorite

place in the world. Even when the grey clouds loomed over it, these streets glistened with a scintillated haze. It must have been the affluence of the area, the large shops, the idiosyncratic alley ways, the kitsch boutique and restaurants, falling out of the narrow lanes onto intrigued tourists, and local residents anaesthetised to the historic marvelous surroundings, foraging through the crowds, trying to get on with their day to day lives. Islington did not smell of London, and on any sunny day, you could have been in Paris or Milan. It's a part of London to be celebrated with its diverse richness, admired for its flagrant opulence and humbled by the legions of thespians, dancers and actors roaming the streets, making their way to the world famous saddlers wells and beyond. It's a place where I felt safe, wanted and at home.

"I love this high street," I tell Jon, gripping his arm to show my support.

"Yeah," Jon muttered dejectedly with his head bowed.

"You ok?" I asked. *Oh God, please be ok, I need you to be ok. What has that bastard done to you?*

"Look, Phoebe, I know what you're trying to do. I am not discussing it. And I am especially not discussing it with you?"

"What is that supposed to mean," I snap, yanking his arm back and physically stopping my macho man brother. I stare at him, full of concern, "Well?" I yell, passersby momentarily break their routine and stare at us.

"No offence, you are a nightmare. You can't hold water if you tried, and this, well, it's a private matter, and I don't want to share it."

I stare at my brother incredulously. "First of all, I can hold water very well. Secondly, and more importantly, when your dick head of a partner physically attacks you in a public car park for all to see, that rubbish is not private, it's very public. For God sake, I am your sister."

"It's none of your business, we just need time to work it out."

"Jon, I saw what I saw, so you can act like the battered wife who pretends that her husband is not beating her, but we," I point to Jon and I, "know different."

"Are you for real, battered wife, is that the best you can do?"

"What?" I stare at my brother. "Are you seriously getting upset over the fact that I have called you a battered wife, like really, Jon? I saw Jack hit you, and you did nothing. I saw him," I pause, "and you did … nothing." I can't help it I look at my brother confused.

We came to a natural stop at the pedestrian crossing. I looked at my brother, who is completely transfixed on my favorite eatery on the High Street Browns. He is deep in thought somewhere far away. I too concentrate on his gaze, and for the first time since we're out, I can feel the cold air on my nose. The mahogany furnishing and fancy Victorian chandeliers are inviting.

"Let's get a coffee," Jon sighs. I smile, grateful that he read my thoughts.

"Ok. Sounds great."

I am so fatigued from the emotion of it all. It has just been too much. First with dad, then Maddie, and now this. What else? I sit twiddling my thumbs. I am nervously observing my brother at the counter. My mind is racing, there are so many questions that I need answers to.

When did the abuse start? How often does this happen?

Why is he still in this relationship? Who else knows? I know that I am going to have to tread carefully.

My mind races bask to Beeches Primary School, when we were kids. Jonathan always looked out for me. I was proud that he was my brother. He always protected me. At the age of eight, when Adrianna Fitz John punched me in the tummy and pushed my face in the muddy puddle, it was Jon who ran across the playground and kicked her as hard as he could in the arm and dragged her off me.

When my first love at thirteen dumped me for my so called mate and broke my heart, it was Jon that waited for him at the bike sheds and gave him a whopping black eye. Even as a teenager, boys thought twice before approaching me, as I was always Big Jon's little sis. What happened to that guy? When did he go from being this mammoth tough guy to such a sniveling wimp? It's not right, none of this is right. I start to feel my skin tingle with anxiety and my mind is racing. I could feel that I couldn't control myself. Try and be sympathetic, say nothing. Hold your tongue, sister dear. How dare he treat my brother that way? Tears swell in my eyes. I am going to make him pay for this. The question is how?

For the first time in a long while, I see my brother. I mean, visibly and emotionally see and read him. He is tired, I cannot decipher whether this is due to mum dying, or whether he is brow beaten, literally, by that maniac of a boyfriend of his. A pang of remorse sweeps through me like an electric shock. I feel the energy race through all corners of my body. As I observe my brother, he is just as vulnerable as I am, and in need of someone to hold him through this time. A large tear escapes from my right eye. I look down and swipe it from my face before it barely catches my cheek. He is at the bar, and I see that our coffee has gone out of the window, and a bottle of Malbec and two glasses are making their way towards me. Jon's face illustrates the picture, he needs

THE JOURNEY

Dutch courage. I know that whatever I am going to hear, I will hate every word of what he is going to tell me.

Chapter 8

Confessions

This is not happening; of all the people to witness my mess, it has to be my undiagnosed bipolar narcissistic sister, who has always had the ability to find drama on a tranquil day out in the country. How could I have let that happen? It was my fault. I shouldn't have made him angry, and now he's lost it, and mouth almighty is here looking at me like I am sodding Tina Turner. Christ, how am I going to explain this, without looking like a complete tosser!

"Well?" Phoebe whispers, her eyes are full of pity and disappointment.

Well? Well? Well what, well mind your own business and get a life, better still find yourself a man, preferably one that does not abuse you. Find yourself someone to occupy that perfectly honed and toned body. Someone to appreciate your precisely filed manicure, pedicure, and fantabulous weave. A man to kiss your sweet heart lips and to love that hard to love exterior, which we all know is an act.

"Jon, what is going on?" she begs.

The cat is out of the bag, so what the hell. If I don't tell her, she will just make it all up, as she always does.

"You know what's going on, you said it yourself, my boyfriend is knocking me about," I say sarcastically. I could not keep it out of my voice. *What is wrong with me? Why am I upset at Phoebe?*

Phoebe looks disgusted by my frankness.

"Duchess, you said that you want the truth, here it is". I play the camp card, trying to shield my shame.

I see her try to temper her annoyance, "How long?"

"How long what?" I scathe. I look the other way, as I just can't face her anymore.

"Jon," she whispers and edges closer to me, she touches my arm, and when I look at her, my defensive armour dissolves. I am visibly touched by her emotion. It was real, there was no agenda, just genuine concern. Her eyes are searching my face, and I hate it. She sees me wince away and pulls my face close to hers. Her

THE JOURNEY

warm tears wet my cheek.

I cup her head in my hands and push us apart. I take her hand, when I look up, she is still crying and searching my face for answers. I sigh, "It started shortly after the Christmas from hell babes."

"Really," she shrieks. Other customers look over. "That long?" she looks visibly shocked. She is right, a day is in the life of Jonathan Mallard, is far too long.

"Shhhhhhh, yes!" I whisper, the embarrassment rushes through me, I blush uncontrollably.

"That's been like years, Jon, decades," she wails, "rea-lllllllly?"

The two women at the next table give me the filthiest look.

Phoebe notices the awkward glances and tempers her tone to a whisper, "Why do you, you know, put up with it? Babes, you could really hurt him if you wanted to, look at the size of you." Her eyes are piercing through me, "How could you? You know..."

"No, I don't know, what?" *what is she accusing me of. This was a bad idea.*

Phoebe held her head down.

"What? Phoebe?" I am starting to get agitated.

She looks at me and can see that I am angry.

"Look at me?" I shout. "Like what?"

The two women look over at Phoebe and ask in an aggressive manner. "Are you alright love?"

"She's fine," I yell back, starring at my sister and visibly showing my annoyance. "Now, if you don't mind, mind you own bloody business," I snap.

They both look at me, wanting to take the matter further, but can see that I am in no mood for rubbish. They mutter under their breath, finish their last swig of wine and leave. On the way out, I wonder if they are reality stars, as they both look super imposed, wearing the latest fashion. Botox up to the hilt with their pretty Frankenstein stares. Their unnatural jet black hair, fake boobs, and high gloss make up represents the glamour model look, or dare I say it, expensive hooker glam, but I could be wrong. I turn back at my sister. "Like what?" I ask in a quieter voice, conscious that I am causing a scene.

"How could you allow him to do this to you?" she whispers, looking anywhere but at me.

The emotion rips through me, my eyes swell and burst their floodgates. "Is that what you think?" I ask in disbelief. "You think that I allowed this? Want this? Deserve this? Enjoy this?" I point to my new swelling above my right eye.

"No Jon," she whispers, regretting the words as they come out. "No. No Jon. It's just that physically you're stronger than Jack. You could easily, you know, kick his him down."

"It's not me, and you know it. I hate violence."

"Screw violence, John, this is self-defense, and you know that." She looked at me irritated and angry. "Why? Why do you stay?" she snaps at me.

"I *love* him," *it sounds pathetic, and I hear myself for the first time. I am a battered husband.*

I put my head in my hands and let out a few sobs, I wipe my eyes, embarrassed that I cannot keep my emotions in check. I discretely scan the room with my puffy blood shot aching eyes. No one is looking, no one cares. I feel the intense gaze of my sister and know that I am going to have to disclose this part of my life once and for all.

I sigh. "Ok babes," the tears roll down my face. "My life is a lie, I am not this confident, strong man. I am weak, battered, tired, and lonely. I have not felt great about my relationship for the past 15 years. It's just so awful," I whisper, "I mean, just awful." I sniff. "Do you know I can live with the physical abuse?" *I register the look of disdain she throws at me.* "No, Phoebe, I can. I can, it's the verbal and physiological stuff that is harder to recover from.

"What do you mean?" her eyes are filled with pity and sorrow, she squeezes my hand.

"He is a terrorist, when I step out of line, he punishes me," I throw my head in my hands.

"Huh?" Her expression turns to rage.

This is the first time in twenty years that I have opened up. For the first time in twenty years I say the words out loud, and listening to myself offends me.

"What, like a child? What do you mean?" Phoebe looks at me in annoyance, I am not sure if it's at me or what I am telling her.

"If I do anything that offends him, he will either attack me, sometimes he even takes my allowance away," I chuckle, but can see that she does not find this funny.

She cuts me off abruptly, "Wait, what do you mean? What allowance?"

"Our wages go into a joint account, but Jack controls the account, he checks all my transactions online every day. If I take out ten pounds, he wants to know where I spent the money. I can't do anything without his approval. He buys my clothes, tells me how to cut my hair, what food to cook, even down to the underwear that I wear." My eyes automatically connect with the floor.

I was surprised at the ease that I disclosed my hideous life to my sister. Just seeing her face and listening to me made me realise that I was in a living hell.

"What happens if you disobey him Jon? I mean, how bad has he hurt you?" *Wow, she is really concerned.*

"He has really hurt me in the past, babes." Yet another tear breaks free as I say the words.

"How bad, Jon?"

"What does it matter?" I whisper, my eyes find the floor for solace.

"You're my brother, of course it matters," she snapped angrily. "What happened to you? She let go of my arm and distanced herself from me. Her spine straightened and she tilted her head at me. *I knew what this meant. The ice queen is back.* "You were such a hard nut at school, how can my brother be reduced to this?" She waved her arm at me, like I was a plate soiled mussels from her favorite restaurant 'The Pont de la Tour'. The disgust in her voice was recognizable and cutting.

"What?" I ask, wounded. *I cannot believe that she is being like this.*

"Look at you, you're pathetic. This is just utter bollocks. Are you telling me how your sick looking fragile boyfriend beats the living crap into and degrades you at his leisure? And you do nothing about it, nothing to defend yourself. You sound like a ... like a..."

"What? Phoebe what? Tell me?" another disobedient tear sashes down my cheek.

THE JOURNEY

The real Phoebe emerges like a phoenix, ready to cast what little self-respect that I have left under the bus. Her eyes narrow, she sucks in her breath and stares me square in the eye. She spits her words out like an ex con in the prison yard, "Like a pathetic snivelling bitch. You disgust me. You could have defended yourself, but instead you've chosen to take this crap."

Aghast I stare at my sister, all I could do is blink in her words. "You don't mean that?" I whimper. *The last of my confidence shatters into a million pieces.* Each word delivered with its poisonous venom was like being attacked around the heels by an angry cobra. Her words are in repeat in my head. *You are a pathetic sniveling bitch. You are a pathetic sniveling bitch. You are a pathetic sniveling bitch.* This feeling sweeping across my spirit takes me back to my childhood. She is my little acid tongue sister, who always pulls me in and strikes straight for my heart in battle. I am that powerless eleven year old, who is different, vulnerable, frightened, and homosexual. I am weak, I feel weak, I am useless, I feel worthless and I am nothing. Once again, my family is right, there is no point to me. *I am pathetic.*

"Thank you for your support as always Phoebe," she rolls her eyes and I walk out of Browns. This time my tears are on free flow, and no one or nothing can stop them. My wound is open, and it's critical.

Chapter 9

Maddie is Home

January 13th 2005 7.09 pm

"Father God, help me to stay safe from harm. Keep me strong during this time, as I need to be strong for mum and dad. Purge my impulses away and curb what I say and do. I have been hiding through the darkness not realising that my family is my truth and the light. I need to deal with my demons. I have to confront me fears, make my peace and hold my enemies to account. With you, I am strong, do not let evil enter my life again. I have committed to you my life and will make it better for all people who are suffering without a voice.

I have wasted so much time, and, as a result, I have lost so much, but I am back now to say my goodbyes. I have to make things right with mum and dad. I know that they are disappointed in me. I am now on your path, and the change in me has been a miracle.

Father God, I ask that you welcome my mother with open arms and take her to your bosom. I know that you will look after her, and she will like you to watch over us. Give us all strength to deal with the loss to come. In particular, give my father strength to carry on. I promise you that I will help and protect him, love and nurture him through this time".

"I didn't know you became religious," dad asked, embarrassed to intrude with my time with God.

"Oh, my gosh, daddy, you frightened me," I said, with a start.

"I am sorry, love," dad looks so apologetic.

"No sweat pops, I'm good," I say. I smile. My father looks so old and unkempt, which is totally not his thing. In fact, you can tell that mum is unwell. She would have read him the riot act. I look at my dad, he seems so sad,

THE JOURNEY

so very alone and scared.

"You ok, dad," I ask.

"I am trying to take this thing minute by minute, it's so bloody painful, though. By far, this is the most humbling experience I have been in. I still cannot believe that she is leaving me. That is the hardest part. I feel that she is ready, but she was waiting to sort out some things first."

"Like what dad?"

"I'm not sure," he laughs out loud. "Maybe I am just talking rubbish, you know me," with that, dad walked from the door and sat down next to me. He leans over, strokes her hair and kisses her forehead. I watch him intently and can see the awkwardness all over him. I cannot remember a time when he kissed her face or held any part of mum's anatomy. Mine were not the parents to show affection to one another. They were warriors, soldiers at war, if they were not fighting one another, they were fighting the world. It was never easy growing up in our house, but despite everything, there was a sense of love and home. They may not have expressed this, but as I have grown older, I have appreciated that what we have as a family is not broken or fragmented. We all have our demons, we all have our drama, and we may even from time to time have wars. What we believe that divides us does not divide us at all. At the end of it all, we are still family. My father had his issues with depression, which made him respond to us the only way he knew how. I did not feel neglected or abused, just different at school. Being an addict opens you up to a world that you believe only exists in the movies. It shows you how wretched humanity can be. How thoughtless and loveless we are, and the depths of the gutter to which you can sink, believe me, there will always be someone lower than you lying on their stomach, stinking in their own stench, ready to pull you down into their pit of sullenness. I have seen the best and worst of people these last seven years. Some days, we may not act like family, even at our worst, we are not as despicable as some of the characters I have met along the way.

I too stroke mum's hair and rest my hand on her shoulder. I look at dad, who is now crying silently. He is trying to be stoic, but it's not working.

"How have you been dad?" My voice is low. I recognise my nakedness in my father's eyes. He sees me, all of me. My pain, my sorrow, my fear. I cannot hide.

"Oh, you know. Half right and half left," he said with a wry smile.

He clears his throat and wipes his eyes like an errant child. "Maddie, how have *you* been?" He searches my face, looking for clues. I lower my gaze, fearful he will see what had become of me. Knowingly, he changes the subject to hide my shame.

"Knowing that your child is homeless, makes sleeping a luxury." *Again that glare.* "I drove around this city to the most undesirable of places, searching for you. I nearly got arrested for curb crawling, can you image that?" Dad chuckled.

I giggle, "No, dad, I can't imagine, you don't even like driving at night." Guilt sweeps over me like a cold breeze.

He smiled tight lipped, "When your baby girl is out there, doing god knows what with god knows who, then of course, I pounded the streets looking for her. In fact, both your mother and I would take a drive most evenings after 11 pm. It broke her heart to see the real London at night. It's not a safe place if you don't know what you're doing."

"Dad, what do you mean doing god knows what and god knows who?"

THE JOURNEY

"We heard that you lost your job, and you know, in order to make ends meet and to feed your addiction, you were doing night work."

"What?" My eyes are so wide that I feel the muscles strain in resistance. "Night work?" my voiced cracked from the emotion.

"Yes," dad said, looking to the floor, clearly embarrassed by the whole ordeal.

"Dad," I say softly, "look at me, please, daddy, look at me."

Dad raised his eyes, but his head was still sunken into his shoulders. "I never ... ever ... sold myself, and especially not for alcohol! Where did you hear such trash?"

"Really, you were not a prostitute?" Dad asked confused, but completely relieved by my admission.

"No dad," I say with authority. "I may have been an alcoholic, but even we have standards."

"Maddie," dad said, straining to keep his composure, it was all too much, he cracked and burst into tears. "I am so very pleased to hear you say that." He takes a long pause and clears his throat, drinks his water and pulls his handkerchief and dabs his eyes. "Very pleased indeed. Do you hear that my darling?" Dad bends over to kiss mum, he slightly raises his voice so that mum hears. "She wasn't on the game after all. Phoebe got it wrong love. Isn't that good news? Eh, Winnie, good news." He strains a smile through his happiness and grief.

The pressure in my temple feels like it is going to explode. *Why would my sister tell my parents that I was a hooker? Oh, she has a lot to answer for, and trust me, I will make sure that she answers for everything this time.*

"Come on Maddie, calm down. This is not the time or place." I kneel down next to my father, who is seated next to my mum, and hold his hand.

"How long has she been like this?" I ask him, forcing my mind to the present glum situation.

"Like this, a couple of days," dad whispers. It's as if he only wants mum to hear good happy conversations. I smile inwardly, as I know that she is hearing everything.

"You look tired dad. Do you want to stretch your legs or something?"

"No love, I'm fine. I will just get a drink and come back."

"Dad, stretch your legs, you could do with the walk and call the family and let them know how she's doing. When was the last time they had an update?" I ask. Not wanting to send him away, but I crave alone time with mum.

"That's a point, you always think of everything. I will call them outside."

I smile as dad leaves the room. He closes the door in slow motion, so not to make a noise when the door creases align. "Finally, I have you all to myself," I say in my most cheerful voice. My mum looks old and small. She is off colour, that is the only way to describe her. The shadow of death is looming, and I can see that we don't have much time. I hold her hand and squeeze it, praying for the miracle that I know will not come.

"Where have I been, I hear you say. Truth? Ok, I have been in rehab for the last 90 days, before that I was living with my artist boyfriend, Franco, in Italy. He lived in a little village outside Lake Como, lovely man mum, he really was lovely when he wasn't drunk." I laugh. I feel the emotion of the moment wash over me. "Mum, if I could turn back time, I would have handled so many

THE JOURNEY

things differently. I can hear you now, you have to stop running from yourself Madeline, learn to feel life as it's happening around you and to you. Stop suppressing every emotion and go with it." Tears roll down my face. I carefully place mum's hand in mine, and I kiss it lovingly, not wanting to disturb her, I place her tear soaked hand on the bed. I feel her presence and look up and see her looking at me. She looked thinner with her eyes closed.

"*Water*," she croaked. Startled by the weakness in her voice, I momentarily froze. I grab the bottle of water with a straw and carefully raise her neck so that she can drink. "Hi, Mum," I say, as if the last seven years haven't happened.

Mum raises her eyebrows at me, searching for signs of my alcoholism.

"I am clean mum, and you are not dreaming. I have finally sobered up, it's taken me seven years, but I am clean." When you are dying, you command the truth, it's the least the person who you require it from can give you in this moment. I have not spoken to my mum in over six years, and considering that this is our first conversation, it is filled without judgment and wrapped in the gloves of sincerity and integrity. I can sit here shameless, as I have overcome my demons, and this time it is not a lie.

"Am I dead?" she asked, with her new dry raspy voice.

I smile broadly, "No, mum, you're not dead, as I am alive, kindda." I reply in my chipper London accent.

Mum smiles, "Good," my heart swells with pity, I can see that it's taking a lot of effort to talk.

"Oh, by the way, I was never a prostitute," I blurt out through the tears. *Maddie, happy face, normal voice, the last thing she needs is you falling apart. I take some prolonged deep breaths.*

Mum looks at me and nods her head once, as if to tell me that she already knew. Maybe she heard the conversation.

"I asked God to let me see you again, and you're fine," mum smiled.

I am so glad that I made it back in time, to see her face, and for her to look me in the eyes and know that all is well. "For sure mummy, I will not go back to that place again."

"You *promise*," mum asked, searching my face with her eyes.

I start to cry, mum looks upset as well. "I promise, mummy, I promise you that I will not have another drink as long as I live."

"You need to …" her chests heaves, and her throat wheezes as she tries to breathe. "You … need … to … forgive … Yourself. I Love you," Mum smiles, "I'll see you."

"What?"

"I will see you."

"It's ok, mum, I am not going anywhere," I tell her. She looks at me annoyed with disgust, she knows that I understand her, and I am sitting in this moment which belongs to her, and I make it about me.

"But I am," she says, then looks out of the window.

"Hold on mum, for a little while longer. I need you." She looks at me, pained, as she knows that she is needed, but there is nothing more for her to do. Her time is running out.

She mouthed, "Love you," and closed her eyes.

THE JOURNEY

I sat there completed in the moment that I spoke to my mother again, but cheated that this was all the time that I have had with her. Why did it take me forever to figure stuff out? I could have been here with my family. They needed me, and I was out there being needy and dependent on the bottle. I stand up and smell the peachy fragrance in the room. I look out the window, past the gardens, and see people walking about their daily business. A beautiful young woman's arms are looped with her boyfriend. She seemed carefree and genuinely happy. "Are any of us genuinely happy?" I ask.

"What was that, love?" Alice said. I spun around, and Nurse Mckee was taking mum's vital signs and completing her chart. "Are you family?" she asked apologetically," It's just that I have not seen you before?"

"Yes, I am," I smile. "Are you mum's nurse then?"

"I am one of them. My name is Alice. I would shake your hand, but I need to administer more pain relief to your mum's drip," she said apologetically.

I nod appreciatively, "How is she doing?" I ask looking at mum.

"She is where she needs to be on her journey."

I motion Alice to come over to the window, "What does that mean? She just told me that she is leaving. You know, like she knows that she is going to die soon. Is she close?" I whisper.

Alice looked at me, "Give me a minute please, and we can talk outside." She looked at mum and then at me. I nodded as I understood the need for us to have this conversation outside of the room.

Alice completed her checks and stroked mums arm. "Are you alright, my love?"

Mum liked her, she smiled at her, not wanting to be a burden and points to her chest.

Alice leant down, "Is it burning or just aching, my darling."

"Buuuurrrrr..."

"It's burning. Ok, I will ask the Consultant to come and have a listen. We may need to alter your pain relief," she said sweetly. "I just want to ensure that you are as comfortable as possible. Are you happy for stronger drugs?"

"Nooo," mum said defiantly. "I .... " Mum starts to wheeze again "need to say ....goodbye." Alice took mums hands in hers and said with compassion, "I understand poppet. I am going to place your mask on, so that you can get some more oxygen in those lungs," she nodded whilst she spoke.

Alice walked out the room. "One moment love, I just need to talk to the Consultant, and we can have a quick chat," I nod at her and sit down next to mum.

"Well, you have her trained," I say. Mum did not open her eyes, she just smiled and raised her eyebrows. She clicked her machine a few times and drifted away.

The Consultant returned a few minutes later with Nurse McKee. They spoked quietly, and he listened to mums chest and reviewed her chart. He looked at me, not with pity or sympathy, but in the knowledge that my mother would soon pass away. I read his face, he could see it and removed his gaze. He despised this part of his role, I could tell. He walked towards me. A tall chap, mid-thirties, quite handsome really, with his thick brown hair and blue eyes, he was in fact striking. His lips were thick, his jaw rounded, and underneath his shirt he looked quite well built.

THE JOURNEY

"I understand that you are Edwina's daughter? You're family?" he asked, unsure of my status or relationship to his patient.

"I am her daughter, yes. I arrived this morning."

"My name is Mr. York, Oncology Consultant."

"I see..."

"Where is the rest of your family?"

"Taking a break," I mutter.

"I am sorry to report that your mother's condition has worsened. I would strongly recommend that you contact your family and tell them to be close by." He patted my arm, "You will need to prepare yourself."

"How long?" I ask mortified.

"It's not an exact science Miss George, but I would predict that she may pass away within the next 24-48 hours."

"That quick," I snap, tears form immediately.

Mr. York nodded apologetically and swiftly left the room.

Chapter 10

Rock Bottom

January 13th 2005 7.54 pm

"Are you alright mate?" a older woman asked me, as I wiped my eyes.

"No, I'm not, I have had some bad news, but thanks," I say.

"Bleeeeeep, Bleeeeep," I look at my phone, and it's the hospital.

"Hello, it's Jon, is she ...."

"Jon, its Alice, where are you?"

"On the High Street, is she..." I try to suppress the panic and emotion from my voice.

"No, love," Alice informs me.

Gratefully, I exhale loudly.

"Edwina's health is declining, and you do need to be here, get back here as quickly as you can."

"I'm on my way." The moment she hangs up, I look

THE JOURNEY

around franticly for a taxi or a number 21 bus.

"I don't mean to be rude, but you look like you've had a shock, can I help," my random stranger asks.

"To tell you the truth, I have had a hell of a day. My mum is in St Augustus, and my sister has just witnessed my long term boyfriend attack me. She has proceeded to tell me that I am nothing more than a sniveling victim bitch, amongst other things." I am taken aback by my candidness. I look at my stranger apologetically, I do not care that I am emotionally naked, it's the truth, if she didn't want to hear the answer she should not have asked the question. I see her reflection looking at me, she seemed genuinely concerned. I regain myself for a moment. "I am sorry, I should not have said all that, I need to get back," I tell her flatly. I see a black cab in the distance, "Taxi," I shout and put my arm out. The driver took one look at me and drove straight past even though he had his light on.

"Really you fucking tosser!" I scream at him as he pasts me with my middle finger erected for all to see.

"I have a car, and you don't seem like a serial killer. I am just parked less than one hundred yards away. Let's go."

I hesitate, "Its fine, I can run there."

"You can, but I will get you there quickly. Let's go, it will take a few minutes at this rate."

"Thank you, you are very kind, and you too do not look like a serial killer," I smirk at my good Samaritan.

She smiled. "Sam," she stretched out her well-manicured hand.

I look at her, mid-fifties, I would say. Very polished, old money, maybe an actress, definitely a thespian of some sort. "Jon," I reciprocated, I suddenly became very conscious of my state of dress, hair, breath, and general stank demeanor.

My good Samaritan glided through the traffic in the latest model of her Land Rover Range Rover sports estate. As promised, she delivered me to the hospital in only a few minutes. "Good luck Jon," she said kindly.

"Thank you, I will always remember your kindness," I smiled at her and left her car, feeling that my faith had been restored in mankind.

My limbs are weighted with grief, and it's becoming physically harder and more laborious to walk and to keep my body upright.

I walk into mum's room, she looks peaceful, her night gown has changed. She has her post sky blue satin and lace number on.

"What's with change of bed clothes," I ask quietly.

"Mum left me strict instructions to ensure she said goodbye in a decent nightgown," dad said, his lips quivering.

We all smiled, "Trust mum," I laugh quietly.

Dad, Phoebe, and Maddie all give a pity stare.

"What?" I ask demandingly, already knowing the answer from their stares. I look at Phoebe, who averts her gaze, and looks at anything else but me.

"This is not the time," dad said. "I am so sorry son, I should have been a better father to you."

"What?" I try to laugh it off. "Dad, what are you talking about?"

"I told them," Phoebe cut me off. "They all know that you are a battered fag hag."

THE JOURNEY

"Eeeeeek," I slam my hands to my mouth and felt my knees buckle. My dad and Maddie run to my aid. Dad catches me before I fall and holds me tight. I am safe and for the first time in twenty two years I feel home.

"I got you son. I got you. I had no idea. It my fault, my pride got in the way of me being your father. I should have been there for you. I should have protected you. I was too interested in protecting my image in the community. I am going to make him pay for what he's done to you." My father kissed me over and over again on my cheek. "My beautiful, beautiful boy."

"Jonathan, we are here for you, I am here for you," is all that Maddie could say. "We will get through this, you have to leave him, and I will help you, you're better than this situation, and you know it," she could barely speak through her tears.

I hold them both close to me, my eyes are closed and my head is throbbing. The love that I have for them both in this moment is greater than anything that I have ever experienced. I look up and Phoebe is smirking at me. My mother is awake and is looking pained, as if she has experienced the whole thing. Maybe she has. I let go of them both and walk towards my mother. I kneel down and take her hand.

"Mum, I am ok, do not worry about me, look," we both look at Dad and Maddie, "they are going to help me get through this. It needed to come out. I needed to be free of the shame and guilt. "Do not worry mummy. I am going to be ok," I kiss her hand, she smiles at me, tears streak her face, she looks at me lovingly and blinks slowly. "I love you mum, when you're ready to go, you just leave, we are going to be fine."

Mum looks at Phoebe.

"It's ok," I tell her, "we are going to take care of her as well." Mum looks at me and nods slightly and slowly closes her eyes.

My sister looks at me and feels the burdens of her behaviors weighing heavily on her shoulders. She raises her handkerchief to her eyes and runs out of the room.

Maddie makes her way towards to the door.

"It's ok, Mads. I'll go, stay with Dad and Mum," I say calmly.

I chase my sister to the corridor, and drag her to the stairwell. She looks at me full of regret.

"Jon, I …. I don't know why…"

I slap her so hard she falls into the wall. She holds her cheek and gives me daggers. "Now you find your backbone? Shame you can't demonstrate this level of aggression with Jack," she snarled.

"That wasn't for me," I say quietly. I point to the room. "Your mum is dying Phoebes, get it? She is in the last stages of her life, and even now all you can think of is getting one up on me. You have tried to make her death about you. How can you be so selfish?"

"No, I didn't, I told the truth and look, everyone is still in love with St Jon, so why are you complaining?" she yells.

I look at my sister with renewed eyes. Even now, she is contrite and unapologetically cruel. My voice cracks under the strain, "I just had to give her comfort right now, so that she can *die* in peace. Have you *no* conscience?" I yell. "What has happened to you that you feel like you can act like a poisonous cobra in everyone's life?"

Her face softens again. "Jon, I am sorry. I didn't mean to. I don't know why I do…"

"Bullshit," I interrupt. "You a grown woman, you're not a

child anymore. You swore to me that you would not say a word. You offered me support, then you do what you always do, you kicked me as hard as you could when I am weak. I met the most delightful human being, a stranger. She offered me more compassion and understanding than you."

"I am sorry," she whined like a child. "It just happens, I don't know why, but it does, I don't mean it." She was trying to reason with me, but no more.

The door to the stairwell swings open and slams into the wall. It's Maddie. She is looking at Phoebe with a hate filled glare.

"Oh, get lost, Madds, no one invited you to this party. It's between me and Jon," Phoebe snarls.

"My perfect little sister, so pretty and sweet. Who would believe that she slept with my Pete?" Maddie said in a childish rhyme like chant.

"What?" I exclaimed. I looked at Phoebe for some sort of confirmation that she has gotten this seriously wrong, but her face said it all.

"What gives you the right to out Jon like you're a saint. You should have outed yourself first. You're real good at telling other people's secrets and a master at keeping yours to yourself, or so you thought," Maddie says quietly.

"Madd, I .... I ....."

Maddie walked up to Phoebe, I started to brace myself that I am going to have to drag them apart. "You ruined me." She whispered. "It has taken me seven years to get over what you did. To deal with my broken heart, to acknowledge that you went out of your way to wreck my relationship with the only bloke that I have ever loved." Phoebe stood there just wiping tears from her eyes, leaning against the wall. "You did that. What did I ever do to you?"

Phoebe was really sniveling, "It wasn't like that. At the time, I ... I know it's inexcusable, but I thought that he loved me."

"He was not yours to love," Maddie screamed at her. She then threw her hands up in the air, angry at herself. "Today cannot be about you. Jon is right. I am here for mum, dad, and Jon. You can jump off London Bridge as far as I'm concerned. You are so dysfunctional, all this," and she pointed at us in the corridor, "is just another day in paradise for you. We will have our day sister dearest and yours is not going to be today, but it's coming. That much I can promise you."

I look at my sister, I am speechless, my mind is racing. I am aware that she was very competitive and jealous, but not to this extent. This was just foul, even for Phoebe.

"Madds, why did you run out on everything three days before your wedding?" I ask not wanting to know the answer.

She looks at Phoebe, "Go on, tell him what you were doing with Pete in *our* flat?"

"What?" Phoebes eyes were wild.

"Tell him," Maddie responds angrily.

"You were there?"

"Yes, I was, and I heard everything," Maddie informs my sister who is looking grey, as all of her colors has drained from her body. "I was in the loft, that's where I hid his wedding present. I heard you laughing at me, both of you. What was it that you called me? Poor, pathetic, maggot Maddie, thinking Peter will be her child's daddy."

THE JOURNEY

Phoebe shakes her head, "Look, I'm sorry, we were high."

I could not take it in. I sit on the stairs and put my head in my hands.

"Madds, you left because of her?" I spit out the words, desperately trying hard not to slap my sister again.

Maddie nodded. "You know what bro? I have missed the last seven years with my mum because of her. You know what I know now? They were not worth my exile. I missed out on my family because of you, and it was not worth it. You and Pete, you're the ones that are damaged. You're both worthless, and you have the integrity of a worm, but I owned it, and for that, I won't forgive myself, as I am here, wishing that I had the strength at the time to confront you both. Today is not about you, it's about mum. You're nothing to me. We are done." With that, she left.

I sat there in silence. I feel completely useless, and all I can do is stare at my sister. "This is the worst day of my life so far." I shake my head, still trying to process the last few minutes.

"Jon, I can ex..."

"Forget it Judas," I abruptly interrupt. "That ship has sailed. We are meant to be family, but your actions make me place you in a different category. To hell with you. After the funeral, I am done with you. Truly. Be spiteful, bitchy, and wicked to your cats. I choose not to be fucking bothered. Your energy taints all that is pure. Deal with that." I looked at my sister and walked out of the stairwell and back in the room. Maddie's right. We have to focus on mum and dad right now. This bullshit has no place in my reality.

"Alright, son?" my dad embraced me as I walked into the room.

"Yes dad. It needed to be said. Now let's just concentrate on mum."

My father nods.

"Here. Here," Maddie chimed in.

We sat quietly praying with her. She was somewhere else now, we could see that. Her demeanor was changing, her breathing was raspy, we could visibly see that she was slipping away, I could feel her spirit leaving us. I wanted to scream, make a pact with the devil or God, the universe, anyone and anything. But I know it's fruitless. It was all fruitless. This was her time, and I have to just grow some balls and accept it. I thought that there are not many things in life that one has to accept, as there is always an element of choice. Today is different. This moment is bigger than us, and we need to embrace it for what it is. Mum is leaving us and is never coming back. Its final.

I look up, Phoebe is sulking alone by the far wall. This was all her doing, she has made her choice.

THE JOURNEY

Chapter 11

Revelations

She is beautiful. I lay in my bed, lifeless but perfect. How I wished I had the vision to see how beautiful I was then, and to relish in the freshness of my youth. I have been gone for some time, as I must be at least 15 years old now. My hair falls on my shoulders, and only a trained eye would notice the slight imperfection on the bridge of my nose. My limbs are lithe and sculptured, far more than I recall.

It's early, the fragrance of dawn creeps through the open window. I sit on the window ledge. This room has changed since the last time I was here. It's fit for a princess. The colour scheme was lime and cream, not bad Grand mama, Good Housekeeping would be proud. My balcony doors are shut, the extra-large queen size four poster bed represented opulence, the floors were a deep red mahogany, polished to perfection. When the sun started to rise, I saw the reflection of my face staring up at me. I look terrible, my burdensome body seems to be ragged and unwell, my skin has turned grey, and I feel weaker than I have ever been.

"Winnie," I whisper.

My younger self sucked in all the air in the room and sprang up to the perfect right angle, breathing heavily, eyes wide open, desperately trying to focus on what or whom was next to her. After a few seconds, she realised that I was no threat to her, her eyes narrowed, "Edwina?" she asked in a muffled voice.

I smiled at her, "Hey, kiddo, it's been a while."

"I thought that you were a figment of my imagination", she pinches me hard. "Are you dead yet?"

"I don't think so." I whisper.

"Where have you been," she barks at me with angrily.

"I'm not sure," I say apologetically.

"Why are you back here? It's been five years. Why now?"

"Five years," I say, although I guessed the length of duration, it still takes me back.

"You're like all the rest," she said with venom.

"The rest! Who?" I ask, my little self was real feisty back then.

"Mima, my mother and now you. You all leave me in the end, all of you abandoned me and left me in this hell."

I want to cry but am no longer producing tears.

"Am I expected to feel for you? Look at my life, it's miserable. I am in this big and beautiful home without anyone that loves me. Tell me that my life gets better, that I am happy and loved."

I stare blankly at this young girl, not knowing what to say, she searches my face for clues relating to her future like I am so old gypsy woman.

"Tell me," my younger self yells.

"If you insist. Your future is wonderful, you meet your husband and have the most wonderful marriage. Your life is filled with love, laughter, and three beautiful children. Voila ..." I stand up and take a bow.

My younger self stares at me. "Then I ... am ... happy," she eyeballs me as she asks that question.

"You certainly are." I smile, hoping that it will hide the doubt in my eyes.

"You're sure?" Winnie asks with a poignant glare.

I nod and swiftly change the subject. "Where is Mrs. Mack?"

"What do you mean where is she? Don't you remember?"

"No," I snap.

Winnie looks pained at my shortness. "On the 6th of November, 1947, she went to see her sister in Trinity Ville. She never came home, both villages searched for her for days it was like she vanished into thin air." Tears filled Winnie's eyes, but none fell out. "She protected me, and he *killed* her for it."

"Who did?" I whisper. I started to tremble, fear washed over me.

"You know who?" she said in a low voice, she was enjoying torturing me. I cannot recall being this spiteful as a young woman.

I close my eyes, a torture type pain surges through my spine, whilst injecting all of the abominable, bloodcurdling, execrable memories of my childhood back to that part of my brain where they were carefully locked away in a vault. Lying on the bed next to my younger self, I feel her glare on me. Winnie stretches out her hands and clasped them in mine. I open my eyes, and she looks at me with sedate sobriety. "I can see that you're remembering, aren't you?"

The pain was too intense, I do not know whether it's from the cancer or being here, but it's too much. I open my eyes, I notice that my face is moist. I am hot and clammy, I know that my time on this earth is coming to an end soon. I focus on my mini me and, for the first time, have nothing to say. Everything aches.

"Our father is a loathsome son of a bitch, isn't he?" Winnie whispers in a voice so deep, it was barely audible. I let go of her hand, turn away and gently nod my head. I have the familiar feeling of giddiness. *Noooooo, not now, she is furious with me, she thinks I have abandoned her.* As I travel through time, multiple memories flood through my mind's eye. My body begins to feel light, I am floating on the ceiling, it's no longer a liberating feeling. *I can't go back, Lord, take me now, but do not let me go back.* I float through time, and I'm in the same room, five years earlier. Mrs. Mack is making my bed. She is talking to me, I am sat on the window ledge, looking at the plantation. Her voice is so high with excitement that I cannot help but tune in.

"Oh Winnie my darling I am so thrilled. My sister Sarah has given birth to a lovely boy. Fit and strong, just like my daddy. I cannot wait to meet the lovely sweetheart."

Feeling her joy, Winnie clasped her hands together. "That's great news Mrs. Mack. When can I come and see the baby?"

THE JOURNEY

"Hmmmm, not sure. I will speak to Dr. Barnett about a little visit later on in the week."

Winnie is sat on her white bureau chair looking through her school books on the table. She stares at me as if to say, "What are you doing here?"

I raise my finger to my mouth, to remind her to be quiet. She nods silently.

"You ok, sweet pie?" Mrs. Mack enquires.

"Yes Ma'am. I was just wondering what they will call the baby. Please, can I come with you? I don't want to stay here by myself. Also, grandpa is not home, so they will be mean to me."

Mrs. Mack picked Winnie up off the bed like she was a doll. Her hair was arranged in four perfect groups of ringlets, each one tied with yellow satin bows. Her cream knee length dress, with accompanying kremlin petticoat, was a site to behold. She looked stunning, a child borne to wealth.

Mrs. Mack placed me on her lap. "Listen, Sweet Pie, I will be back in the morning. Ok? I will prepare supper, and cook will help you this evening at bedtime." She lovingly kissed my head. My heart skipped a beat. I felt the love in her kiss and saw the adoration in her eyes. No one heard daddy enter the room. He stood at the doorway, looking exceptionally distinguished, yet, smelled like a well fermented vineyard. The atmosphere within the room plummeted, even though it was November and well over 30 degrees. Both Mrs. Mack and Winnie jumped to their feet and stood to attention by the beds. The once defiant Mrs Mack was no longer around, she was trembling. She held Winnie's hand to reassure her, but her display of calmness did not fool either of us. Winnie looked at me pleadingly, as if to say "Do something."

"Child, come to dad-dy and give him a kiss," he said, slurring his words.

Winnie looked at me pleadingly again, wishing that I had some magical powers to strike her father dead.

"Child!!!!" daddy screams.

"Go on, Winnie, give your daddy a kiss," Mrs. Mack instructed her.

As Winnie gets closer to her father, his demeanor changes. Daddy raises his left hand high, Winnie stands still, anticipating the blow, he delivers a hard slap across her face. Her poor little head is thrown back. He grabs her hair with his right hand and pulls her down, as he drops to his knees.

"Daddy, no," I scream. *What type of monster is he?*

Winnie lets out a blood curdling scream. The whole household comes to a standstill. He moves to punch Winnie, but Mrs. Mack grabs his fist, and her skirt engulfs the punch. She pushes daddy hard, and he loses his balance, so is forced to let go of Winnie's hair. They both topple over on the ground, and daddy hits the floor hard, as Mrs. Mack's weight falls onto him. She grabs her skirt to make a run for it. Even though daddy was drunk, he was the first one on his feet.

He swings towards Mrs. Mack head, but she jumps backwards.

She raises her hand, "Calm down, Sir ... She is just a little girl. Hasn't she been through enough?"

A sensation of fear dominated us all, for each of us knew that it would not end well for Mrs. Mack. Winnie ran to her bed with her hands at her ears.

"Daddy, please no," she screams, tears streaming down

her face. "I'll be a good girl, I promise. Please don't hurt her, she's my only friend. I'll be a good girl, daddy."

I ran to the bed and put my arms around her. After last time, I knew I was powerless.

Both daddy and Mrs. Mack looked at Winnie, his face softened momentarily. We all silently prayed that Mrs. Mack would get a warning, even Mrs. Mack. Suddenly, with raging vengeance, daddy punched Mrs. Mack square on the nose so hard, as she landed on the floor she was unconscious. Winnie leapt of the bed to run to her, "Mrs. Mack," she screamed. Daddy turned his head, his face was unrecognizable with rage. "Get away, you little bitch!!!" he screamed at Winnie. She stopped running, rooted to the spot with fear.

Within a matter of seconds, Mrs. Mack started to come round, she raised her head slowly. "Win ... Winniiiieee," she held her head, blood was dripping from a cut under her right eye, and both her nostrils were filled with blood.

Daddy walked towards her and was laughing. "No one here to save you now, you old hag."

"You only beat me because my husband is away with your daddy. Please ... Please, sir," Mrs. Mack pleaded. "I will not say a word."

Daddy looked over at Winnie, but I would have sworn he was looking directly at me. "Get on the bed," he snarled. Winnie ran as quickly as her legs could carry her and jumped on the bed. She went into the foetal position, "Please, don't," she whispered over and over again.

I cradled my younger self, "It's ok," I cry. "It will be ok, I promise. Don't turn around, ok?"

"What is it about you, always meddling in my business?" he yelled.

Mrs. Mack, still dazed, was on all fours, "please sir," she whimpered.

Daddy grabbed her hair and pulled her to her feet. "You think that you are better than me, but *I* am a gentlemen, a man of position, I am respected here. But you, a common bush girl, a descendant of a slave whore, think that you are better than me, don't you?"

"No, sir. No, no, no, no," she pleaded, tears strolling down her face.

"Yes, yes, yes, yes ..." He pushed Mrs. Mack to the wall, he pressed himself up against her. He leered at her, "You know something, woman? You are passable. There is something about you, I am not sure what it is, but it's passable". He glanced over to the bed and saw that Winnie was sat on the bed, her back to him. "Winnie, get out!"

Winnie turned around and starred at her father. She shook her head defiantly.

"Winnie, I will beat you black and blue today if you disobey me. Get out!"

Winnie looked at Mrs. Mack. Not wanting to abandon her friend, her eyes were pleading not to be sent away.

Mrs. Mack looked at Winnie reassuringly. "It's ok, darling, daddy and I are going to have a little chat. Ask cook for some lemonade and pineapple cake, I soon come."

Winnie cautiously walked out the room. As she was about to go through the door, she looked deep into her friend soul and asked "You promise?"

"I promise baby," Mrs. Mack said, her voice breaking as she was trying to sound positive.

THE JOURNEY

"Why have you turned my only child against me?"

Mrs. Mack said nothing, she just looked at Barrington with hatred.

Daddy pulled her skirt above her waist, Mrs. Mack tried to save herself, but was greeted with a hard punch to the stomach.

"Arrgggghhh," she gasps for breath.

I witnessed the revulsion in her. I stood by filled with loathing as I watch my father hit my only friend repeatedly, she tried to defend herself but was met with a barrage of slaps and punches. Daddy rips off her panties. She doesn't cry out, she no longer struggles, she lies lifeless on the floor. My father's fumbling attempts to enter Mrs. Mack become laughable. She lies there waiting for the unwanted intrusion, and ... nothing. He tries again, and again, and again, with the same response. Mrs. Mack sits there motionless, with each failed effort, she smiles.

Her ferocious aggressive attacker is no more, instead there is a drunken, unstable, hesitant young man. He rolls on the floor, silent and panting. Mrs. Mack did not move or say anything. She lay silent, crying and smiling.

The situation in the room seemed explosive, yet sedate. My father got up off the floor and went over to Mrs. Mack, she did not flinch, she still had that smirk for a grin. My father walked towards her, he lent out his hand. Remarkably, she took it, and he pulled her to her feet. She winced all the way up, but she was standing, thank God. Upright, holding her ribs, she just starred at my father with that same smirk on her face, and hatred exuding from her eyes.

He apprehensively walked towards Mrs. Mack. She puts her hand up in front of her "Stop!"

"Keep your mouth shut, and we can forget about tonight," daddy says.

Mrs. Mack is silent.

Daddy walks to the door. "Mrs. Mack, I mean it. If you don't want a repeat performance of …."

Mrs. Mack burst out laughing. "Repeat performance of *what*?" she waved with disgust in the direction of his private area.

Daddy looked fatally wounded, "I mean it. Say nothing to Mackie."

"I could never tell Mackie any of this, he would hang if he knew what you *tried* to do," she was angry and defiant.

"What did you say?" daddy demanded.

"You heard me the first time. Maybe I am just too old for you. After all, we all know how you like young little girls." She was angry with him and could not hide it.

"Shut your mouth!" I could see the vein bulging in his forehead. I sit on the bed, hand over my mouth trying not to scream. Even though they could not hear or see me, I wanted to be sure.

"Or what, sir? You going to tickle me with your broken bamboo stick?" Mrs. Mack starts to laugh heartily, she fell so far in her own joke, she did not see the aggression reemerge on daddy's face.

Daddy walked towards Mrs. Mack, she did not flinch, he head-butted her so hard, she careened to the side of the bed.

"Nooooo," I scream.

The emasculated man had gone, the barbarian rapist that I had become accustomed to, who always delivered his punishment, was back. He threw Mrs. Mack on the bed, raised her skirt above her head and raped her.

I feel weightless, I am on the ceiling, before I had time to turn, I am spinning in a vortex, lights are flashing, I can hear multiple voices, I cannot make out what they are saying. I land with a thud on Winnie's bed.

"Edwina, are you feeling alright? You don't look too good," Winnie asks as I open my eyes.

"I am dying child, I should look terrible," I tried to smile at my younger self, but could not muster the energy to do that.

"You've been asleep for a while. I was wondering, what's it like?"

"What?"

"Dying. Are you ready for it all to end?"

I look at my younger self. "I am not sure that I am, it's funny really. My body is ready for the journey, but my mind it's still as sharp as ever. Mentally, I am still 21 years old, but with more wisdom. Does that make sense?" I ask.

"No," Winnie giggled. "No, it doesn't."

"It will. Do you remember Mima?"

The sound of her name pained her face. "No, I don't," she whispered.

"Then let me tell you what I remember. Our grandmother was a strong beautiful woman. She was married to Grandpa Vincent for many years. They were so in love, even after all those years."

"What was he like?"

"I don't know, I never met him. Mima would tell me a story about him every day, and it was funny. She was a gateway to his life and the connection between the two of us. I know I was young, but she kept his memory alive so vividly, it did not feel like he was dead. He lived on through Mima."

"How did he die?"

"I don't know," I lied.

"Why are you lying to me? I am you, remember? So I know when you're lying."

"Drop it, Winnie. I said that I don't know how he died."

"It was him, wasn't it?"

"I honestly don't know," I try to sound as sincere as possible.

"Look, Winnie, there are experiences and things that you need to learn in your own time. I cannot rob you of that, it would not be fair."

"Ok, well, answer me this." She looked so serious.

"Honey, if it's about how Grandpa died, that is not going to happen."

"Why?" She looked really annoyed. I gave her the 'I am your mother, don't mess with me' look.

"Ok... I am not impressed with your reasoning, but ok." I was so serious back then. "So what about Mrs. Mack? How did she die?"

I inhaled hard, then held Winnie's hand. "Don't ask, if you can't handle what I am about to say, kiddo."

Her eyes became red and moist almost immediately. "I can handle it," she whispered.

THE JOURNEY

"When I went back to sleep, I saw what happened. Daddy raped Mrs. Mack. Although, I did not see him kill her, you and I know that he did it. He could not risk her telling Mackie. He just couldn't."

Winnie closed her eyes. "Thank you for telling me, we … I need to get ready for breakfast."

There was a beautiful porcelain bowl on the dressing table, with cold water in it. Beside it, was a face cloth. Winnie methodically washed her face, she stripped and wiped down her whole body with the lemon fragranced soap as her aid. I sat back and watched my mini me dress herself, the opulence was staggering, even for that time. My curly ringlets nestled snuggly by the nape of my neck. My corkscrew fringe was bade with a green headband. I put on my undergarments and a light cream sleeveless over shirt, with a bright green skirt that matched my head band. I slipped into my Channel pumps and opened the door.

"Morning Miss Edwina," the maid said. Holy flip. The maid was stood outside her door.

"Good morning," she chimed in her cheerful voice. I watched her with suspicion. I have just told her that our father raped and murdered her one and only friend, and she doesn't flinch.

"Breakfast is served Ma'am, are you ready? Your Grandma and Papa are in the breakfast room."

"I will be there in a minute," she replies politely.

The maid seemed surprised by that.

"Yes, Ma'am."

Once the door was closed, Winne looked at me. "Tell me," she said with brute force, as if she was talking to the help. "Do I fall in love? Am I happy? Do I have an amazing life, is this hell worth it?"

"Well, I'm here at nearly 70, so what do you think?"

"You have not answered my question."

Taken aback by her tone, I say gently, "Winnie, it's worth it, trust me."

She smiled, "Ok, let's go to breakfast."

I walked across the circular landing, and was taken aback by the beauty of the handcrafted mahogany staircase. The grandiose oil paintings were of past ancestors on both sides. As I walked down the stairs, I watched slave owner from each generation bid me "Good day". I suddenly felt clammy, to be back in this house, knowing all the pain that it had caused my family, let alone the poor slaves of centuries gone by. I was the decedent of slaves and its owners. I am not sure how I feel about that. I sat on the step to catch my breath.

Winnie stopped and looked at me. She gave me a concerned glare. I waved her off. "I'm ok. See you in a minute."

"Good morning, darling girl," I heard a rapturous, deep southern voice behind me.

Winnie grinned wider than a Cheshire cat. "Grandpa, good morning, and how are you on this beautiful, yet illustrious morning?"

"Darling, now that I have seen you, I am just fine."

He propped his elbow out, and Winnie took it and they headed down the wide beautiful mahogany staircase, with the Ming rug stapled in place perfectly. Feeling better I followed them into the Breakfast Room.

This room was the size of my downstairs house. I counted six double doors which led to a balcony that could oversee the whole plantation from each direction.

"Wow," I say.

"It's beautiful," Winnie bellows.

"What is?" Grandpa enquired.

Grandma Phyllis and my father momentarily look up from their papers.

"The day, grandpa," Winnie looks at me awkwardly, then smiles.

Winnie walks to the food station. There are three maids dressed immaculately, just waiting.

"Good morning," Winnie says to them all. They all smile, they like her. "I will have some salt fish and ackee and breadfruit with avocado, thank you," Winnie walks to the table.

I laugh, "Winnie, I forgot just how much money we all have."

"What are you smiling at girl?" grandma Phyllis barks.

Winnie lowers her eyes and her smile disappears. "Good morning grandmother."

"Well?"

"Grandmother, I just felt like smiling for a change. Aren't you tired of my frown?"

The room stood still. There was a defiance in her eyes.

My father starred at Winnie. "What did you say Edwina?"

Winnie looked at her father cautiously and, like a sweet piece of plantain, said. "Daddy, I asked grandmother whether she was not tired of my frown."

"Well, I for one am pleased that you are smiling," grandpa said. "It brightens up my day that's for sure." He looks at Winnie and winks at her.

"Thank you grandpa."

"What do you have planned for today?" he kept my gaze, as he knew that the others were seething at my impertinence.

"I thought that maybe I could go into town to do some shopping". I look at my father and ask "Is that ok, daddy?"

"It's out of the question. Don't you have your riding lesson this morning?"

In her sweetest voice Winnie says, "Yes daddy. I was hoping that I could go afterwards with you. We don't spend any time together, and I was hoping that we could have some father daughter time."

My grandmother dropped her spoon on the plate. As we only ate out of the finest China, and all cutlery was solid silver, it was quite a clash. Daddy was caught off guard and starred at his daughter. I could not help it, I just laughed. Winnie, my little actress, was perfect. She kept a straight face. The silence prolonged for a few seconds more.

"It's ok, daddy. I know that you are very busy," she lowered her eyes and continued to eat her breakfast, head bowed.

Barrington rarely showed his emotions. He was choked for a few seconds. Barrington Senior looked at him and nodded to his granddaughter's direction. Even grandma Phyllis appeared to thaw.

"Winnie, I would be honored," Barrington said his voice was soft and tender. "What did you have in mind?"

THE JOURNEY

"Anything you pick will be just perfect daddy," Winnie smiled her eyes wide with a devious twinkle.

"Ok ...." daddy was caught off guard for a second time. "Ok, I will surprise you," he smiled. A few seconds later, he swiped a stray tear from his eye.

Seeing my father like this, vulnerable and kind, was a rarity. For the first time in my life, I realised all my father wanted was unconditional love from his daughter. Nothing more. As he continued to eat his breakfast, he would glance over at his only child, the emotions in his eyes reflecting nothing else than pure love in its own twisted way.

What I did not count on was another sentiment at the table. That was my grandmother's. Hers was not one of happiness, but of pure jealousy.

I smiled to my younger self. *"Well played my love"*.

Winnie looked up and starred at me. I knew what that look meant. She was going to make them pay.

I sat to the west of the plantation, cautiously observing Winnie and daddy on horseback, they were in a slow canter across the paddock area. My tension soon wains, as I notice that my father is actually talking to me. He does not bark, slap, punch, or kick me. He appears to be interested in his daughter. Winnie is talking to daddy, waving her hand around, a trait that I did not lose. I smile, the warmth of the sun radiates across my body, and somehow neutralizes my aches and severe pains. I stroll slowly to them both. Winnie was observing me from the corner of her eye.

"Daddy, who taught you to ride?" Winnie asks.

"Grandma Phyllis," he smiled.

Winnie gives him a shocked expression, as if to say

really.

"Yes," daddy says with hilarity in his voice. "You know, she wasn't always this uptight. Cut her some slack Winn."

Winnie lowers her eyes. Startled by her reaction, daddy immediately interrupted her thoughts. "I was not chastising you, so take your eyes off the floor," he said gently. "I am just trying to point out that grandma is quite cool when she wants to be. I know that she can be a bit mean. But it all comes from a good place."

"A bit," Winnies whispers, her eyes rooted to the floor.

"Listen, I have not been the perfect father, and your grandma had not always been very …grandma-like, but that does not negate how much we love you. I …"

"What daddy?"

"Nothing Winn," he looked away, trying to somehow reassert his masculinity.

"Then why does she hate me daddy?"

"She doesn't, Winn, I promise you." Daddy had to crunch hard on his teeth, as his emotions were getting the better of him.

"Then why does she treat me like an animal?" Winne bleated.

Daddy looked wounded, "She does *not* do that Winn." He sounded hurt.

"She does, and you know it," my poor younger self sobbed uncontrollably.

Daddy jumped of his horse in one move, he was quite the athlete and pulled Winnie from her saddle and hugged her. He pushed Winnie away from his chest and cupped her face, "You are my blood. She could not hate you if she tried."

Winnie had her eyes firmly closed. "Look at me Winnie," he said with authority. "My mother does not hate you. Her blood, my blood runs through your veins. Hating you would be like hating herself. It just is not possible."

"Then why does she behave the way that she does, daddy?"

"It's complicated. She was not always like that. I promise you that."

The horses trotted to the corner of the paddock, where there was a bale of hay and water, both stallions rehydrated, seemingly bewildered by the conversation around them.

Daddy took Winnie's hand and led her to the house. As he pulled her close, she rested her head on his chest and my father did something that I could not recall at my old age: he kissed me on the head and held me close. He was being my parent.

After a short rest they both bathed and prepared themselves for their first father daughter lunch. She looked stunning if I say so myself. Her hair was free from ribbons and any hair band or debris, and her curls just nestled with grace and sophistication around her face. She was wearing a beautiful lace two piece that her grandmother had ordered from her dress maker in the United States. The colour was rose, which complemented her complexion. The sleeves ended just past her bicep, and the shirt was fitted, showing off her curvaceous figure. Her skirt was long and greeted her leg in between her knee and ankle bone. Winnie had a white Chanel bag, accompanied with Chanel Kitten heal shoes. I look at my younger self and smile I was beautiful. I looked like a movie star.

My father had impeccable manners, and that came to the fore front on this day. I think it took both Winnie and I by surprise. He was waiting at the bottom of our beautiful mahogany staircase. In a lovely Navy Blue suit, with a crisp, whiter than white shirt, no tie, and a white silk handkerchief in his pocket.

"Daddy", Winnie squealed. "You look very handsome."

Grinning like a Cheshire cat daddy pulled Winnie close "And you look beautiful," daddy whispered in my ear. "Now, I hope you're hungry," with that, he looped his fingers in mine and walked prideful out the door.

The Crystal Hotel restaurant was delightful. The waiter approached the table. As Winnie was familiarising herself with the menu, he was familiarising himself with Winnie. Daddy starred at the poor young chap so hard, he became clumsy.

"Winnie. Drink? What will it be?"

"Oh, daddy, there is too much to choose from. You choose for me, please." My father was touched by this and softened his stance momentarily.

"Alright," he looked at the waiter and became acid. "Boy! Two mango and pineapple juices."

Startled by his approach, the young man looked at daddy. "Y-Y-eess, Sirrrr."

"You alright, boy? Do I need to write this down for you?" he snapped at him like an aggressive alligator.

Embarrassed by my father's etiquette, Winnie lowered her eyes to the table cloth. The boy scurried away like a field mice.

"So." Daddy reappeared all smiles. Winnie looked at me. All I could do is shrug.

THE JOURNEY

"Daddy, why did you embarrass him like that?"

"That boy was salivating and undressing you with his eyes."

"Daddy" Winnie said, genuinely aghast.

"Winn, I do not mean to be so crude, but I know what these peasant boys are thinking".

I look at Winnie and say flatly, "that is what all men are thinking."

"Daddy, that is what all men are thinking," Winnie repeated looking directly at her father.

"What do you know of such matters?" Daddy snapped.

"I read about it," Winnie says, indignantly trying to hold her ground.

"Really?" he asked sarcastically.

"Yes."

"What have you read that describes men in this fashion?" he asked smiling at me now.

Winnie's smile broadens, "I am reading Tess of the d'Urbervilles."

We all laugh. Our drinks arrive by another waiter. I look at Daddy and say "See, you're a bully."

They both smile.

"Winnie, thank you."

"For what?"

"For handing me the olive branch."

"Daddy, I have been handing it to you for many years, you were just too ... preoccupied to notice."

Daddy's eyes filled with tears, "I am sorry."

"Anyway, daddy, this is a father's and daughter's lunch. No sad talk."

They both smiled and daddy grinned, "Agreed."

"I have to tell you, daddy. Most of the women in this room keep glancing over to you," daddy laughed so hearty. "Seriously daddy. Look," Winnie whispered.

Daddy smiled with such heartfelt happiness. "They are not looking at me, my child, they are looking at you. You are *beautiful*."

"Really," Winnie asks, needing approval.

"Yes, really."

Blushing, Winnie took a sip from her juice. "Why have you not married? You are a very handsome and eligible bachelor."

Daddy spat out his juice with laughter. "What?" Embarrassed by his lack of etiquette he immediately reached for his napkin.

"It's just a question. You are." Winnie giggled uncontrollably. She found it quite sweet that her father was shy.

"Erm ... Well, I ... I ... I suppose that I have not met the right woman yet," he was grinning from ear to ear.

"Oh" Winnie looked disappointed. "What about my mother?"

My father's eyes grew wide, his expression changed, he started to look emotional.

THE JOURNEY

I chime in, "Winnie ask him if he loved her."

"Did you love my mother?" she questions.

Daddy cheeks flushed red.

"Winn, I ..."

"Please, daddy."

He lowered his eyes. "In my own way, I adored her?" he said very quietly.

"Why did you not get married then?"

"It was complicated. Parents. Families. It was just not meant to be."

"Why? Was it because she was poor?"

"Come on Winn. Lucy and Vincent would not be described as poor, but it was just complicated. Also, I was not in the best place. To answer your question, I loved her. If I could go back and change ... change the way ... I behaved, I would."

Wide eyed, Winnie asked "What does that mean daddy? Did you hurt her?"

"Winn, I have the tendency to hurt everyone." He looks directly in his daughters eyes.

She ignores his response, "What was she like?"

"She was a lovely girl. She had shiny black ebony skin, it was so smooth to touch. Her brown eyes were extremely large and almond shaped. She had beautiful lips and the whitest teeth I have seen on any woman. Her hair was like yours, but afro, it was so soft and thick. She was a very sweet person. I did love her. Sometimes I am unable to show my affections."

"Daddy, what did you do?"

"Winn, it's not important. It was such a long time ago."

"It's important to me," she looked emotional, and daddy could see it.

"I did not treat her well."

"Why?" she asked sharply.

"I was young, arrogant and foolish."

"Did she love you?"

"Yes Winn. If I could change the outcome, I would. To answer your question, I just do not think I am the marrying type."

"You are Daddy. When you're loving, you are loveable."

Daddy starred at Winnie, "Thank you."

"You're welcome." She smiled and showed all her teeth. Daddy laughed. "Daddy, I think that you should meet a nice woman, who will open your heart, and give you more children, maybe a son. I think this would be good for you."

"And would you be ok with that?"

"Daddy, I am 15 years old. In a few years, Grandma will have me paraded to all the suitors in Kingston. I bet I will be married and a mother by 21 years of age."

"Nonsense," daddy barked.

I laughed, which made Winnie laugh, then daddy laughed.

The laughter came to a screeching holt. A woman in her late twenties walked towards my father. She had a light peachy complexion, brown eyes, and thin reddened lips that drained the colour out of her face. Her straight hair flowed to her back. "Barrington, who is your new whore?" she demanded in her lady like demeanor.

Daddy stood up with such force, his chair fell backwards. Clinching his fist, the woman flinched as she recognised that she had just run over daddy's line, let alone crossed it a mile ago. I too thought that he was going to knock her head off her shoulders. "Winnie, do something quickly."

Winnie stood up and stroked daddy's arm. Then turned to face the rude woman. She walked around the table, towering above her and stretched out her hand, not leaving her gaze.

"Who are you?" Winnie asked with a regal type curiosity.

"Who am *I*?" This woman was clearly one of daddy's floozies.

"Let me tell you who I am. My name is Edwina Barnet."

Horror crept over the rude woman's face.

"If you are too ignorant to work it out, let me explain I am the granddaughter of Dr. Barrington Barnett and," she looked at daddy, "the daughter of Barrington Junior. Now who has chosen to address a Barnett so disrespectfully?"

"Oh, Barry, I am so sorry," she looked at me. "Let me apologize my dear. I had no idea."

"Clearly," Winnie said with a streak of her grandmother in her voice. "What's your name?" she snapped.

"My name is Sylvia Edwards, I … I … I'm … friends with your daddy."

"Oh, really, Sylvia? I could have sworn I heard jealously

in your voice, which in my estimations, would have made *you* one of his whores."

Sylvia looked pained, "Barry, I ..."

"Would you not agree daddy?" Winnie asked without removing her gaze from Sylvia, who had diminished to a sweaty mess.

"I would." daddy chimed in confidently.

"Now Sylvia, under different circumstances, I would have asked you to join us. However, having met you, I choose not to lunch with whoremongers. You may go!" with that Winnie waved her hand.

Daddy looked at his daughter with bemused astonishment.

Sylvia gave daddy a begging plea. "You heard the young Miss Barnett. Leave us to dine in peace."

Once out of earshot, "Daddy, is she really your lover?"

My father looked poignantly at his daughter. "No. I go to her when I want the company of a woman. After today, that will never happen again. Edwina you are more like your grandma than you realise," he laughed out loud, "Whoremonger?!"

Winnie giggled, "I heard grandma use the term once."

They both laughed. "Well, after all that excitement, my child, I am ready for lunch. You?"

"Yes, daddy."

My life was being played out to me like a soap opera. Anyone observing them would have thought they were a strong family unit. How wrong they would be ... This relationship was as fragile as broken glass, and as sharp, too.

THE JOURNEY

After tucking into their pumpkin soup for starters, chicken rice and peas for main, both were sated by the delicious food. It had been a lovely afternoon, and they had talked like old friends from school.

"Daddy, can I ask you a question without you getting angry?"

"I don't know if I can promise, but I can try."

"Why did you drink so much?"

Daddy exhaled, "Winn, I cannot answer that."

"You can Daddy. You choose not to answer."

"It's complicated."

"Alright."

"Edwina, it is complicated. I have been drinking heavily for nearly thirty something years. I have not had a drink in over five years, and I feel great. Sometimes, sometimes I regret my behaviors after being so drunk that I lose control. No good can come from it."

Winnie and I both look at each other, nothing is said, but we come to the same conclusion. After he murdered my only friend, he knew that he had to stop.

The conversation moved onto other topics. I had stopped listening to them. Instead, I was watching the young man, eyeing up my younger oblivious self from the bar. It was Harold, he was our awkward waiter. Bless him, he was really handsome and so very young. Fresh faced, his whole life ahead of him. With me.

I have drifted into a deep, deep sleep, I am back at the plantation, it's evening. I hear the sounds of crickets' echoes, the sounds of the night garden. The sweet aroma from the apple, lemon, and lime trees encase the lining of my nostrils.

"Edwina, wake up," Winnie gently rocks me.

"Hmmmmmm"

"Wake up. Where have you been?" Winnie was excited about something.

"I have been here."

"No, you haven't. I have not seen you in weeks," she snipped.

"Really?"

"Yes. Where were you?"

"The last I remembered we went for lunch, which for me was like yesterday. Actually, it feels like that occurred earlier today."

"Well, you are here now. There is so much to tell you."

"Like what?"

"I met a really nice young man."

"Really? Who is he?"

"Remember the waiter that daddy was really rude to?"

"You mean?"

"Yes, at the Crystal Hotel. It's him."

"Daddy is going to lose his mind when he finds out," I warn her.

"He's not going to find out, is he? It's not like *you* will tell him. Nothing is happening, I just like him, that's all. We talked a few times."

"How is that even possible?"

THE JOURNEY

"Daddy and I have lunch there every Thursday. There are some places not even daddy can follow me to."

"Such as?" I arch my eyebrow with disapproval.

"The Powder Room."

"You meet in the Powder Room?" I laugh.

"Nooooooo. There is a small store cupboard, and we sneak a few minutes each week with each other. We exchange letters, and he kissed me yesterday. It was just scrumptious, his lips were so soft. He really cares about me. I think he might even love me."

We did not hear the door open. "Who might love you?" grandma Phyllis said with a quizzical glare.

"My daddy," Winnie spat out the words with such venom, both grandma and I was taken aback.

Grandma walked towards the bed where Winnie lay. Suspecting that her grandmother may take this as an opportunity to beat her, Winnie jumped off the bed and stood her ground by.

"So, you think your daddy loves you?"

"I know so."

"You gullible, naïve child. Your father is incapable of love, he is damaged goods. You can thank your mother's family for that?"

"What does that mean?"

Realising that she had said too much. "Nothing."

"My father loves me and you can't stand it can you?"

"You know nothing of love."

"I knew the love of my grandmother before you all killed her. That was real love."

"Lucy was a ..."

"What grandma?" Winnie was shouting at my Grandmother.

"She was a lying, deceitful old peasant, who deserved to die like a dog."

"Nooo," Winnie lurched towards her grandma fist raised.

"Mother!" Daddy screamed at her from my bedroom door. "Get out!"

"Barrington, darling, thank God you're here. This insolent little street urchin."

"ENNNNOOOOUUGGGHHHH!!!!" Daddy screamed at my Grandma. She stop dead in her tracks and slowly backed away.

Winnie was lying on the all fours, her head on the perfectly polished mahogany wooden floor weeping her soul out. Daddy grabbed his mother by her shoulders and walked her forcefully out of the room. He sat down on the floor next to his daughter. He attempted to hold his daughter close. Winnie pulled away and slapped her father hard in the face. "Grandma is right. You murdered my Mima like a dog," Winnie spat the words out.

"Edwina" daddy was crying. "I ...am so sorry."

"Get out!" Winnie screamed. "Get out!" They were both on their feet, Winnie's fists were clenched and in motion, she was driving them into her father's chest as hard as she could. Barrington stood his ground and allowed his daughter to pound him hard repeatedly until she was tired.

"Get out! Get out! Get out!" Daddy walked out and

slammed the door. Winnie sobbed on the floor for hours. I tried to comfort her my little self, it was no use. Grandma Phyllis had just ripped the scab of this wound, and it was bleeding heavily.

Chapter 12

Barrington Barnett Junior

What in the world possessed my mother to be so rancorous? Come on, Barry, how can you make this right? I run down the staircase, through the corridor and out of the house. The night air is warm and pungent with the smells of the plantation. Too angry to confront my mother, I walk towards the main road. It's at least a mile, this should give me time to think. I look up, the moon is full, a light breeze washes over me and proceeds to cool my temperament. My initial stomp has been traded for a rhythmical walk to the melody of the swoosh and churn of miles of sugarcane, which are enveloped either side of me.

I shake my head, not knowing how to mend this fragile bridge between my daughter and myself. All of my emotions swell around my body, yet, I feel the heftiness of the burden in my chest. The pain is indescribable, but this is the closest I have been to heartbreak. *How could my mother inflict a wound so deep into her only grandchild? It's just so ... cruel.*

I arrive to the main road and am surprised that I have travelled so far in such a short time. *Well, Barry, this is progress, five years ago you would have shot your mother in the face.* I smile at my sick sense of humour, although it is not amusing, I feel like laughing at the situation. I have travelled an arduous emotional road to get here and do not wish to return. I turn around to walk back, I see the plantation, unable to face the confrontation which lays ahead of me, with a heavy heart, I walk deep into the sugar cane fields. I find a spot in between the perfectly manicured rows and lay down, gazing at the clear night sky. It was truly magnificent, each star that I focused on seemed to shine and twinkle brighter. I think fleetingly of the spirits I have released from their waking bodies: Angeline, Lucy, and Mrs. Mack. I cannot help it, nor do I want to control this. I weep for all the pain that I have caused. I weep for displacing the only person that I have loved without fear, but most of all, I weep for myself. As I look into the night's sky, I feel God's presence over me. *This is bigger than me, Edwina, my mother, and all the others. I can do better. I will do better.*

I awake with a start. It's deep into the night and I am cold. It's been raining and I am soaked through. I walk to the house and see that most of the lights downstairs are on. I walk with haste, fearful that something awful may have happened in my absence. I open the door and my father, mother, and Winnie run out of the drawing room.

"Oh Barry, you're ok!" my mother exclaimed with sheer relief in her voice.

My anger cannot be sustained. She runs to hug me and I push her away hard, she nearly topples over.

"Barry!" she yelps as she steadies herself on the paisley armchair by the wall.

My father steps forward, I put my hand up and look at him, "Don't!"

"Have you been drinking?" my father asks annoyed.

"No father I am sober." They all looked relieved.

"I just needed some time away. I was angry and did not want to do or say anything that I would later regret." I look at Winnie, who seems tired.

"Are you angry with me Daddy?" Winnie asks in a shaky voice, she is beautiful in her white night dress, her hair all unruly.

"No Winn. I have no issue with you. You were being human, reacting to information delivered by your Grandmother's acid tongue. You were … are wounded, I accept that. It was a normal response, nothing more than I deserved under the circumstances."

Winnie looked pained as she searched her father's face for clues as to what he was thinking. "Daddy, I am going to bed, now that I know that you are safe… Goodnight." I could tell that she thought about kissing me, but decided against it. Things are awkward between us. The swell in my chest rises. There was only one person to blame for all this pain.

Before she leaves the room she looks at mother, she smirks I think. I am not sure if I am overtired. We all watch my beautiful child as she disappeared around the corner. I cannot contain my rage. I looked angrily at my mother and father and walked into the drawing room.

"Barry, look, I am so very sorry for my indiscretion," my mother quickly walked around the armchair in the opulent room. She was fidgeting with her hands, and both my father and I could tell that she was nervous. "It was thoughtless and ... and ... and ..."

"For a woman with so many words, I am surprised that you are finding it difficult to find the right one. *Cruel* is the word that you are looking for," my message is delivered with authority. *I am no longer the puppy, led by his throat. I am a man, my own man, and tonight she will see this.*

"Yes," she mutters almost inaudible, she barely looks at me. She senses the sea change in me, she feels my new energy resisting her. The relationship has shifted. I am in the driving seat.

"Sorry, mother, what was that?" *I can't help it. I need to see her squirm.*

"Yes. It was *cruel*, and I am truly sorry." She is searching my face, wondering whether this pathetic excuse is enough.

I stare at my mother for what seemed like an eternity. I did not realise that I had started to cry again, not until the tears fell off my cheek.

"Barry, I am so"

I put my hands up, and my mother stopped in her tracks.

"You are a deceitful, treacherous, conniving, miserable, cruel, wicked old bitch mother. That is what you are.

THE JOURNEY

You have manipulated me for far too long."

Both my parents look aghast at my disrespect. "I am the way that I am because of you. I have committed hellish acts because *you* are my mother. You have been able to wind me up, and I foolishly have created havoc in your name. You said those things to *crush* my only child. Your *only* grandchild. You said those things because you are jealous that we have fostered a relationship despite the odds."

"Nooooo, Barry."

"Shut up and do not interrupt me. You said those things because you, my friendly serpent, prefer me drunk and wanting, in need of your assistance. Were you trying to get me to throw myself in a bottle again? I will never forgive you for this mother. You have taught me that I have misplaced my trust in you. A mother who loves her son does not behave in this way. A Grandmother that loves her Grandchild would not dream in hurting them like this."

The room fell silent, and my mother was wiping her eyes. She looker old and small.

My father looked at me and nodded. "I am sorry for you son," he had not called me son in many years. "I don't say this often. Irrespective of what you have done in the past, I am proud of you and the way you have turned your life around. Man to man, you have my respect. At least, now you can see your mother for who and what she is." My father looked at his wife. "I expect you in my room in the next five minutes. I suggest you go and prepare yourself."

A cold chill ran down my spine. I knew how my father kept my mother under control these days, I did not like it, but now I see that it was perhaps a necessary evil.

It has been a long time since I have craved for a drink

like this. The pull is so strong that I know that, if I stay, I am going to fall off this five year wagon of sobriety, and I may never get back on it. It's been a struggle every day. Some days are better than others. The last twenty four hours have been the absolute worst.

I just need to get through tonight, and tomorrow is a new day. I laugh at myself and with myself. I relay the evening in my mind. My heart is overcome with emotion. My father is proud of me, the man that I have carved out of the gutter. I momentarily flash back to whom I was. I push the old Barrington away. It's safer for my sobriety that way. My eyelids are like iron clads. I cannot keep my eyes open any longer, and I fall into a deep and peaceful sleep.

It's dawn, I feel the warmth of her soft naked skin next to me. I turn, and Donna is tucked under my arm. She is plainly beautiful in her own sort of way. I find her enchanting, loyal, and ruthless. Had she had been from different stock, I may have married her. She has been my sole stabling force for the past five years. She was my savior and salvation, and I will love her to the end of time.

I lay awake, restless, looking aimlessly at the ceiling.

The night sky was slowly creeping away.

"Good morning, darling," she whispered and kissed me on my forehead. This was how she greeted me every morning for the last five years.

"How are you?" she asked, her face full of concern. Her big brown eyes searched mine for a sign, any sign.

"I am hurt, sweetheart, really hurt," I scrunch my eyes closed like a child.

My lover entwines her body with mine, and my head lay in her full breasts. Comforted by her womanly curves, I

THE JOURNEY

hold on to my love.

"Barrington, it will get better. This is storm, and it too will pass. We will all get through this." She delivers the message like she always does, with conviction and sweetness.

I look at her, "How?" tears wet my eyes. "How can you be so sure? She hates me, and so she should. I am a wicked, vile human being." My voice cracks, "I have done unspeakable things."

"That man is now gone, you are a different person. It's your mother who is vile and wicked," she snapped.

I look at her cautiously.

"Darling, this is not your fault. This is not ... on you."

"How can I fix this?" I nestle my head in her chest, she holds me tight.

"You can't Barry. You just have to give her time and space."

"I don't know how. We have come so far. Finally she is talking to me, and now it's ruined." I close my eyes and roll over.

"Then go somewhere, take a break, you deserve it. A break may just cool the temperature down for everyone?" She raises my head and looks at me "What do you think darling?"

"I will only go if you come with me," I tell my beloved.

"That could never happen you know that."

"A break will do us good. It's time to stop with the charade. Let's be together. I need you by my side as my woman, my wife," I say quietly.

"Your mother would have be strung up," she laughs, "no, thank you."

"Why?" I ask insecurely. "Do you want to get rid of me?"

"Never," Donna proclaimed with delight. "Never," she whispered again. With that, her hot mouth reached mine, and she sedated my quest for alcohol two successive times.

Chapter 13

The Blooming of flowers

THE JOURNEY

Our plantation library was a place of wonder. The 14 foot walls were covered from wall to ceiling with deep oak wood shelves that glossed and sparkled. Every inch of this room housed classics, from Proust, William Shakespeare, the Bronte sisters, and Tennyson. I lay on the 60 foot Oriental rug, so opulent you would be forgiven thinking that it came directly from the Ming Dynasty. I feel so very sober. These years that I have blocked out, erased all memories, irrespective of whether they were happy or not. How I robbed myself of the core of me. Like it or not, this was my legacy, and I gave it up for love? Or did I? Was I an unruly teenager in the throes of puberty? Or did I make poor choices? Now that I have seen my father, I can see that he is truly remorseful for his crimes. I have filled my heart with hate for this man, when all I feel is love for him right now. Maybe I could have made this relationship better. He was right, Harold was not good enough for me. This love has taken all that I have to keep this marriage together. Why? Why did I just not leave? I could have had a different life with Courtney. I have never longed for, yearned for, and loved a man with more passion, than I did him. Yet, I stayed. I was a coward.

I was a wife and mother. I chose Harold all those years ago. My choice nearly cost him his life. My family made me indebted to him, trapped like an animal at times, and here I am. Full of regret that I did not pursue the love of my life.

"Edwina, what's wrong?" Winnie asks.

I roll my eyes. There is not much to say, "Nothing, I am fine," I tell her with dejection in my voice.

"You're not," Winnie chimes in.

"No, Winnie, I'm not. I am dying of cancer. Three weeks ago, I was diagnosed with Terminal Stage 4 Malignant Melanoma, which has metastasized to my brain and chest."

Winnie looked scared. "What does that mean?" she whispered wide eyed.

"It means that the tumors have spread from their original primary site in my breast and have developed in my brain and chest." My younger self looks crushed. "Winn, I am only here because I am dying. This is not a figment of your imagination, it's real. I am here when I should be with my husband, beautiful children, my friends and I cannot understand why I am reliving this, this painful chapter in my life. I shut this out a long time ago and never thought that I would revisit it. Now I am here. I cannot do this." I cry, but no tears fall. The pain in my chest seizes me, and my body becomes rigid, and I collapse on the floor.

"Edwina, Edwina, please don't die, you're not ready." Winnie falls to her knees and holds my head in her lap. She kisses my forehead. "You are all that I have. Please stay." As her tears wash over me, I feel ease through my body. I look at her.

"I cannot do this anymore. I want to die, it's *tooo* much Winn. I just need to go," I plead to her and God, wanting them to take me to a place where I am pain free.

"You cannot leave yet. There is much that you need to do first. It's not quite your time," she said, looking very mature and grown up.

At the corner of my eye I saw a figurine at the door. "Winn," I say looking at the doorway.

Winnie swung around.

"Who are you talking to child? And what are you doing on the floor?" Grandmother Phyllis asks. She hesitantly walked into the room and looked around the corner, under the table and behind the book shelf.

"Answer me, who were you talking to?" she carefully

THE JOURNEY

stepped towards the drapes and pulled them apart, to ensure there was no stranger lurking in the room.

"I will not tell you," Winnie wails then looks at me "Please, don't leave me," she looks deep in my eyes. "Not now."

"What?"

"I will not tell you," she sobs openly at her loss.

"What is it child?" my grandmother looked shaken by my display of emotion.

"*You* would not *understand!*" Winn was still hunched over, cradling my head.

"Get up," grandma Phyllis commanded.

"I can't grandma. She is dying, can't you see her?"

"Who?" grandma turned pale. "Edwina, there is no one here?"

"I am here. Look harder. It's me and I'm dying." Winnie is hysterical.

"Ed … Edwina, please, get up, dear." Grandma is really concerned, she kneeled down next to me and pleaded quietly for me to get up. Fear washed over my grandma, she ran from our room. "Barrington!" she yelled, "Barrington, come quickly! Come quickly!" her voice became shrill and high.

My miniature self, on the cusp of womanhood, whose primary emotion since the age of five has been grief and loss, looks at me, begging desperately for guidance. This cancer is ravaging my insides, the fight is nearly over, and I am starting to feel relieved. She helps me to the sofa, lovingly. I want to reassure this young girl before me, but I just can't. She looks at me, "Don't die! Who will I talk to?" I weakly squeezed her hand, she looks at me. "Listen, Winnie, do not tell them about me. They will think that you are mad. Please, stop talking. Ok?"

Winnie just nodded.

Lying on the sofa chair did not ease my pain, but enabled me to feel better. I could sense myself drifting back. "No, I need to stay," I willed myself.

"Winn." I hear Daddy shouting my name as he ran towards the library taking giant steps at a time. Grandpa was next, and grandma Phyllis a few seconds behind.

Winnie sat on the floor, leaning up against the sofa chair. Daddy immediately scooped her up and put her on the bed.

"Winn, darling, talk to daddy. You ok? Who is here with you?"

"No one," Winn sobbed.

"Barry, that's not what she said, I swear," the words tumbled out of Grand mama's mouth.

Daddy picked up Winnie's hands and kissed them. "Baby, tell daddy, what is it? What's going on?"

"Daddy, please, don't ask me," she threw her head in his lap, he stroked her hair, trying to reassure her.

"It's ok. No matter what you say, I promise I won't get mad. I will not react. Is that what you're worried about?"

"Pleeeeaaasssseee...."

Daddy held his only child, as if she was about to die any moment.

"Tell me, Winn, what is it?"

THE JOURNEY

She looked at daddy. "They are here with me."

"Who is, darling?" grandpa asked and stepped forward.

Winnie threw her head on her father's shoulder. The others looked at each other, confused.

"Who, Winn? Mother says you were crying and saying that someone is dying. What is going on?" he sounded desperate.

Winnie points to the lounge chair by the patio doors. "Mima is sat right there." Daddy's eyes grew large, and all three of them stood with open mouths. On the chair is Mrs. Mack."

"Mrs. Mack!" Grandpa exclaimed. "What?"

Grandfather walked cautiously towards Winnie, daddy took at least four steps back, both hands ran through his hair. He clasped his fingers and locked them at the nape of his neck. He starred at Winnie, incredulous at what she confessed. Daddy and grandma Phyllis were locked in the same shocked gaze.

Grandpa sat down on the chair next to me. "Princess, look at me." He said quietly.

As Winnie looked up, she saw the disgusted look on my face. She smirked at me.

"Princess, how long have you been hearing voices?" grandfather asked.

"I am not hearing voices grandpa. They are here. I can see and hear them."

"What are they saying?"

"Mrs. Mack is asking me to tell Mackie that she is ok. She's found peace." I look at daddy. "She has a message for you too. Do you want to hear it?"

Simultaneously, daddy said "yes" and grandma Phyllis screamed "no".

"Tell me," daddy demanded. He was pale and looked like he needs to vomit.

"Mrs. Mack says that, to this day, she doesn't understand why you had to rape her. She did not deserve that. She would never have told Mackie, the shame would have killed her. 'You did not have to murder me,' she says, 'I would have taken my own life sooner or later, as I would not been able to live with what you did to me'. She says that you will rot in hell, and no peace will follow you until you die."

"Enough!" Grandma Phyllis screamed. Daddy ran to the corner of the room and threw up his breakfast. He was on his knees.

"Barry, really, the girl is delusional. It can happen when one has had a shock," Grandpa tried to explain.

Grandpa took a moment to soak up the emotions in the room. The air was thick with fear. "Barry, Barry .... This is just .... Barry, Phyllis. What aren't you telling me?" grandpa's voice became quiet.

Grandma Phyllis walked to the balcony window.

"Father ... I ... What Winnie says is true, I did those things and ..."

"No, Barry. No. No. How could you do this to her, to Mackie? My god you *are* an animal. My Grandpa had tears streaming down his face. "I begged Mackie to stay after Lucy. He was going to leave and take his wife with him and I begged him." My grandfather faced turned red, he was in shock shaking his head, tears sprang from his eyes. He stood there looking at my father, "you have stained your soul son, damn you, damn the both of you. Damn and blast both your rotten souls to hell" he then stormed out of the room and slammed the door with such velocity that the field hands could have heard it.

"Tell Mrs. Mack that not a day goes by that I do not regret that night," daddy said, "and", his voice cracked, "your Mima, tell her that I am so very sorry for all the pain that I ..." daddy pointed to Grandma Phyllis, that we have caused her."

"What did grandma do, daddy?" I ask, feeling sick before he could answer.

He looked at me. "I am sure Mima will tell you at some point. *She* killed your grandpa Vincent, it wasn't me."

"No," Winnie sat on her chair, looking at her grandma with sheer horror.

"How?" I whispered.

"The how does not matter. What's done is done and cannot be undone," grandma Phyllis said quietly.

"Oh Winnie, what have you done?" I ask her. "You have opened Pandora's Box, and I do not think that even *you* can put this right."

Winnie looks at me. She gives me a chilling stare and whilst looking at me says "Grandma, she has a message for you too."

"Who?" Grandma was as white as a sheet.

"She says that she knows that you see her in your dreams. She wants you to know that you will never have peace, not even in death. Neither of you will have peace."

Any lasting pigment left in my Grandmother's complexion completely drained away. My father walked out the room with his bowed head and quietly shut the door. Grandmother swiftly followed him.

"Winnie," I exclaimed. "What were you thinking?"

"Me?! You have sat here, with your boohoo depression, talking about how terrible it's been. I am doing something about it. I am going to make them all pay. All this family does is destroy people."

"Well, you definitely fit in now, don't you?"

"What? Do you not remember how he killed Mima? You told me that he raped and murdered Mrs. Mack. Remember, she was *our* only friend. What do you expect me to do? Nothing? Not going to happen. I will destroy them as they have destroyed me, as they destroyed you. How can you live your life not remembering you childhood? How can that be possible?"

"This is not the answer. Daddy was distraught," I snapped.

"So was Mima, so was Mrs. Mack, and the countless others that he has killed, raped and destroyed," she shouted. "They are both culpable, and I am going to make them pay for it. You blocked it all out, as it was too much to bear. *It is* too much to bear. I know, I am living it."

"I am too weak Winnie to fight with you. You have to be prepared. This will not end well my dear. I roll over and fall into a deep sleep."

"Edwina, don't go! What am I going to do? Edwina. Edwina."

THE JOURNEY

The sun rises and sets on my lonely heart. It's been weeks since I have seen Edwina. I don't know whether she is dead or alive. Oh Lord, please don't take her away from me before I have the opportunity to apologize. She has to understand. I have to make them pay for what they have done to me. They robbed me of my grandfather and Mima. The only woman outside of my family that loved me enough to nurture, sing, and play with me was Mrs. Mack. What did my father do to her?! He rapes her, and then he kills her. I am going to make them regret the day they snatched me from Mima.

The last few months have been glorious with daddy, but a few months cannot put right all the death, pain, and hurt he and my grandma Phyllis have caused me. The math just does not add up. I should not feel like this. I have done nothing wrong. It's them.

Grandpa had avoided everyone. He is staying in town, in a flat above the surgery. I heard the maids whispering that daddy has started drinking. I didn't want him to drink, he is a nasty drunk, and when drunk, he is unpredictable and dangerous. I just wanted him to hurt. If he cannot control his demons, that has nothing to do with me. Grandma Phyllis won't look at me, each time she sees me, she is touching her crucifix. It's not avoidance, it's terror. I am more alone than I have ever been. Maybe Edwina was right. I have unleashed the madness. Loneliness and solitude is something that I have been used to. The difference between then and now is that I had someone to make conversation with. Even snidely conversation is better than this. Now I have nothing. I did not think that it was possible to feel anymore alone with so many family members around me.

My oversized closet is every woman's dream. I dress as a lady should. I put on my lime dress, I wet my hair and crunch my curls, and slip a matching ribbon around my curly bonnet. I wear my Chanel white heals. I look at myself in the mirror. I look tired, but then, I feel really warn out. This emotional conflict that I am experiencing is taken its toll on me. I may not have the maturity or the strength to see this through, and I am really scared. I have unhinged them. I look at myself in the mirror again and apply some pink lipstick.

"What would Edwina say?" I ask myself out loud. "Hmmm she would say 'You started this. So finish it! Be strong, decisive, and honest.'" I smile to myself. "Oh my God, how can I be so foolish?! It's you, Edwina. I *am* you. I make it. I actually make it, and that won't change. Edwina is living proof of that." I review my image in the mirror. "Give them all hell! I can. Whatever is to come, I survive," I laugh loud and smile at myself.

I run downstairs, as I was positive that I heard voices. I put in my best act as I bounce into the breakfast room.

"Morning, father, grandmother."

"Morning," they say at the same time.

"You look nice," grandma Phyllis declares in a sweet voice. I actually think she meant it.

"You ok?" daddy asks me, looking around the breakfast room for signs of life outside of me.

"I will be when you stop drinking, daddy," I say. The maid in the corner of the room raised her eyes from the papers she was arranging and looked at me.

"What?! How do you know that?" he asked alarmed.

"Don't worry daddy," I giggle. "I did not get a message. I overheard one of the maids last week. If I look tired, it's because I am worried about you. Besides, you're a mean drunk."

THE JOURNEY

"I slipped once," daddy explained quietly. "It's ... it's been hard to process these last few weeks. There's been a lot to take in."

I felt a huge pang of guilt. I look up and see grandma Phyllis smiling at me.

"I was thinking that maybe I should go away for a few weeks," daddy tried to play it down.

"Really, where?" I am surprised, but hide it well.

"Anywhere except here," daddy muttered. His light was gone.

"Barry, you need to be here for ... for ... Edwina. You can't leave now," grandma pleaded. What she really meant was that you cannot leave *her* with me. Not now.

"Daddy, I will be fine. I am ok, I promise. I think grandpa was right. I must have been delusional, as I have had no more visits." I smile at them both, desperately trying to reassure them.

"How long do you think that you will be gone?" I say, too bubbly for everyone's liking.

"Not sure, maybe a month," daddy tells me, eating his scrambled eggs.

"Ok. Where will you go?" I ask, more sedate this time.

"I was thinking about going to see some of Daddy's family in the United States?"

"Daddy, that would be great. Please go. Besides, it will give grandma and I time to actually have some girl time." I look at my grandma, who appears to be disgusted at the prospect. "How does that sound?"

She glances at daddy, "It sounds divine."

I give grandma a smile, she can see that I know that daddy needs this time of solitude. "Settled, then."

"When will you go?"

Daddy hesitantly looks around the room, "Tomorrow."

"Daddy, can I go into town?" I ask.

"What for?" grandma snapped. I eye her like a swordfish with my curt side eye.

"To visit grandpa. I have not seen him for a few days." I look suspiciously at the maids, trying to choose my words carefully. "So can I go, please?"

"Of course. You know, Winnie I am constantly in awe at how thoughtful and kind you are. Always thinking of others. Who would have expected that I will have such a lovely daughter?" daddy smiled.

"It's easy daddy. I have all your best bits and mummy's good bits," I got up and kissed him on the head. "Thank you daddy."

"You're welcome, Winn."

"Grandma, do you have any message for grandpa, or would you like to send him any fresh clothes?"

"No dear, thank you," my grandma eyed me suspiciously. I smile to avert her gaze.

"I will ask Mackie to drive you," daddy said.

"Is that wise," grandma chimed, immediately after he said it.

"Hmmmm."

"Daddy, it's fine," I leaned in and whispered in his ear. "I am *your* daughter and your secret is safe with me. I am a Barnett after all." Daddy looked at me and smiled. He looked proud.

He cleared his throat, "It's fine mother."

"But, Barry!" she exclaimed.

"It's *fine*, mother. Mackie will drive her. Besides, ironically, I trust Mackie with my life. He will take good care of my little girl."

I flash my grandma a big smile. "Grandma, can I get you anything from town?"

"No dear," she looks at me with hateful caution.

"Ok daddy. I will be ready to leave in ten minutes. That ok?"

"I will call Mackie now," and he left the table.

As soon as daddy was out of earshot, "What are you up to little girl?"

"Wouldn't you like to know, grandma?"

"Careful now, that is my son you're playing with. She stood up and walked towards me.

I straighten up and looked my grandma in the face. "I am not playing, believe me," I say quietly, as we have given the maids quite a show already.

"Just because you have your daddy wrapped around your finger, do not think you can do the same with me," grandma hissed, through her smiling face and gritted teeth.

I laughed and deliberately throw my head back. "I do not want you wrapped around any part of me, grandmamma," I snapped spitefully.

"You become more like Mima every day," she says quietly.

"Then you should watch out."

"Me. Tut-Tut. I *destroyed* her. Remember!" Grandma suddenly became aware where she was, and that we had an audience.

I stretch to the sky and cock my head at a right angle, "That was then, grandmamma. There is new, young, energetic fresh blood in the house old woman. You will find it hard to keep up." We both stare each other down. "Have a nice day, grandma. I will give your regards to grandpa."

The morning sun hazed my view to the extent that I had to squint to see Mackie. He was stood by the car. Over the years, his body had thinned, his chin appeared closer to his chest than I remembered.

"Good morning Miss Edwina," Mackie said with a smile.

"Good morning, Mackie." I avoided eye contact, as I felt choked with guilt at what my father had done.

"You look a vision this morning," he whispered blushing, as he opened the door.

"Thank you," I reciprocated in the same secretive tone as his.

We sat in the car and I look out, and the plantation was luscious green, yellow, and honey. It was the rainy season, and everything felt as if it were in bloom. We drove slowly along the dirt mile road. I sigh aloud.

"I know it's beautiful this time of year," Mackie broke my train of thoughts.

"How did you know?"

THE JOURNEY

"Miss. Look at this," he waved his hand across the windscreen to the view behind it. "Only a blind man would not appreciate the beauty," he chuckled.

"Mrs. Mack used to say that to me all the time."

He smiled, "Yes, sounds about right. She was the one that taught me that saying."

"I miss her," I say gently and quietly.

"Me too my darling. Me too," he looked out the window for a few seconds while driving. Mackie's shoulders drooped and he frowned. He wiped his eye quickly and cleared his throat and inhaled with speed.

"Mr. Mack, I am sorry. I just didn't think…. I did not mean to upset you. I just wanted to…."

"No, Noooooo, it's ok. I get like this sometimes. It's that time of year. It was Maggie's favorite time, the rainy season."

I giggle, "Wow."

"What?" he asked his eyes fixated in me.

"All these years, and I never knew her name?"

"Really?" he sounded surprised.

"Yes" I smile broadly.

I mist up. I can't help it. "I loved her, you know, she was is my only friend in the world."

"I know how you feel. She was the only person I could rely on," he tells me and means every word. "I just wish I could either find her or figure out what happened."

"With what?"

He looked at me "Something happened to Maggie. My everyday pain is that I have no closure. I have *no* peace. When someone dies you say goodbye. I didn't have a chance to do that. I am stuck in the not knowing."

"Are you sure that she is dead?"

"I know it," he tells me with conviction. "We have never been apart, not one day, and it's just not her style to go off. We ... loved each other. It's not like some of these people who are married that had to stay together out of duty. I only wanted *her*. I only loved *her*. That has not changed."

"Is that why you have never moved on?" I ask.

"Yes and no. I cannot move on, as I am stuck in the past. I have no closure. It's not fair to bring all the hurt, anxiety, and fear that I have about Maggie's death into something new."

"What about you? You are such a nice looking man. I know that you are good and kind, as Mrs. Mack would tell me so, all the time."

"Really?" Mackie smiled.

I nod and lower my eyes "I often wished you were my father instead of ... him."

He looks at me through sad eyes and shakes his head. "That sounds like my Maggie. She would always praise the good in a person."

"You can meet someone else. You can find love again, marry, have children. Mackie, if I was older, I would marry you," I blurt out.

Mackie laughed out loud, "You would would you?"

"Yes, I would. Mrs. Mack told me what a great person you are. She was hoping for a child one day. She was soooo good to me."

"Darling, *you* were our child. You are still my child, and we loved you as if you were our own blood. Especially ... when you first arrived. You were so ... wounded."

His words seep through my pores like a sponge. I look at Mackie, tears in my eyes, he pulls into the layby on the highway.

"You ok Miss?" he enquires.

"No," I whisper.

"Now it's my turn to apologize. I should not have said that to you. I am sorry."

"Mr. Mack, you tell no lies so don't apologize. You have done nothing wrong. My father is the culprit here, and *he* is to blame."

Mackie's eyes fall to the gear stick. "Miss Edwina, I loved your grandmother with all my heart. She and your grandpa Vin, they were *good* people. Whenever I go to town, people, neighbours stop me and still ask after you, all this time. 'How is Mr. Vin's and Miss Lucy's granddaughter?' Do you know how many warnings I get for you?" he laughed. "Warnings, I kid you not."

"I don't understand," I giggled.

"This person and that person say 'Make sure you look out for her in that house!' For poor Maggie it was worse." he laughed.

"What was she like?" I ask.

"Who, Maggie?"

"No. I mean yes, but I was referring to my grandmother Lucy."

He smiled. "Your grandmother was a pioneering woman, she was wise before her years, and she was talented with a sewing machine. Oh my, Lord knows that I tell the truth, she used to make Mrs. Barnett dresses and gowns. That was when your grandma was a looker. She could turn a blind man's head."

"Really?"

"Yes, she was beautiful," Mackie nodded.

"No, not about that. Mima made grandma's dresses? Really? I did not know that. Hmmm, Mima worked for grandma."

"Yes," Mackie said, realizing that he might have said a little too much.

"Mackie, don't stop. This conversation is between us. No one talks about her, and it's really hard. I know that I have this love for all of them but do not know why, and my childhood memory is so limited."

"Your grandpa Vin was an amazing man. He was a good friend to my father. They were neighbours, at the plantation."

"What, *our* plantation?"

"Yes, his father was a slave, as was my great grandfather."

"Then how did he get to the big house?" I was fascinated by my family history.

"It was largely due to your grandmother. She was a wealthy woman at one point, from all her dress making. She made a lot of money from dresses for weddings, christenings, and that sort of events. Her clients were wealthy whites in Kingston. There was a war on, so imports from Europe and the US were nonexistent, and

THE JOURNEY

your grandmother could sew. She worked hard and made enough to buy that plot of land. Vincent was not happy. He wanted to be the provider, but he soon came around. They represented the dream of every slave and plantation worker. Ownership of land meant ownership of your time, ownership of you, the man. Do you know what that means for a black man like me? It meant everything. Your grandmother, when she started to build that house, some people did not speak to her, as they felt that she wanted to be better than them. Miss Lucy put them right. She started to tell them that the white house was not just for her and Vincent, it was for the community. When your grandfather discovered that Vin owned land with his wife, he evicted them."

"What?" I asked shocked.

Mackie's voice changed, it was harder, "Yes Miss. People like us, in their minds, must always be subservient and grateful."

"Mackie, I had no idea. I am always remembering her being so capable. How did my grandfather die, Mackie?"

Mackie starred at me as if I asked him to sleep with me.

"Mackie, how did he die?"

"Miss ..., I am not going to lie to you. I know exactly how he died, but it's not for me to tell you the ... how?"

"Then who?"

"Miss ..., I think we need to get going, Miss."

"Does it involve my father?" I ask.

Mackie's eyes were dead straight on the road.

"My grandfather?"

"Miss, it does not matter how many times you ask, I have

told you my stance on this position, and it will not change," he said gently.

The rest of the journey was in silence. On arrival, Mackie got out and opened my door. As I got out of the car, he reached his hand to help me. He looked at me. "You look like her, you know?"

"Who, Mima?"

"No darling, your mother."

Tears sprang to my eyes. "Really? I don't know what she looks like. I have not seen any picture of her."

"Miss, she was a very beautiful person and had the kindest heart. Your grandpa Vin called her his butterfly. She was delicate like Lucy, but she was strong."

I hug Mackie. "Thank you."

Mackie gently pushes me off him, looking around to ensure that gossiping mouths do not get the wrong idea. "What time shall I pick you up?"

"I would like to spend the day, so do not rush back, please," I ask. "And Mackie."

"Yes, Miss."

"Do not ever call me Miss again. Its Winnie to you, ok?"

He smiled, "Ok, Winnie."

In all the years that I lived with my grandparents and father, I had not once visited the Barnet's Medical Centre. I had driven past it, waited outside of it with my grandma Phyllis, yet we never entered. I walk up the steps and knock on the door. There is movement inside, thank goodness, or I would be stuck. A tall, thin, beautiful mature woman walks towards the door. She has her hair in a bun, and a lovely pale blue, mid length

THE JOURNEY

skirt and matching short sleeve shirt. She looked very sophisticated.

She opens the door and stares at me.

"I am sorry to disturb you, I am looking for my" before I could finish, she cut me off.

"Grandfather," she says, her eyes were misty. "I know who you are. Come in, Winnie." She took my hand, it felt so familiar to me that I did not withdraw it. I allowed her to lead me through the surgery, up some stairs. At the top of the stairs was an enchanting open plan room. It was so simple: Beachwood floors, open shutters, a sea view in the distance, sophisticated cream lean furnishings. It seemed so modern. The bed overlooked the window, and the view of the village, with the blue sea protruding out of the tree tops, was enchanting.

"This is breathtakingly beautiful," I exclaim.

"Yes, it is," my mystery woman agrees with me.

"Now I understand why grandpa spends *so* much time here. It's delightful. Where is he?"

"He is out with a patient. She is very unwell and may not survive the day, so…"

"I see, well, I can leave."

"No. No." this stranger woman says, "Please stay". She looks at me, intently drinking in every element of my presence.

"I was about to make lunch. Can I get you something to drink? Juice, water, anything cool, Winnie?"

"How do you know my nick name?"

"I know you. My name is"

I abruptly interrupt her "Rene. Is your name Rene. Are you my auntie Rene?"

"Yes, Winnie darling" she leapt into my arms, and we held one another for a long time. She kissed my face, neck, and the backs of my hands, all the while, her wet tears caressing my skin.

"My darling, my beautiful, sweet honey pie. My sweet darling. How I have longed for this this moment. Look at you! Perfection, just like your mother."

My aunt Rene made us iced tea, we sat in the living area.

"How are you?" she enquired.

"I am well, thank you?" I say politely.

"Are you?"

"Aunty Rene, I think you used to come to Mima's. Is that you? Have I remembered the right person?"

"Yes, Mima and I were sisters. Not blood sisters, but sisters none the less."

My heart skipped. I feel weak. "Today is a strange day?"

"Why?" my aunt Rene looked concerned.

"Mr. Mack and I were talking for the first time about Mima and grandpa Vin," I smiled.

She smiled, "How is Mackie?"

"He is well. I love that man so much!"

"He and Maggie were ... *are* good people," she corrects herself.

"Hmmm," I nod, whilst fidgeting with my fingers.

THE JOURNEY

"Winnie, as I said, your grandmother and I grew up as sisters. Your grandpa Vin and I were like brother and sister. I am the closest family that you have here."

I snap at her, "Then why am I not living with you?"

Surprised by my rude outburst, she explains, "I tried to take you, to raise you, but your father had rights. He was the father. I tried everything, but they were too strong for me," she says regretfully.

"Who was?" I snap.

"Your grandmother, your father."

"Hmmmm," I continue to fidget. I am feeling very warm all of a sudden. *Rene keeps staring at me, which unnerves me.*

"You are such a stunner. I heard that you had blossomed, but this is ... you are lovely," she smiles.

"Hmmmmm," I look out of the window.

"Are you ok?" she asks.

"Aunt Rene, why are you here? I mean in grandpa's private residence."

"The *truth*?" she sighs.

I nod, "Yes please." I want to be suspicious of her, but I can't, she seems so familiar to me.

"You grandfather and I have been lovers for twenty five years."

"Really?!" I gasp. I am annoyed at my response. I am momentarily unnerved, but intrigued, there are so many gaps for me. I intend to get answers, and I think she can close them all.

"Aunt Rene, this is a lot to take in." I chuckle, whilst reeling from my shock.

"I know, but for me it's wonderful to see you. I missed you," she says quietly.

"There are so many gaps that I have with events, people, and reasons why things occurred. Can you help me?"

"Sure," she says.

"Aunty Rene, I need answers, not platitudes," I look at her seriously "Will you *really* help me?"

Aunt Rene got off her chair and came and sat next to me, she cupped my face in her hands and looked me in the eyes. "If you ask it. I will tell the truth. All of it. Even the bits that are hurtful. I will not leave any of it out. I promise you."

Tears starts to roll down my face. "Tell me everything. I want to know about my mother and how she died. I want to know what actually happened between her and daddy. I heard today that Mima and Phyllis had a relationship. I need to know why grandpa Vin died at the hands of grandma Phyllis, and, finally, how did Mima injure her arm. I mean, if she was a seamstress, that was her income? Can you do that for me?"

She sighs hard, "Yes, I can." My aunty got up, walked to the bedroom, opened her dresser drawer and took out two white handkerchiefs. She then walked to the kitchen and grabbed a bottle of rum and two tumblers.

I hold my hands up. "I do not drink."

"No. But after I answer all that you have asked, you will need one," she says seriously.

She sits down and tells me everything. "My head is

pounding, aunty Rene. I cannot take any of this in. I am decedent of pure evil. My father raped my mother. My grandfather Vincent goes to rip my father's head off, quite rightly, and ends up dead because grandma Phyllis stabs him. As if that was not bad enough, my father, on the same night, hacks away my grandmother's shoulder with a machete. My mother then dies in childbirth, and years later, when they find out about me, my father kills my grandmother. Now, that's a family tree to be proud off." I look at Rene, "You must really love my grandfather."

"I do," she says quietly.

"He is really pure". She beams.

"Really? He *threw* my Grandfather off his plantation when he discovered that he bought land with Mima. That's terrible."

"Yes, he did those things, but regretted that decision and made peace with your Mima and Vin. Who do you think delivered you?"

"Grandpa?" I gave her a questioning glance.

"Yes, and he kept that secret, he never said a word. He would visit you every week."

"I … I don't remember. I had no idea."

"You had a lot of protectors," she says proudly.

-Bang –

-Bang- Bang-

"Is that the door?" we both jump out of our skin.

"Yes, it must be Mackie," I say.

I notice the time. It's after 6 pm, I look outside and it's

dark.

My aunt flies down the stairs and returns with Mackie. I am still lying on the sofa, looking ruined.

"Miss Winnie, you alright? You feel unwell?"

"No, Mr. Mack, I am fine. Just exhausted with my family. I know the truth now, all of it. I do not want to go home tonight. I *will* not go home tonight. Tell grandmother whatever you choose, but I will not go home. I need to speak to grandfather. Please tell my grandmother that I will be home tomorrow."

"Miss Winnie, she will not accept that," Mackie says, with a worried frown. He looks at Rene with disdain.

"I do not care about that. If she wants me, she can come and get me. I will be home tomorrow, after I have spoken to my grandfather," I say with annoyance.

I fall asleep after 8 pm, my aunt was right, I needed the rum, it definitely took the edge of the emotion. Deep in an alcohol induced sleep, I hear my grandpa calling my name. "Winnie, princess, wake up," he says. He looks tired and concerned that this day had tipped me over the edge.

"Princess. Come on, how much rum did she drink?" he yells angrily at Rene. He quickly understands that I have lost the use of my limbs and am clearly not in control.

"She had two glasses," Rene told him.

My Grandfather shakes me hard, "Winnie, wake up!"

"She is not a drinker," he says scornfully to Rene.

I stand then throw up all over the beautiful beach flooring. Grandfather hands me a handkerchief. Rene runs to the kitchenette for water.

THE JOURNEY

"I am so sorry," I moan.

"It's ok, Winnie, you're drunk. This is a natural reaction. I must get you home," he tells me, as he attempts to move me.

"Noooooo," I moan.

"Yes," he shouts at me angrily.

"I need to talk to you, please grandpa."

"We can talk in the car" he gave Rene a filthy look.

"Barry, she can at least stay the night. Poor dear is unwell," my aunt tries to reason with him.

"And whose fault is that?" he yells at Rene.

"Barry!" Rene exclaims.

"Shut your mouth!" he shouts back. I was shocked to hear my grandfather speak to anyone like that.

"Please grandpapa, you're scaring me." I had never seen this side to my grandfather, and I was starting to worry for Rene.

She tried to reassure me, "It's ok, see you soon," and waved bye.

My grandfather pulled me off the chair. I had the water in one hand, he had a bowl in the other. We entered the car. "Please don't be mad, she was just trying to help me."

"I can see that," he snapped. He sees that I am fighting the tears and looks at me. "I hear it's been an eventful day for you," he asks softly.

"Yes, it's been pretty awful," I wail.

He pats my knee "I would have told you everything when you turned 18 years old."

"Hmmmm," I give him the look of liar. "Grandpa, I need help. I don't know how long I have left in that house, with them, but I will need money. I will get a job and look"

My grandfather cut me off. "You will not get a job. No matter what, I will take care of you. I will make arrangements, you will never want for much," he said in his southern accent.

"Thank you," I smile, "I like Rene."

My grandfather smiles. "She is impossible, but I love her."

"I will tell you now, your day cannot get any worse. I plan to divorce your grandmother, and I am in the process of changing my will. They won't benefit from anything. I leave this all to you and Rene. Mrs. Mack it was the last straw. I cannot continue to pretend anymore. I love you, but I am fearful. It's the lies and secrecy that kills me. Your grandmother is your father's conspirator, she should never have helped him bury the body."

"Oh grandpa, where is she? She deserves a Christian burial. If not for us, for Mr. Mack, he is stuck in time, it's cruel."

"I don't know where she is. I am still trying to understand the how and why." He looked at me with sad eyes. "I will have an account set up for you by the end of the week. Ok?"

"Thank you." *I leap and dance inside.*

"Also, now that you are aware of everything, I must tell you that you've inherited Mima's estate. I can arrange an appointment with my lawyers, and we can meet to discuss how you proceed. You are already wealthy. Your aunt Rene has been managing the farm, plantation, and oversees all the sugar contracts. You can leave tomorrow and be independent. You don't need your father, or me."

"Really, grandpa?"

"Yes, Winn. You don't need any of us, that's why they have been trying to control you. *They* need you."

"No matter what, I will always need you," I tell him.

Chapter 14

Circumstance defines you

It was June 1955, and the piercing Jamaican sun beat down on Harold's neck and back, his skin shone like a precious onyx stone. Now 19 years old, his body was sculpted, and his muscles were rippling with every movement he crafted.

Winnie watched her man in the field. She smiled at the thought of him.

My butterflies creep into my abdomen and my man friend awakens in longing. I love this woman, and one day she will be mine, all of her.

Harold was so proud of his beau, she left her grandparents' house three years ago, and never looked back. Restoring the big house to its glory, with Mackie at her side, her farm was the most successful business in these parts. She had surpassed the plantation financially. *She was happy, we are happy and one day she will be my wife.*

"Harold you want some water boy?" Mackie offered. I take the copper cup and drink my fill, this was thirsty work.

"Hey boy, stop looking at the Mistress. You see how she is in the house and you are in the field? It's not going to happen," Calvin, my jealous younger brother, joked.

"Shut up fool," I snapped.

"It's been like forever, and you are still in the shade. It's like she is embarrassed to have someone like you as her man." he twisted the knife.

"Calvin, you would not know, as you have never been with a woman," I jibe, the other men laugh.

"Well, you have not been with the grand duchess over there, so we are even," he jabbed back. The men laughed louder and harder at my situation.

"*ENOUGH,*" Mackie bellowed, and immediately commanded quiet. "I have known many of you a long time, some of you all your lives. The next person that makes a dirty remark about the Mistress will not be able to work this farm ever again, nor, will they work any other farm in this district. Understand? I expect you to respect her. Not only when she is in front of you, but also when she is not. Understood?"

Murmurs of compliance from the men were received.

"Good," Mackie said with finality. "Harold, a word." the remaining men looked at Calvin, who bowed his head from my gaze as I walked past him, as he knew *yet* again that his reckless mouth had gotten someone, this time me, into trouble. I followed Mackie out of the thick of the cane field for a few minutes onto the road. It was clear that whatever he had to say to me he did not want any one hearing us.

"What is wrong with you?" Mackie demanded.

"Mackie, I ... look ..." I stutter.

"Do you feel that insecure that you have to talk about her like that to them foolish boys?!" he barked.

"Mackie," I try to laugh off my embarrassment, "listen, my brother, he's ..."

"I am not talking about your brother boy," Mackie stepped towards me.

I feel the fear in my gut rise to my throat, he was serious, his eyes narrowed, muscles flexed, and he was looking straight through me.

"I am talking about you." He lowered his head to my face, I could feel his warm breath. I cautiously step back, everyone knew that Mackie was not a man to be trifled with.

"Mackie, you know that I love Winnie," I complain.

"That's it boy, I don't know. How can you allow those fools to even put her name in their mouth like that, and you not slap it out?!" he yelled at me. I am grateful that he led me away from the flock, as I would never live this talk down.

"Listen Mackie." I try to interject, but Mackie had not finished with me.

"You say that you love her, but you do not honor this woman. Just look at what she has done in the last three years! She has restored this great house." He points aggressively in its direction. "You now have work, so does most of your family and village, and this is how you repay her?"

I look at Mackie, he is boiling hot, and I start to appreciate how remote we are. "Listen Mackie" I plead.

"It's Mr. Mack to you *boy*. Until you start acting like a man, you do not refer to another man by his name *boy*. Do you understand me?" He stepped forward, and every muscle from his jaw to his toe flexed. I feel his restraint. I sense his anger. I do the only thing a man who wants to see tomorrow could do, that is, I put both hands up. "Mr. Mack, I am so sorry.. You're right". I step back again, I am trying to get as close to the road as possible.

"She is a Barnett, and, for thirteen years, she has lived in privilege and comfort. Before that, Miss Lucy treated that girl like a princess. Lucy and Vincent are like our motherland's Royal Family. There are so many expectations set for her: where she will live, whom she will marry, how many children she will have. Half of the wealthiest families in Jamaica seek her hand in marriage. Yet, she is here, entertaining the village idiot, who is not man enough to command respect from his peers, let alone his family. Boy, if you love her, let her go as you are *not* man enough for her. If you insist that she is the one for you, and you truly want to be with her, *earn* her!" With that, Mackie stormed through the sugar cane field from where he came, breaking and spiking many of the canes as he ploughed through.

I look up to the sky, the sun penetrating through the cloudy haze onto my skin, like blue flames on a fire. I look at my feet, my shoes are battered, I did not even own them when they were new. Every piece of clothing that I own is as a result of a family member purchasing something new. Why would she choose *me*? *I* wouldn't. I am the son of a field hand. I have plans to move to England and make my fortune, but I am in love with a woman who has already inherited a fortune and is managing her successful business without me. I am not worthy. She is a Barnet, after all.

I walk back, my heart heavy, filled with fear and

hopelessness. I hear Dexter, Winnie's beloved dark brown thoroughbred neigh in the distance. I know that damn colt doesn't like me. As she canters towards me, I notice the horse saddle and blanket, even Dexter is dressed better than I. She jumps down and leads Dexter my way.

"Hello stranger, are you ok?"

"Why wouldn't I be?" I snap. *My God, she is beautiful. Dressed in her blue khakis and white shirt, her body is firm, her breast swelling with innocence.*

"Winnie smiles at me. Well, I saw Mackie and you go off in a storm, and now Mackie is marching to war in my cane fields, shredding my profit with his thighs as we speak. Everything alright between you both?"

"Did he say anything?" I try to enquire, without sounding too desperate for the response.

"That's the funny thing, he has said nothing. Is everything alright between you both?" She looked beautiful when she was concerned.

"It's good. Man talk, you know," I tried to sound like someone in authority.

"Really? Ok," she giggled.

"Why are you laughing?" I ask annoyed. "You don't think I am a man? Or because you have this plantation, and your grandparents are the richest people in St Thomas, do you think you are the man?"

Winnie dismounts with such athletic prowess, she swings her right leg and pushes her body out of range, "*What*?!" she enquired, more than annoyed, but not enough to temper her anger.

"You heard me!" I shout at her now.

"Harold, I am *not* one of your street girls," her acid tongue appeared.

"Well, if you think I know street girls, I must be nothing more than a street boy."

"Harold, my job is not to make you feel better about yourself."

"Look at me, I am in rags, working for my woman's plantation like a farm hand. I am a joke. I should be *with* you, running the place, not working like a dog for you." I was right in front of her. She just stared at me.

"What are you suggesting Harold? That you, you move in?"

I nod, my confidence waning as I see her expression.

"For what?"

"I am your man and I should be *with* you. Winn, look at it from my perspective: I am your man and I am in rags. I have no status, and everyone takes me as a joke."

"I see," that's all she said.

"You say you love me, but my life has not improved because of this love. I am not better off. I am just here, working for you, seeing you when you can, hiding from your father and grandmother. I am a laughing stock. Your house is big enough for my family and I to live with you in comfort, but *no*, the man you love and his parents and siblings, we are still out in the cold."

"Well, we cannot have that, can we?", she replied sarcastically.

"Don't talk down to me?"

"What?" she was vexed now, I could see the vein in her forehead popping out.

THE JOURNEY

"You heard me!" I yelled.

"Me. You are the one doing all the talking," Winnie glared at me.

"Well, what are you going to do about it? I am your man and you need to treat me as such," I demanded. *She needed to step up. If she wants me, she needs to make my life comfortable. She is worth a fortune, we all could have a nice life. My mother could move in and run the house, my youngers could give up working as kitchen help, and we could send them to school.*

She stared at me, "My *Man*! Ok, what does that involve?"

"What?" I did not understand where she was going with this.

"You being my man, what does that involve?" she was being funny now, and I did not like it.

"I am here for you. I help you with the business. I take care of you," I tell her. *Why can't she see that she needs a man around?*

"Hmmmmmm, is that so?" she glares at me again.

I look down at my clothes. "Look at me Winn, I am dressed like a beggar. I do not even have any decent clothes, and here you are looking like Princess Elizabeth from blasted England." I was starting to show my annoyance and impatience.

"So." she said with spite in her voice, "this is about money?"

"No. It's about respect. If I had all the money you have, I would not have to suffer like this," I tell her.

"So you're suffering now?" she looks to the sky and crosses her arms.

"Yes" I stare at her. *How can she not see this.*

"Horse shit, and you know it!" she screamed.

Dexter, her chocolate brown Colt, grunted and bolted up right.

"Winn." I try to explain, as I can see that she is angry.

"Shut your ungrateful mouth! How dare you try and manipulate me?! You clearly think that I *owe* you!" she scathes at me.

"No, that's *not* what I meant," I try to appeal to her.

"Yes, that is exactly what you meant. I owe you. I live in the house that my grandfather am grandmother built, and am running their plantation, so that means that I am responsible for making *your* life better?" she looked at me, tears in her eyes, but no tears flowing.

"I'm just saying...." *I feel her hurt, what have I done?*

"I heard you Harold. I should be taking care of you. You, who have had no input, have not slaved to build this house or this plantation, should just be able to sit in grandpa Vin's chair because what? Oh yes, because I claim that I love you. You believe that you are entitled to *all* of this this in the name of love. If that is not enough, you also think that I am now responsible for your whole family, and because you have told me that you love me, it is now my responsibility to feed, clothe, and house all these people, as I have so much space."

"You make what I said sound cheap."

"I didn't do that my love. That was *you!*"

"Whilst I was falling in love with the man, the man was falling in love with my fortune and counting the days until I would share it with him."

"No Winn! No!" I walk away from her, my hands on my head.

"Yes Harold. I have had to endure a lot and"

He interrupts me "Endure?! What have you had to endure, Princess Winnie? You have never gone hungry. You do not know what it's like to be poor."

"No, I have never been poor, but trust me when I tell you, I have endured. My grandmother was murdered in front of me. I have no mother, she too is dead. Until recently, I lived in a house with my alcoholic, abusive father." Winn grabs my hand and puts my finger on the ridge of her nose. She looks me in the eye. "Feel that ridge! That's where after my father shot my grandmother in her head, he punched me so hard, he broke my nose. I was..." her voice broke, "I was six years old." Her tears started to flow.

"Winnie, baby love..." I try to pull her close to me.

"No!" she screamed and wrenched her body from my grip. "No Harold. I thought that you were the only person that wanted to be with *me* for *me*."

"I *do*," I try explain. "Oh no, look, I didn't explain myself well."

"Harold, I would rather be dirt poor, but with a family that loved me like yours any day of the week. My father did things to me that were unspeakable. My grandmother is a hateful hag and loathes me to this day. I just wanted to recreate and live Mima's dream. I wanted to provide hers and grandpa Vin's legacy for me, you, and our children." She looks in the distance.

"Winn, I just feel that you treat me like a farm hand," I say quietly.

"You *are* a farm hand. I cannot promise you what I

cannot give. I don't want to give you what you want," she tells me, her words like acid are burning my skin.

"Why not?" *I cannot believe she has said this. She is ashamed of me.*

"The moment you become visible to my father, you, your family, are all dead men walking. My father will hunt you down and kill you. He's dangerous Harold." She says quietly.

"I can take on your father." I jokingly tell her.

She slaps me hard.

"I cannot believe that you hit me!"

"Wake up, Harold. You are not the Lone Ranger, this is real. My father will destroy you, he will destroy us and what's left of me. Is that what you want?"

I raise my hand, Winnie steps back. There was not fear in her eyes. It was war. I run through the corn fields, frustration and anger resonate through all pores. My tears are hot with fury. People like me never get what they want. *Maybe it's time I become the man. Maybe I earn her, just like Mackie says.*

THE JOURNEY

Chapter 15

Awakening

I cannot believe that fool. Who does he think he is? Why would I take care of him? His family? Lucy and Vincent worked hard for this land, they spend years building this house, and he thinks that I am just going to give this to him. His family, and whoever he feels is deserving, just because he is my boyfriend. We have not even been intimate yet. This is crazy!

"Brrrrhhhh" I pat Dexter.

I know, Dexter. I stroke his neck, *thank you for agreeing with me.*

I smile and start to gallop. Thoughts are racing through

my mind.

This cannot work. I have been kidding myself for quite a while now. He's right, we are still the same virginal teenagers that met three years ago. He should understand that, if I commit to him like that, he will have to be my husband. I do love him. He is so sweet, but he is naïve, stupid at times. He is a dreamer, he does not have a clue how hard it is to run this place and what's involved. He thinks that he can get a seat at the table just like that, contributing nothing to earn this. He is a fool.

"Arggghhhh!" I scream out loud. Dexter slows to a canter, as if he can sense that I need more time in the field to work these thoughts through. I yank the rains and gallop in the opposite direction from where I have just come.

I ride and ride around the plantation, dusk is upon me, and I still am no closer to a resolution of this anger that I feel.

This position that has been burdened on me. I have to make this work, as without it, I am back under the wicked watchful gaze of grandmother. Also, having my own business provides me with an income, so I am not reliant on anyone, and that includes any man. I fear the future, he is not quite ready to be a man of mine, and is no match for my daddy, that's for sure.

I dismount Dexter and gently hold his reigns to show him that we need to keep walking. Dexter stops. I look at him and stroke his nose. He leans his neck on mine. I look deep into his eyes. Dexter snorts through his nostrils. "You're Right, honey. It's time to go home" I rub and kiss his nose.

"Where have you been?" my aunt Rene yells at me as I walk into the back door of the kitchen.

THE JOURNEY

"I have been riding," I tell her calmly.

"You have been gone a while." Mackie eyes me suspiciously.

"Oh, I just needed time to think on things." I say trying to sound casual.

"What things?" Rene walks over to me and immediately wraps her arms around me. I shrug her off aggressively.

It's too much. The emotions of the day erupt, and I cannot keep this to myself. I feel like crying, but I can't. I am so disappointed, but more importantly, I am furious. *How dare he?!* I shake my head. I walk to the cooler and take out a bottle of ginger beer.

"Winnie, what happened?" Rene asks, concern written all over her face.

I look at my aunt, "Nothing I want to discuss."

"I did not ask you whether you wanted to discuss it young lady. What is wrong?" she asks, there was no messing in her voice.

"I think Harold and I are over," I gulp the remainder of the ginger beer. Sweat beads were on my head, I wipe my brow, look at my aunty Rene, who is just staring at me.

"Why?" she asked quietly.

"He ... he is just a free loader. He's telling me that he wants to be running this place with me." I start pacing in Mima's kitchen. I notice the door is open. I walk briskly and close it. I look at Rene, who is now sitting in my grandpa Vin's chair.

"Is anyone else here?" I enquire.

"No, my sweet darling, it's just me."

I smile, she always reminds me of Mima, when she calls me that.

"I love him, but I am not sure whether that's enough for him. He wants and needs so much more than I can give," I tell her.

"Like what?"

"Well, he thinks that he should be here with me, full time." I look down, as I am embarrassed by what I am about to divulge "you know...."

Aunt Rene looks at me suspiciously, "No, I *don't*."

"Like man and wife."

"He asked you to marry him?" aunty asked confused.

"*No,* he says that he should be with me in the house. He is upset that he is a field hand, he wants to be running the place with me."

"What experience does he have with such matters?" Rene asks angrily.

"That's it," I say.

"Does he think managing a business is easy? What skills does he bring to the table?"

"Exactly," I exclaim.

"Does he think that marriage is his way in?" she asks.

"Well, he did not ask me to marry him," I say with embarrassment. "He just wants us to act married."

"Oh. You mean that you're not already?" aunt Rene ask surprised. Her eyebrows arched as she tried to hide her amazement to the situation.

"No, I don't mean that. I just wanted to wait. You know.. for marriage."

My aunt nodded her head apologetically, I could see that she was still reeling from the information received.

"It's like." I hesitate.

"Yes. Like what darling?" she was all ears.

"It's like he wants me to take care of him and his whole family. He started to tell me how his whole family could come and live in this house and there would still be space. He tells me that he is suffering, and I am here looking like Princess Elizabeth. I mean, it's like he wants me to save him. I am just not prepared to make such a commitment. Everyone thinks this is easy, and it's not. I honestly thought that he would be happy, grateful even, that I have given him and his family jobs. Instead, he resents me. He seems more worried about his friends' and brothers' opinion, rather than recognising that I am just trying to do my best. This is grandma Lucy's and grandpa's Vin's house. I am just babysitting it. I cannot just open it up to him and his people. I love him. I really do, but he is making me responsible for him. I just cannot do it, can I?" I look at my aunt for reassurance.

"No, you can't," my aunt said quietly. "If you do not feel comfortable, then you will have to do what your gut is telling you. If it does not feel right, then baby, it's not right."

"Rene, I do not have the energy to save him. I am just learning how to save myself. I feel. I feel so ... so..."

"Trapped?" aunt Rene asked.

"Yes," I gruffly whisper. There was so much sadness in my voice.

"That's ok. If that's how you feel then you should end this

now."

"But I love him," I say, the emotion building in my voice.

"*Do* you?"

"Yes," I snap.

"Then sacrifice everything, and do what he asks of you," she said quietly looking at me.

I can't believe that she is asking this of me. "Aunty, I love the way he is when he is with me, he's ..."

"What about when he is *not* with you? When other people are around?" she asks.

"Huh?"

"When there are other people around? What is he like then?"

"What are you getting at?" I ask.

"When it's you and your friends, how is he?" she asked very matter of fact.

"I don't know what you mean?" I look at her confused.

"Do you feel that he loves you when he is with his friends and brother? Does he hold your hand, kiss you? Touch you?"

I look down "Well, you know he's shy." *Why is she doing this?*

"What does *that* mean? Are you saying 'no'?"

"He is attentive." I protest.

"Ok," she is staring at me, and I am now very hot.

THE JOURNEY

"What is this?" I snap.

"What?"

"This interrogation, coupled with your questions. I love Harold," I tell her, but neither of us believe it.

"Oh sweetie, I do not doubt your affection," she said. "Your dinner will be ready in an hour," she tried to change the subject.

What is this woman trying to do to me? She knows that I love him. Harold means everything for me. I just can't be rushed. I won't be. He needs to live his dream, make his way. I cannot give him my way, he did not earned this. I do love him, but I am no fool. I know that I may be young, this forever thing, is not all that it's cracked up to be. I don't want to end up like my grandmother Phyllis, in a loveless relationship.

"Aunty, this is unfair. I know that you don't feel that he is good enough for me, but I earn my own money and am capable of making a living for me. I am not reliant on him or anyone. That does not mean that I need to save him." I stand up, not knowing what else to do.

Aunty Rene stepped away from the stove "Do not put words in my mouth. I never said that," Aunt Rene bellowed. "You need to be honest with yourself. This is your beau? Right? Yet, your beau has not touched you, caressed you. He works on your farm. You have no immediate plans to move the relationship along at all. Ok. I understand that the young man is reaching, expecting to run this, and have his family up in here. But-"

"What?" I interrupt her, raising my voice more than I expected.

"It appears to me that you are the one full of doubt. He's ready to be part of you and your business. He wants to integrate you in his family," Rene tried to defend him.

"No, he wants to live *off* me," I tell her curtly.

"You're sure of this?" she asks.

"Of course! I was there, not you. Whilst I was busy falling in love with him, he was busy falling in love with my fortune. You're wrong. I don't have reservations. I love him."

"Then what is stopping you?" she asks me exasperated.

"You know what?" tears fill my eyes and fear swells my chest.

"What?" My aunt looks confused.

"My father. You know that when he realises that Harold is my beau, he will kill him, just like he has destroyed anyone and everyone else that loves me," I say.

"Then why put him through this? If you love him as much as you claim, end it." Rene looked pained by my revelation.

"What?"

"So you are comfortable with the idea that Harold may be murdered in one of your father's jealous rages?" anger started to swell in her chest.

"No, of course not."

"Then, if you love him, end it!"

"You're twisting my words".

"Me? No, I am trying to show you that you are not as serious about Harold as you claim. He is your security blanket, your play thing, nothing more. Stop being cruel, drown the puppy, club it, but for God sake, put it out of its misery. If you don't, this puppy will follow you everywhere and will continue to shit in your shoes."

"That's hideous, you're hideous. Now who is being cruel?"

"It may be hideous, but it's true and you know it. Just think about what I have said."

She's wrong. I do love him. Harold has been amazing to me. I don't have to want to give him my everything for this to be real. I just feel like I am being pushed into a corner, and I cannot have that. I am not responsible for him. So why do I have to be his everything. He is not mine. If anything happened to Harold, I would die ... Or would I?

I want a man who is strong in his love for me. A man who would declare to anyone and everyone that he is mine. That's not Harold. Harold lives for his family. He is directed like a puppet and dances to their tune. This is why I am in this situation. It's not his doing, it's his family's doings. They crave to live a better life, yet they are not prepared to work damn hard for it. I will not dig out my gut for him. He has not proved his worth to me for such a sacrifice. A man should be able to stand on his own. Not expect his woman to give him the world. If only he was more like Mr. Mack. He is strong, courageous, and his own man. Even though people thought he could do better than Mrs. Mack, he loved his wife and she loved him.

I love Harold, but not enough to be his everything. I have responsibilities and need to take them seriously. Being a wife and mother is a luxury I cannot afford. I need to be a successful business woman, like my grandmother. My father controlled my every move up until now. I am just about to have financial and psychological freedom. I am not the slave of this plantation. I am its Mistress.

P.D Lorde

The plantation has turned into a well-oiled machine. I have the right people, in the right roles, doing just what I require them to do. My vision over the next two years is expansion and to become the supplier of choice in America. The village is thriving, I have hired over eighty percent of the population. The church has a new roof, and, for the first time, the children have a real school building, rather than a rundown shack. My grandparents would be proud of me. Even grandma Phyllis congratulated me in my efforts.

THE JOURNEY

Daddy, I know he's also proud. He has not told me so, but he will tell anyone who will listen. "Have I told you that Edwina has just completed building the school? Fine work, I say, fine work."

Life is good and God is great. My father and I are on the firmest and strongest ground ever. We talk every other day. We dine twice a week in Morant Bay. He is a shrewd business man, and even though we are competitors, he wants the best for me. I see it now, through his narrow lens, he loves me with all his heart, and I know that he will do anything to defend me and my honour. In a strange way, I do find that sweet. He loves me and wants to protect me. I have come to terms that he is a different man to whom I first met, but I cannot and will not forget our history.

We talk now, I mean about everything, or almost everything. He is my best friend. He even told me about Donna. I am trying to convince him to bring her from the back of the closet to the lighted dressing room. I think he could be considering this, he loves her and radiates every time he mentions her name. It makes him vulnerable, more human, like the rest of us. I had contemplated telling him about Harold. However, aunty Rene and my grandfather advised strongly against it. Deep down, I know they are right. He still has the capability of being unpredictable, which makes him extremely dangerous.

It's been at least two weeks since I have seen Harold. I have played this evening in my head and just need for it to be over. Harold left me a note asking to meet me. When I agreed, my heart sank. I need to be brave, he has to recognise that this, whatever it is, is just not working. My aunt is right, I have to let him go.

It's Saturday, my field workers have left early and have gone home for the day. I have bathed and am ready for bed, but need to reorganise my thoughts for my conversation with Harold.

I put on my beige khaki skirt and blue cotton over shirt. I look at myself in the mirror. I am tired and have lost weight. I smooth coconut oil through my hair and pull it back into a ponytail. I slip on my pumps and sit on the veranda waiting for Harold. I go into the kitchen and boil my kettle. There is a medley of fresh lemon, lime, and crushed ginger in a small muslin bag in my teapot. I pour the hot water in the cup, and when I turn around, he's there looking dapper, with a pair of new black trousers and a crisp white shirt and flowers.

"Harold, you startled me," I jump back.

"Sorry baby," he looks embarrassed, as he can see that I am taken aback by his demeanor.

"No, it's fine. I was not expecting you so early," I relax, a little flattered that he made such an effort.

"I couldn't wait to see you, and it's warm, so did not want my flowers to wilt, he beams at me. "Here." he thrust the flowers at me.

"Oh, thank you," I blush. "What's the occasion?"

"They are a peace offering. I behaved" he paused trying to find the right words, "badly," he said, his eyes on the floor.

I smile. "It's ok. Let's go on the veranda and talk."

As we pass through the kitchen and long corridor towards the front of the house, Harold smiles at me.

"What?" I fix my hair "Do I look ok?"

THE JOURNEY

"You look perfect," he smiles.

I sit on the large hand crafted wooden chair, with bullet holes in the arm ledge. It is still here after all these years, with my grandmother's cushions, we both sit down and look across the veranda to the plantation.

"This is beautiful Winn."

"I know," I smile. "This is my home, I feel safe here." I notice that he is melting under his new Sunday best attire. "Oh Harold, I am sorry. Where are my manners? Do you want a drink?"

"Oh, ok. Anything cool," he wipes his brow embarrassed.

I rush in and pour some cold lemonade in a glass. As I walk back to the veranda, Harold is on his knees with a small red velvet box in his hand. I stop at the doorway, and the bile in my stomach pushed its way up to the back of my throat.

"Edwina, I ..."

"Stop Harold. Please stop!" I feel sorry for him, he's so nervous. I rush over and put the lemonade on the table.

"Edwina" there is a brow of sweat prickling its way to the surface, "will you?"

"Harold stop!" I grab him under his sweaty arm pits and wrench him up to his feet. He looks at me completely crushed. "What are you doing?" I barely whisper, looking around the plantation to see if anyone was watching this spectacle.

He glared at me with wounded pride. "I was trying to

propose to you baby." he barely mumbled.

"Why?"

"Why?!" he snapped. "Because that is what men do when they want to declare their love for their woman. Why? Because that is what you want? Why? Why? I love you stupid?"

"Oh" I look out to the plantation. This evening was not going how I had it planned in my head.

His body language became defensive. "Why won't you allow me to ask you?"

"Because tonight I only agreed to meet with you so that I could end things between us." I was trying to be kind, but my words sounded so cruel.

Harold stepped back, he put his hands to his eyes. "No. No baby, you don't mean this."

"Harold, look, I have had time to think and we're not ready. I am not ready." I try to explain.

"I'm ready, that's all that matters, and I love *you*, and only you."

"That's the problem Harold. I am not ready. I don't want to be married right now, and I don't want to be married to you. I have so much to do here. I have responsibilities to the community, myself, my grandparents, who built this place."

"Your grandparents are dead Winnie. They would want you to live your life."

"Yes, they would. Harold, being married to you would not

be living my life. I don't want these things that you talk about. I just want to be Winnie, living my life without restriction. Not answering to anyone. I am a free spirit and I want to remain that way for as long as possible. I have been a prisoner for far too long."

"What?!"

"I don't want you. It's not you. *"he needs to know the truth* "I love you, but I am not *in* love with you." I stand back and watch him absorb the news, my aunt was right, I needed to let this puppy go free.

Harold's eyes brimmed with tears. "I heard you, but I cannot believe what I heard. Wait, do you think I will keep you prisoner or something? You make this proposal sound like prison," he yelled. He was angry now.

"No, that's not what I am saying. I just can't marry you."

Harold walked towards me and grabbed me by the waist. "Why?"

He pushed himself on me. "Maybe I should have treated you like them gully girls."

I push him off with all my might. "Harold" I scream. "No! It's over. I will not feel guilty for my life, my wants, my dreams. I am not responsible for you. I cannot be responsible for your family. That's not my job." I tell him curtly.

"Is this what it's about? Hmmm, I am your big black buck, but my family is too black for you?"

"No, that is not what I said."

"You want to marry a light skinned man with money right? Hey, some man with class, standing? A man who does not work in a field, a man who has a name?"

"I will marry the right man for me. Harold I don't need to marry for money. I have more than I require, and you know that. I just cannot marry you. I'm sorry."

I walk to the house and feel him grab me and push me inside the door. We are in the foyer. His eyes are wild, he looks like he wants to hit me but is thinking real hard about it.

"What you gonna do Harold? Show me what a man you can be?" I point to my privates "Is this what you have become? Some field hand rapist?"

"Maybe." He grabs my neck and forces me to kiss him. *I need to get away, or else who knows what he'll do.* I turn my head. "*No!* No, get off me! This is madness."

"I love you Winn! After all this time, you can't just walk out on me. There is no me without you. Please don't do this. Let's talk … Let's-"

"No" I push Harold off.

"You don't know your own mind," he grabs and pulls me again, and I struggle to push him away.

"Get off her!" a woman stood in the corridor by the kitchen. She was youngish, I would say late twenties. She was well dressed, jeans and a t-shirt. Her afro was short, her curls soft, her face familiar to me somehow. We both froze. She walked towards us, brandishing her machete at Harold.

THE JOURNEY

"Boy, I think you outstayed your welcome. Don't you?"

"Leave this house! This is private business." Harold yelled at her.

"Well, the way I understand things, this," she points to the house and plantation, "does not belong to you. I heard the Mistress tell you to leave, and you're still here. So, the way I see it, you boy, is the only person who has outstayed any welcome. I am a reasonable woman. I will ask you once more, and if you are still here when I start to move, tonight one of us will meet a relative we lost a little while ago." She meant business.

Harold looked at me and sucked his teeth.

"Winn." he looked at me.

What did he expect me to do? Throw her out? "You heard her. Now leave and *never* come back. You and your family find some other fool to hire you and take care of you all. I am done!"

Harold walked out of the door and slammed it behind him. I ran and locked the door then hurried to the kitchen and locked the back entrance. I turn to my young warrior. "Thank you," I say. "He's not like that normally, I have driven him to this."

"What? You have driven him to *abuse* you?" she snapped.

"No, you don't understand. I have just broken his heart, so he is hurt," I explain. I walk to the cupboard and take two cups-"Tea?"

"Do you have something stronger?"

I shake my head, "No."

She smiles at me. "Yes please, tea will be lovely then." my rescuer answers.

I turn around and she is sat in my grandpa Vin's chair, shoes off, crossed legged, as if she had been there her whole life.

"Comfortable?" I look at her slightly annoyed.

"Very," she exclaims laughing at me.

"What's your name?"

"Just call me Saint."

"Saint." I laughed. Is that really your name?"

"Yes, my mother named me Saint. Think of me as your female living 'Saint Christopher'."

I laugh out loud, "You cannot be serious."

"I am." Her face was stern. When Saint realized I was observing her she smiled broadly and winked at me. I gave her the tea, and she examines the cup and smiles again. "Thank you Miss Winnie." For a machete wielding vigilante she was incredibly polite and very familiar. We drink in silence for a while, but it felt natural.

"So what's your story Miss Winnie?" Saint asked.

"You know me? Have we met?" I enquire.

"Maybe? Though everyone knows *you* Edwina Barnet," she says sarcastically.

THE JOURNEY

"You seem so familiar to me that's all." I tell her.

"Hmmm," she smiles broadly. "I knew your grandmother when I was a girl and would play with you as a child."

"Really? Ok" I smile at the prospect that we were play mates, although she would have been considerably older than me.

"You." she points at me aggressively "Needs to meet a nice man. Not someone from round here. Broaden your horizons, you can do better than the village idiot."

I laugh. "You sound like my Aunt Rene."

Saint smiled. "Maybe your Aunt Rene is a wise old bird." she said seriously eyeballing with every word. "You should listen to her."

"Who told you she was old?"

"Winnie, I'm from round here, so I am familiar with a few of the villagers, this included your Aunt Rene and Mima." she smiles.

"Ok" I look at her trying to place her face and voice.

I hear a car in the distance tooting its horn, he must have found out, he was driving like a mad man. I look at the clock on the wall.

"Who's that?" Saint enquires looking uneasy.

"I think it could be my daddy." I walk to the main door and spot his black Chevy. "Please do not tell him about tonight. It's complicated," I say, as I walk back into the kitchen.

"Oh," the door was wide open and Saint was gone. I close and lock the door. I start to panic. I do hope that someone did not see Harold attack me. The bile in my stomach reached my throat again. I feel hot. He pounds the front door like a man on a "urgent" mission.

"Winnie," my daddy screams. "Open this door!" I run to the entrance preparing myself for the full velocity of my father's temper.

"Daddy calm down, I can"

"She dying." he sobs, "She is dying."

"Who daddy? Grandma?"

"No, Donna. She dying, and I cannot save her," he wails.

I stand in the doorway and hold my father as tight as I can. "It's going to be ok daddy."

"Nooooo," he sobs, "It won't. Nothing will be the same again."

My life has changed quite dramatically over the last two months. I miss him, I really do. Harold has indeed been my security blanket. He was the only person to stabilise me. The man that I loved was my best friend, and I feel so bereft of him. My grandfather has been so sweet, although, he did not approve of us, he could hardly insist that I give him up. Not when he's with Rene. It's strange, they seem more suited than he and grandma. He's so relaxed with Rene and is so amusing. I mean, he is a hoot. His stories relating to his childhood in Mississippi, sound like another world. I understand him now, more than he realises. He is more focused as a human being here. He is able to stand freely in the personality that

THE JOURNEY

God has given him. He loves all people, regardless of religion, colour and wealth. My grandfather is a true humanitarian. He recognises that he cannot be his true self anywhere else in the world. Aunt Rene would be raped and beaten to death in his world back in America. Here, they can love and be loved by their friends and family, free from judgment.

The night that Harold proposed weighs heavily on my mind. I am so disappointed that it ... we did not end better. I have not seen him, he has not written to me and won't reply to my letters. Grandfather says that it's better this way. Even though this is messy, it's clean.

The same day that I broke Harold's heart, Donna was diagnosed with lung cancer. Grandfather tried, but he could not soften the impact of the devastating news to them both, but in particular, to daddy. He immediately started to grieve her, however, when her physical condition altered, it reaffirmed his worst fears, and he became inconsolable. She suffered more than any of my animals on the farm would be allowed to. In the end, she begged grandfather for death, and the humanitarian within him did what he knew to be kind, and obliged. On the 24th October, 1958, Donna Grantham, who was forty years old, held onto my father's hand and told him for the least time that she loved him. She promised him that she would be with him forever and she was honored to be the only woman in this life, and will be waiting for him on the other side. My father had moved her out of the service quarters to his bedroom suite, where she had slept every night for the last eight years. My father insisted that the room was filled with purple and pink hibiscus flowers, as they was her favorite. Donna asked to be bathed and oiled, she instructed her nurses to put her in her finest church dress and to tend her hair to make her look presentable. Withered and ravaged by this cancer, she wanted to look and smell nice for her Barry. That day, all her friends and family came and said their last farewell. Kissing her and tearing up at the sight of this once vibrant and spritely woman being reduced to a shell of her former self. That was the tragedy. With dignity she smiled, cried, and, where she could, said her goodbyes, all the while my father was at her side, holding her hand, stroking her face, telling her that she was beautiful, and he would love her forever.

I sat with my father for ten long days and nights. I prayed with him, stayed with Donna when he needed to get air, eat and smoke his tobacco. He was such a rock for Donna, yet, when he left the room he would diminish into a heart broken man. I saw him humbled and quiet for the first time and felt that my own bereavement could not compare to what daddy was going through.

My Grandmama watched from the corners of the room, taking in all the activity. She had loved Donna like the daughter she never had. Donna started work at the plantation over twenty years ago, when she was still a child herself. She had been her chambermaid for the last thirty years. She held secrets for my grandmama, secrets that would die with her. She was more than my her maid, she was her friend, confidant and, in the latter years, both women became very close, especially when Phyllis realised that it was Donna who had effected change in her son. Although, it appeared to everyone else that Phyllis disapproved. For years she observed the young woman's love for my father and watched as she blushed uncontrollably when Barry was in the room. Donna had grandmother's blessing, and, the first night that she spent with my father, it was grandmother who sent her to be my father bed maister, which turned into something far more meaningful to both their lives.

Two days before Donna died, my father left to bathe, sleep and rest. He was exhausted. Donna insisted that he takes a break. My grandmama ordered me out of the room, and when I returned, she was on the bed, Donna's head was in her lap, and my grandmama was stoking her hair with one hand, and her body with the other. Both women were crying, yet, the room was silent. I felt the grief and sadness and backed out silently unnoticed.

That evening was very somber, the air was strong with the scent of death, coconut oil and lavender. Both my grandfather and father retreated to the corner of the room and they talked quietly for some time. Both men looked drawn, but my father was thinner than I have ever seen him. He welcomed the news with a somber nod. The pit of my stomach churned, and I could feel the bile creeping to my throat. I could see that she could not suffer like this no more, and death was a welcomed friend to Donna, and to those who loved her. The nurse summoned my father. My grandmama was present also. Donna opened her eyes, and smiled at my father, "Thank you for the flowers" she told him weakly.

Daddy delicately put her hand into his and kissed it repeatedly, then looked at his love and smiled with her.

"You're welcome darling," he said. They both smiled. "You look beautiful," he whispered.

"Barry" she smiled shyly. My father's tears rolled down his cheek, he swiped them away, like unwelcomed pests. He sat next to Donna, lay down and then maneuvered her head into the crook of his arm. "Are you sure?" he whispered and looked at her.

She nodded weakly. My grandfather took the morphine vials and put them on a tray. He informed them both that he will inject her in the thigh, and soon afterwards she will drift off into a deep sleep. Donna smiles at grandfather. My grandmother, who stood at the corner of the room, ran over.

"Wait!" she held Donna head in her hands and whispered something that made my father cry. Donna expression was pained. My grandmother kissed her sweetly on the lips and left the room. My chest felt full with emotion, my temperature was rising, and the bile was back in my throat.

My Grandfather stroked her leg. On the tray were four needles filled with morphine. He mechanically administered them, one by one, Donna told my father that she loved him, and they smiled. She quickly became drowsy, and then she fell into a deep sleep, her face relaxed, she was now pain free and smiling.

One by one we left the room, and my father and grandfather stayed. I walk into my old bedroom only to find my grandmother sat on my bed.

"Is it done," she asked.

"Yes," I say.

"He is going to need you more than ever," she tells me.

"I know."

"She was a sweet girl, so young," grandmother says,

wiping her tears with a silk and lace white handkerchief.

"I know. That's what I want." I tell her.

"What?" she asks quietly.

"Love. Grandma, I want love, to be loved, to feel love, that's what I want."

"Then find it." she tells me as if she is ordering shoes.

"I don't know how," I tell her without shame.

She smiled, "I do, and I will help you. You are beautiful, clever, smart, independent and a business woman. Men between Jamaica and China will walk on broken glass for you."

I smile at her.

"Leave it with me. I need to rest, both my heart and head are weary."

When the heavy door closes, I lay on my childhood bed and silently cry. My thoughts are of course with Donna, but they are also with Mima, Grandpa Vin, my mother, and Mrs. Mack.

Chapter 16

Butterflies

It's dawn and the plantation alarm clock crows to yields

the morning sun. Life as we know it starts for the day. I am tired mentally, my muscles are sore, and I genuinely feel fatigued. My life is not my own. I am a young woman, with far too much responsibility, and I am starting to feel the strain of it. On top of that, my father is drinking again. Not as much as before, but he has slipped and it's noticeable. There are flashes of the old bastard, and I don't like it. He unnerves me, and I hate the feeling of vulnerability that I have when he is in the room. I am more mature and more able to deal with old behaviors, but his acid tongue burns old wounds and opens up new ones.

The familiar sound of crunching gravel on my driveway startles me. I jump out of bed, rub my eyes and head for the window. It's grandmother's car. I look at the clock, it was 5.15 am, something must be wrong. I grab my jeans and pull a cotton shirt over me. As I open the door, the morning sun is peeking through. The air is cool and fresh, and feels refreshing on my skin. The cold air helps my unaided breast stand to attention.

Grandmother parked the car by the front of the house. "Morning Edwina," she said authoritatively and walked straight past me to enter my house.

"Come in, grandma," I say sarcastically.

"Edwina, I am concerned," she says looking at me. "Your father has not returned home. In fact, this is the second night he's been absent. Have you seen him?"

"He stayed here the night before last, but I am not sure about last night?"

"You look tired," grandma informs me.

THE JOURNEY

"I am." I sigh, looking around my kitchen, trying to avoid her gaze.

"Then take a rest. This place is doing well, you can leave Mackie to tend to things. You need to rest, your beauty won't last forever, and you will not be able to find a suitable man if you look tired and old. A young woman as gorgeous as you are, should maintain her appearance, not diminish it because you're determined to work like a field hand."

My father walked into the kitchen from the back door. "Mother, she is not a field hand and does not need a husband. She has me now."

I look at my daddy. "What does *that* mean?" I asked, worried at what his response will be.

"You do not need to rush into anything, you have plenty of time. Mother, I stayed here last night. It was closer and I got in late."

"You mean you were drinking?" I ask.

"Winn, I had a few, but I wasn't drunk," daddy said without apology.

"Daddy this is becoming a habit again. I hate it when you drink, you are nasty, violent, and unpredictable. I cannot be around that again. I just can't. You have to find a way to get over this. Until then, stay out of my house."

"What?"

"You heard me. Stay away!"

"You can't talk to me like that!." he looked at me with

disdain.

"Why not? The last time you were drunk in this house my grandmother died. I am just making sure that we understand each other." Once I had said the words, I regretted them, but they needed to be said.

My father starred at me, "Last night that was my last drink. I am sorry."

I walk over to daddy and look at him. "Don't make promises you are not prepared to keep. There are too many things riding on this."

Daddy picked up his hat and wallet and left without a word. He got to the backdoor, turned and looked at me, nodded and disappeared.

"Coffee grandmama," I now ask in my stern voice.

"Yes dear, why not," she replied with a half-smile on her face. She looked lovely, in her lemon two piece skirt and blouse. Her hair was in a chignon, very stylish indeed. Her grey strand looked like high lights.

I prepared the coffee under Phyllis's watchful eye. "I have some bun in the larder. Would you like a slice?"

"That would be lovely," she says quietly.

I pour the coffee in a pot, set out my finest cups and saucers, I have a selection of hard dough bread, cheese, ham, tomatoes, and cucumber dressed in lemon and oil.

"This looks lovely Edwina," my grandmama is genuinely surprised.

"Can I be candid grandma?

THE JOURNEY

"You may," she eyed me suspiciously.

"Why are you here today? You could have called me, you didn't need to drive all the way here."

"Yes. I could have, but I wanted to tell you that I have booked us a box at the races and I thought that you should attend with me."

"Ok" I smile "That sounds nice." I think to myself that we could use some cheering up.

"Yes, it would be nice, and the island's elite will be there. You may make some new friends. I worry that you are not enjoying your time. You need people like you, in your own age group."

"That would be nice," I smile more broadly at the prospect of meeting new friends. "Maybe I am a little too serious, you know, for my age, but I just want to make a go of things."

"You have done that already. I don't want you missing out on your youth. Once it's gone, it's gone."

"Ok, when is it?"

"Next week. I thought we could go to Kingston this week to buy something nice, what do you say?"

"It sounds good. Mackie can hold the fort for a couple of days."

"That's the spirit."

"Grandmother, what else are you up to?" I enquire, still not convinced of her reason for visiting.

"Nothing, it's just a nice day out." She smiled to herself.

"Hmmmmm." I watch her like a hawk.

"This is lovely, but I must dash. Lots to do. By the way, good for you!"

"Good for me?" I enquire.

"Barry needs a firm hand, and now that Donna is gone, you may need to be it."

The back door flies open. "Morning" Rene bounds through the door, chirping away about her day ahead. She looks up and stops dead in her tracks. "What are you doing here?" aunt Rene asked through gritted teeth.

"I am leaving, the air distinctly smells of rotting fish," grandmother says.

"Get out!" shouts Rene, her body lurching forward like she was ready to pounce.

"Temper temper whore! I see that you are still an alley cat."

Aunt Rene drops her bags and picks up my solid wood rolling pin. I jump in front of her, shocked at how she is carrying herself.

"Ladies," I nervously laugh, my voice is at least three octaves higher than usual. "Ok, grandmother, you are leaving. And Aunt Rene, the books are in the office. There will be none of this," I point to both of them, "in here. Ok?"

My grandmother turned around and look directly at Rene. "Whore, you and I have unfinished business. The next time you pick up a weapon, be prepared to use it." Grandmother looked at me and smiled and walked out of the room towards the front door. Rene was rooted to her spot, looking like she wanted to rip off my grandmother's face. I escort Grandma to the exit, still in shock with what I have just witnessed.

In the kitchen, Rene is seated head in hands. "What was that about?" I ask genuinely interested in the response.

"Why is she here?" Rene was visibly upset.

"She was enquiring about daddy that's all. And she has arranged for us to go to the races."

"Really?"

"I know, I thought that was quite sweet".

"Sweet?! Winn, don't be an idiot!"

"Excuse me?!" I was put out. *How dare she call me that word?*

"Seriously, are you that naïve and stupid? That woman does nothing unless she benefits somehow. Be careful, that's all I'm saying. She has most probably prostituted you off to some well to do family. All I am saying is be careful."

"Are you sure that you're not jealous?" I could not help it.

"Of her?" she shrieked. "Winn, I know your grandmother personally, she is not one to be toyed with. Be careful! That's all I'm saying," my aunt walked towards me and kissed me on the cheek. "I am sorry for calling you stupid", she said in her normal voice. "I know what I am talking about ... Be careful." With that, she walked back to the office.

Once out of sight, I smile broadly. My grandmother was pretty damn awesome. Not that I should be impressed, but she ripped into Rene without even breaking into a sweat. Now, I don't know what issues they have, what I do know is that it has nothing to do with me. I for one, plan to stay well out of that mess.

My grandmother's organisation of us all, regarding this day at the races is so excessive. Our trip to Kingston embodied numerous trips to "Sally's" Boutique. Sally was the only Boutique in town who catered for the elite. I had three outfits for *Lady's Day*. My grandmother conveniently did not tell me that there would be a Charity Ball that evening, followed by a picnic the next day, and Gala dinner that night.

"It's three days," I moaned.

"So, what is the issue?" she asks. "Edwina, you made a commitment to attend. Are you going back on your word?"

"Yes ... No ... Do I have to go to all these events? I need to be back at the Plantation," I exclaim with annoyance.

"You have to. Mackie is more than capable of handling business whilst you are away. Also, you have at least one hundred and fifty field hands working. So you can and will take three days. You yourself, only last week, agreed that you needed a break. Have one and stop complaining."

The day before we were due to leave for the races, my grandmother surprises me. "I know that you're busy

THE JOURNEY

Edwina, but I wanted to drop off your luggage."

"Luggage, really? I have bags."

"Ok, this is your holdall, dear," the young boy Colin who worked in our house, jumped out of the car and gave it to me. It was a beautiful black shiny leather case.

I have been bullied into going to Kingston the day before the races so that I can rest. Although, I have been resistant to this idea, it is a worthy one. The moment we arrive at the hotel, my body aches with exhaustion. After a delightful shower, I drink what appears to be a gallon of water and fall promptly to sleep in the king sized bed. To my surprise, I nap all afternoon.

"Winn, come on, it's time to get ready for dinner. We are meeting your grandmother's friends from Manchester," my grandpa gently tried to nudge me out of my dreams.

"Grandpa, I am so tired," I moan. "Tell her I am unwell, I just need to rest. My body is aching, and I just need sleep."

"Winn, I am not her biggest fan, but I know that she has put a lot of effort in these few days away."

I look at my grandpa apologetically. "I am sleeping. I am tired and need to lie down. I really don't feel well. Grandmother will just have to understand. In fact …" I yawn, "she was right I do need the rest. I just need sleep, I will be better in the morning."

"Winn."

"Please, I have been working so hard and just need some space to recuperate. Tell her that I have a temperature, anything, but I am *not* going." With that, I slam my head into the comfortable pillow, my curls are thrown into my face, and I attempt to get back to my resting place.

My grandfather sighs, knowing that he is for the high jump. "Sleep tight. We will see you tomorrow."

A few minutes later, I heard muffled voices, and, by the tone of my grandmother, I knew she was furious. I smiled. I did not care, and that was that.

I opened the windows and went back to bed, after a few nonsense thoughts, I was back in the dream world.

"Good morning sleeping beauty," my grandmama barks like a sergeant major, and in one swift move, she pulls the blankets from me.

"Hey, what?" I moan.

"It's time to rise my dear. Lots to do."

"Mother, give her a chance," my father walked into my room. "Morning Winn." He leaned over and kissed me.

"Morning daddy," I hold on to his neck and pull him close, he hugs me back. "Help me daddy". He laughs out loud.

"Breakfast is on its way, then the hairdresser will arrive at 9 am."

"What time is it?"

"7.30," she replied.

"What?"

THE JOURNEY

"Beauty takes time to cultivate," she said with a smile.

"What?"

"We have work to do, now get up," she barked.

I looked at my father who was thoroughly amused. I then looked at my grandfather, who put his hands up in the air to surrender. "You better do what she says. She's serious. Barry, we have time for a quick round of golf?"

"Sounds great dad." Daddy looks at me and mouths, "Sorry," as he walked out of the door.

My grandmother Phyllis stared at me. I slowly realise that today is about her. "Ok. I will be compliant. What's first?"

My grandmother is smiling. It's funny, that's not a side to her that I see very often. She looks radiantly beautiful when she is happy. In fact, today felt like we were family, and I loved it. There was a knock at the door.

"Ah, breakfast is here." Grandma told the room.

I eat salt fish and Ackee, plantain, and boiled green banana with chocolate tea. I look at my grandmother, fully satisfied. "I was hungry."

"You should be, you slept for nineteen hours. Are you feeling better?"

"You know what? You were right, I needed to rest," I tell her.

She smiles, "Well, sleep agrees with your complexion."

"Thanks," I say, as I slip off my bathrobe and walk into

the shower. I wash my hair and body. I then hear a knock on the door. "Yeeesss."

"Monique is here," grandmother shouts.

"Who?"

"The hairdresser."

I slide the shower curtain over and wipe the soap from my eyes. "Who?" I say blinking, trying to avoid the bubbles from stinging my eyes.

"The hairdresser, so hurry up! I will go to my boudoir dear, as my lady is here too."

"Ok," I shout, my voice echoing of the walls of my bathroom.

"Now, she is very experienced so try something ... new."

"Hmmmm ok," I finish off and wrap a towel around my head. Monique is beautiful, her skin is dark and her features petite like she is. Her hair was rolled tightly to her head.

"Ok, Ma'am, I have strict orders, so we need to get started."

"Strict orders for what? And you can call me Winnie," I giggle nervously.

"Ok Miss Winnie. You grandmother would like you to have a natural drop curl style, if I can achieve this."

"Oh she does, does she?"

Monique smeared a serum on my wet hair and combed

my locks through. She then took large cylinders and adequately partied and rolled my hair. Then, I was instructed to sit under this blistering heat on my head and scalp for one hour. I was a hot sweaty mess afterwards.

I took every precaution to cool off. I went to the bathroom and put a face towel underneath the cold water. I wiped myself down and waited for the next gruesome installment.

Grandmother walked into the suite from time to time to inspect her handy work. There were no protesting, she meant business. Whilst I was cooling down with a Coco Cola on ice, Monique went into her bag of goodies and produced at least twenty bottle of nail polish. I chose a blush pink, which was not to my grandmother's taste, however, I did not care, it suited me.

"Ladies, are you ready," daddy asked impatiently.

"Stop fussing, we will get there in time Barry. Meet us in the bar, we will be no more than ten minutes."

"Ten minutes and no more," grandfather bellowed, muttering some nonsense about women making him late.

Monique looked at me. "Miss, you look sensational, you look like a movie star." I chuckle and gaze in the mirror. I was unrecognisable. I did look like a lady. I smile, "Wow."

My hair has soft large curls that fell obediently down my back and shine all over my head. I had a side parting and fringe. I looked so grown up. My dress was off the shoulder, this was the most flesh I have ever showed.

The top was lace and fitted with a sheet satin slip underneath, to give me the modesty that was required; the skirt was embodied with both lace and satin. When I saw it in the shop, I was not sure, but when I tried it on, I knew it was made for me. The colour was white with a hint of pink. I wore matching suede shoes, with the highest heels I have ever worn, and a pink clutch bag to match. I had on a solitaire large diamond necklace, with diamond drop earrings. Altogether, it looked very nice.

Grandmother smiled. "You see, you *are* a pretty girl. With a little more encouragement, you are a superstar. Now let's go mingle with our people, the elite of the elite. More importantly, let's have fun."

We leave the room, and the bell boy, who was in fact a man, was staring at me so much, grandmama had to remind him to press the button. The lift arrived, we walked through the doors and were greeted by knowing stares. Grandmama walked into the bar first, my grandfather and father either did not see me or did not recognise me. Both men were dressed in their black morning suit jackets, white shirts, grey cravats and trousers, and impeccably shiny black brogue shoes.

It was grandfather to spot me first, "Winnie! he sucked in the air "Is that you?"

I giggle with embarrassment.

"You look sensational," he said.

I walk over to my father, who was at the bar, rooted to the spot. "Well daddy, how do I scrub up?"

"You do more than that, you look very, very, very beautiful," he crooked his arm out, "May I escort you

THE JOURNEY

Miss Edwina Barnett to the races?"

I giggle, "You may daddy."

"I need to be here to protect you from all the men that will be trying to talk to you."

"Oh daddy, I doubt that," I tell him.

He stopped and looked at me. "You are *beautiful*, don't forget that. And I can assure you, today I shall be beating these men off with a stick."

Approaching the races, I now realised what all the fuss was about. Even the palm trees looked well-watered and perfectly manicured on each side of the road. Their barks immaculately groomed. *Ladies' Day* was more than I could have imagined. Everyone looked superbly polished. It was here that I recognized the world to which we derived from. We were not just *rich*, we were wealthy, and people knew it.

We approached in a large black Rolls Royce. The concierge opened the door "Dr. Barnett, Mr. Barnett," both men stepped out of the car. The concierge looked at me, "Miss. Barnett, may I help you?" he stretched out his arm. His uniform was immaculately pressed and starched. He wore black trousers with a British racing green strip down the outside of the each leg. His jacket had the same design, and his shirt was crisp white, with matching gloves. I was busy placing this monstrous pink hat that grandmother brought for me on my head without ruining my hair. It had a broad rim which was covered in feathers, however, with my whole attire, it just worked.

"Miss Barnet," the concierge said, "can I help you?" The voice was distinctly familiar, I look up, my heart stops.

It's Harold, his face desperately trying to stay fixed, I am unable to move.

Daddy asks him to move and stretches out his hand, "Come on darling. It's ok, don't be intimidated, this is your world." I crawl out of the car and glimpse at Harold. I see the expression on his face. I look great, and he knows it. I smile. "Ok, Daddy, let's go have fun."

"Atta girl."

We walk through the plush doors, and I feel his eyes burning my back. I shake it off. *Harold is the past, this is my new life. I am going to show him that I made the right decision. He does not belong to me or my world.*

Daddy takes my hand, "you're shaking, Winn. Are you ok?"

"Daddy, I'm fine," I smile, "it's just excitement," I whisper.

My father smiles at me, "You are so sweet."

I look over, my grandmother and grandfather are surrounded by people that I have never met before. My grandmother motions to me and daddy, daddy waves over and they all wave back, eyeing me suspiciously.

Daddy grins, "They are all wondering who this beautiful woman on my arm is?"

I smile.

"You look absolutely lovely," Daddy said.

"Yes, she is lovely," I hear a loud polished accent bellow.

Daddy spins around "Jackson, how are you man? It's

been, what, ten years?" Jackson hugs my father and stares at me.

"Who is this delightful creature," he enquires. "Your wife? You always had great taste in women, you lucky dog, you."

My father looked at me embarrassed, cleared his throat, "Jackson, please meet my beautiful and talented daughter, Miss Edwina Barnett." The older man looked visibly shocked.

"Barry, I never knew that you had a child. When did you marry? Have I ever met your wife?" he quizzed.

Daddy looked at me and beamed. "My wife died nineteen years ago, in childbirth."

"Oh. I am sorry, Barry, I didn't know," he turned to me, "You, my darling are delightful," and he held my hand and kissed it. My father threw his friend Jackson a warning glance.

"My son, Courtney, is here from Miami for the week. You kids should meet," he said looking directly at my father, as if to say 'cool down papa'.

"That would be nice," I reply politely. *I was grateful at my father for protecting my good name. I was touched, he called my mother his wife.*

"Excuse me Barrington," my grandma Phyllis leaned in and literally pulled me from the men. I turned to my daddy, who mouthed to me for a second time, "Sorry." Admittedly, I loved that attention and smiled.

"Dear." I looked hard at my grandmother, she never,

ever, called me 'dear'. "Meet Jackie Boullier, she is an old friend of mine." I smile. Jackie and my grandmother were about the same age. Her son Bradley has just graduated from the University of West Indies as a lawyer and has joined his father's firm in Kingston. Bradley stepped forward. He was a pleasant looking man, with thick eyebrows, and nice lips. He, too, kissed my hand. I look at daddy, who was supervising every male interaction I was having. I smiled. He did too, he looked a little sad.

I spoke to Bradley about the weather, races, and my plantation, which he already knew that I owned.

There were at least nine or ten such introductions. I was talking to a boring young man Royston Northgate, whose father owned the construction company that was currently building all the roads, hospitals, and government buildings in Jamaica. Again, he was lovely, knew all about me and was dull.

"Edwina dear," my grandmother called me, "it's time to go to our box."

"Ok," I wave, "excuse me Royston."

"Can I escort you Miss Barnett," he asked politely.

"Sure," I say, wishing I had the courage to say no.

We walk towards the box corridor, which was carpeted in a thick royal red colour. The thickness of the wool made my heels sink, so I had to lean on dear Royston for support, which he loved. As we get to the reception area, Royston's mother, Marcella Northgate, comes over and introduces herself.

"Oh, my, what a handsome young couple the two of you make."

I look at Royston and immediately unloop my arm. He gives his mother the death glare. "Err, thank you, Mr. Northgate. As we are on stable ground, I no longer require your assistance."

"Oh, my darling, I did not mean to embarrass you both," Mrs. Northgate apologises for her foot in mouth, clearly realizing that she had overstepped herself in the situation.

My father touched my shoulder, I smile, relieved to see him. "Mrs. Northgate, it's always a pleasure to see you."

"Thank you, Barrington," she blushed, "Likewise". I suspiciously look at my father.

"Royston, my, haven't you grown?" daddy said, confidently looking this young man in the eyes.

"Well, thank you for the escort. I can manage from here on in." Daddy loops his arm around my waist and shuffles me towards our box, once inside, we both look at each other and fall about laughing.

"Daddy, did you and Mrs. Northgate have a thing?" I ask.

"A gentlemen never tells, but, as I am no gentlemen, yes, I did," he smiles with a twinkle in his eye. "This is the first time I have seen her since Donna passed away."

"Is Royston my brother?" I whisper in daddy's ear, he bellowed with laughter. All the other race goers in their boxes look at us. By this point, I too could not control my laughter.

Our box was on the balcony, we were in prime location to see all that was going on. The paddocks could be viewed from where we were standing, and, in the distance, I spotted at least thirty or so horses being groomed.

Our chairs were leather, the carpet royal blue, we had an amazing buffet: a selection of lobster, crab, chicken, salad, and an assortment of alcohol.

"You ok, daddy," I ask concerned.

"Yes, I am having a great time," he responds automatically.

"No, I mean with all this alcohol around." My father looked at me, took my hand and kissed it, "I am fine."

"Ok, just checking."

He stared at my head, "What is with that hat?" he laughed.

"Ask your mother," I said apologetically.

"I have an idea," and he took my hat off and put it in the adjourning table behind us. Daddy then pushed his fingers up my nape and ruffled my hair. "I love your hair like this," he smiles.

"Thanks," I giggle.

"I hate the pink lipstick and nail polish," he says seriously.

"Well daddy, I love it and so does all these young men," I laugh. I look up, and notice the royal crest. "Daddy, are we in the Royal Box?"

THE JOURNEY

He smiles, "Yes we are."

"How?"

"We *are* royalty baby, do not forget that. We are premium stock," he laughed. "*You* are royalty."

Harold walked past me with a tray of champagne.

"Boy, come here," daddy said.

"Daddy, it's fine, please don't make a fuss," I look down. I could see that Harold was humiliated.

"No princess, it's not ok," he snapped and starred at Harold.

"Daddy please. Don't!" I plead. Without acknowledging my request, daddy took two champagne flutes and passed me one. I took it and smiled. Harold just stared at me.

My father smirked at Harold. "You can stop starring at my daughter right now. Boy, hasn't anyone told you that you should not hang your cap too high? She is out of your league."

"Daddy!" I shriek.

Daddy laughed. "Oh Winn, I am just playing," he said unapologetically.

Harold looked at my father. "Yes, Sir, I am aware of the saying."

"Good," daddy chuckled and winked at me.

"The young miss is not my type Sir. I have a beau and

am very happy, Sir," Harold informed us, with a smirk on his face. *'What do you mean you have a beau?' I wanted to scream. It was as if Harold hit me in the stomach. I looked at my father, glad of the cap too high comment.*

"Hmmm, I see," daddy smiled, I think he liked his cockiness.

"Winn, are you ok?" Daddy enquired concerned.

"I am just hot daddy. Where is the powder room?"

"To the left. Are you sure you are ok?"

"I just need a minute," I walked briskly to the ladies room. Once inside, I felt immediately better. I look around, this was the most impressive bathroom I have ever seen, and it was cool. A few middle aged ladies eyed me suspiciously.

"Are you alright dear?" a tall, dark skinned woman, with a thick perfect chignon and aqua blue dress asked. Her features were pretty, but appeared pinched.

"I am. It's just very warm."

She smiles. There is some cool water over there, shall I get you some?" she seemed concerned.

"Thank you," I replied, "You are most kind."

She puts the glass in front of me. I am standing before the largest mirror I had ever seen, it was wall to wall, with a thick chrome finish. The wash basins were white and grey marble, with sparkling silver taps. I smile. A young maid walks towards me with a face towel that had been soaked in cold water.

THE JOURNEY

"Here Ma'am," she smiled.

"Thank you." I sit down and put the cool towel on my neck.

"Arrrggggggghhhhhhhhh." I close my eyes. Both women look at me, and we all giggle.

"It's so hot," my new friend tells me. "My poor horse," she whined.

"Your horse is racing?" I asked impressed.

"Yes," she smiled proudly, showing off her perfect white teeth.

"What is his or her name," I enquired, genuinely interested.

"Her name is Carousel."

"Well, that is whom I am going to bet on," I stretch out my hand, "My name is Edwina."

"I know, we are all talking about you. No one knew Barry had a love child, let alone one so beautiful," she gushed without thinking.

I looked down immediately, caught off guard by the comment.

"Oh no, don't do that I'm sorry, I did not mean. My name is Lynnette the klutz with a big mouth." She looked genuinely sorry for her gaff. *'Come on Winn, toughen up!' I command.*

We both laugh. "It's ok, truly," I say quietly.

"I am sorry Edwina. I was not trying to be unkind." Lynnette meant every word.

"Call me Winnie, all my friends do. It's forgotten."

"Well, Miss Winnie, have you cooled down?" Lynette asked, in a very assertive manner.

"Yes". I smile at my new friend, looking her squarely in the eyes.

"Good. Carousel will be racing soon, and I want you to come to my box. We can cheer together." Lynnette looped her arm into mine, and off we went.

On the way back to the VIP enclosure, I spotted Harold in the corner of my eye, pouring champagne in more flutes. He momentarily looks up. I turn away, as I recognise that expression. He is annoyed with me. *How dare he? He is the one that has moved on. Clearly, I meant nothing to him.* Tears momentarily wet my eyes, but I am determined not to cry. Not over him, not anymore.

I walk past our own box, and my grandmother gives me the eye, suspiciously. I smile, elated at the fact that grandmother dearest will not be introducing me to the son of *this*, whose fathers owns *that*.

"Hurry, Lynnette," I hear a male voice cry out. "We're starting."

My new friend drags me into her box and races to the balcony area, she expertly scoops a pair of binoculars from the table and immediately steadies her focus on her horse.

THE JOURNEY

"Crack," the gun snapped and the animals galloped to cue.

"Look," Lynette squeals, "Carousel is number seven, my jockey is the one in blue and purple."

"I see him," I scream over the cheers in the box.

"Come on, Carousel," I chant with the others. I have to say that horse racing was a hoot. Carousel was like lightening, clearly the best thoroughbred in its class, she eased her way through his opponents and won with at least four lengths between her and the second rider.

Everyone was whooping and screaming. I turned around, and Lynette was gone, she had run down with her father to the paddock to give Carousel a big kiss and a much needed drink.

I felt the presence of someone behind me, I presumed it was daddy.

"Hello." Whoever he was, his voice was deep and silky.

I turn round to a divine set of lips and teeth smiling at me.

"Courtney," he said, stretching his long thick hand to me.

"Hmmm," was all that I could think to say. He was a man mountain, with lovely square jaws, white teeth, wide brown eyes and dimple in his chin. I just stare at him, besotted.

"My name is Courtney. I spotted you earlier and could not believe my luck when Lynette brought you to my box."

"And Lynette is?"

He smiles, "She is my sister. And you are?"

"Her new friend," I smile back, "Pleasure to meet you. It's Edwina Barnett, my friends call me Winnie, though you can call me Miss Barnett."

"Nice to meet you, Miss Barnett," with that, he delicately kissed my hand, which sent shock waves through my body. "It seems I have much work to do, if I am to call you Winnie."

"It appears so," I giggle. *Play it cool Winn. He seems too good to be true.*

"Champagne," he snapped his fingers, and Harold appeared. I look at Harold and smile.

Feeling awkward, I ask, "May I go to the paddock? I would love to meet Carousel."

Courtney held my hand, which was very forward, I pulled it away. He looked at me with regret. "I apologize, Miss Barnet. May I accompany you to the paddock?"

We both smile. "I would like that. Please, don't get the wrong impression, I enjoyed you holding my hand, it's just..."

"Edwina, it's fine. I am teasing you."

He stretched out his arm and I took it, he was tall, much taller than Harold. His morning suit was made for a man with his broad and muscular physique. I could tell that he had a fine hard body underneath all those clothes. I start to blush, and not just in my cheeks. On arrival to the

THE JOURNEY

paddock, Lynette runs over.

"Sorry for leaving you like that, Winnie, this is just so wonderful."

"It's ok, your brother has been taking care of me."

"I can see that," she says sarcastically.

They both smile at one another. I catch his gaze, and he gives me a wink. *He seems so confident, I really like that, and I am finding it a very attractive quality."*

"Come and meet the horse," Lynette said.

"Actually, I should go back to my box."

"I will escort you," Courtney replied smiling. My heart skipped a beat, and I had flutters in the base of my tummy.

"Ok," I try to sound cool. As he escorts me to my box, we fall silent. I could not believe that I was tongue tied over this man. *Are you kidding, Winnie?! He is delicious. Not just nice, but adorable.* He changes course at the last minute and leads me to the bar.

"I have a confession. I don't want to let you out of my sight. Can you please have a drink with me?"

"Alright, that will be nice," I smile.

He motions over a waiter, "A lemonade for the lady and a water for me."

"So Courtney, what do you do and who are your people?" I ask, with an air of Phyllis Barnett about me.

"Are you serious?" he exclaims, I am not sure if he was genuinely surprised or offended.

I look confused.

"Edwina, do you not know who I am?" he asked bemused.

"I'm sorry," I blush, "Should I?"

"No." he was the one who is now embarrassed. "Miss Barnett, I am Courtney Du Pille the third, my father is Courtney Jackson Du Pille the second, known to his peers, which includes your father, as Jackson. He is. Well.. We are the founding owners of Jamaica First National Bank."

"Ok then," I say with sarcastic humor, "no need to tell you who I am, as you already know."

He laughed, "Yes, my father and your father are acquaintances."

"I learn something new every day," I smile.

He stares at me for a few seconds. "You are very enchanting, Miss Barnett," he said quietly.

I blush and look down, Courtney puts his index finger under my chin and gently raises my head so that I was looking in his eyes. "Don't be embarrassed, you are lovely. This is how God made you, so embrace the face, body and mind that you have been given. We are made in God's image, revel in it."

I smile, my heart quickens, to my surprise, I feel my panties moisten and my nipples harden. I look at

THE JOURNEY

Courtney, he too is lovely. "You are a very handsome man, Mr. Courtney Du Pille the third," I say quietly, as I did not want to be overheard. He steps towards me and brushes his body on mine. The flutters in my stomach are somersaulting.

"Then it's settled," he says in a low voice, "we will make beautiful babies."

I burst out laughing.

"What's this?" I hear my grandfather interrupt our intimate flirting. He gently tugs me away from Courtney so that I am forced to take a step back. Courtney did not move.

"Dr. Barnett, sir, it's a pleasure to see you again," he said staring at me.

"I can see that," my grandfather replied annoyed. Embarrassed by my grandfather, I look to the floor only to be greeted by Courtney's large feet looking at me.

"Golly, you have boats for feet," I gasp.

"Well, when you sail me, you will never get wet," again I laugh uncontrollably. Courtney too is trying to suppress his laughter, as he can see that my grandfather is less than impressed with him.

"Edwina, come along," my Grandfather curtly pulls me in the opposite direction. As I walk away from him, I mouth, "Sorry," and he winks at me. My heart skips yet another beat, and my panties are soaked for a second time today.

"There you are" daddy whines. "I thought you got lost.

Where was she?" he asks grandfather.

"In the bar," he said disapprovingly.

"With?" daddy asked curtly, suspiciously eyeing me up and down for clues.

"Du Pille's son," grandfather said raising an eyebrow. My father was silent and cracked a shy smile.

"I see," he said quietly, then looked at my grandmother with approval. She too raised an eyebrow and smiled. I, on the other hand, danced inside, I saw it for the first time ever. It's approval. I plan to go full steam ahead.

This day was exhausting, there were so many highlights, but the most impressionable has to be that beautiful man, Courtney Du Pille. I cannot stop thinking about his chocolate cocoa smooth skin, his shapely lips, white teeth, and fine clothes. *Who are you kidding Edwina? It was the body under the clothes.* He was the whole package and more, and I cannot wait to see him again.

Riding back to the hotel. "Good day darling," my grandmother asked, trying to be noninvasive about my meeting.

"Yes, it was lovely," I smile. "Thank you for forcing me to come out and have some fun," I say.

"I see that you met Lynette, very accomplished like yourself. I can see you becoming quite friendly."

I smile, "I think you could be on to something there, grandmother," I note that grandmother and father exchange looks and smile. My grandfather looked grumpily out of the window.

THE JOURNEY

It's 8pm, and there is so much commotion next door. Monique has pinned up my hair. I have on a Chanel dress, which makes me feel quite exposed. However, my grandmother is insistent that this is all the rage. I am wearing a pink chiffon dress, which is strapless, with a sweetheart bodice to cup and corset my bosoms. I have cupped shoulder straps - and they sit perfectly on the upper part of my biceps. To break the dress up, is a diamond encrusted belt sewn into bodice, the skirt is pink chiffon. I inspect myself and look very different. I look so grown up and aristocratic, compared to my usual day to day plantation look. The door separating our bedroom opens, and my father stands there looking at me.

"Daddy, don't just stand there. Pass me my necklace." I snap.

"You look sensational," he smiles, walks over and kisses me on the head.

"Twice in two days," I say.

"Winn, you look better without anything at all, you don't need a necklace. You look lovely."

"Earrings?"

"Show me," daddy asks.

They are grandmother's drop down diamond earrings, I hold them to my ears.

"Bingo," daddy said. "Courtney is going to have a heart attack when he sees you."

"That's the plan," I tell him. Monique was fussing with my

hair, she smiled at me. I look at my father, who is stunned by my response.

"Do you like him?" he asks quietly, his expression becomes very serious.

"Daddy, he has a lot of potential, and I do feel drawn to him. He's nice and is not intimidated by me."

Daddy smiles, "I see, well, you look beautiful. Enjoy this evening. Can I give you some advice?"

"Hmmmmmm," I say, applying more lipstick.

"Be a little unavailable, men like a challenge," he smiled. I look at him.

"How do I do that without turning him off?" I say.

"Do nothing, make him chase you and do not make this easy for him."

"Ok, I will try," I smile to myself. My daddy was a sweetheart when he tried.

"The Royal Kingstonian Gala Dinner" was held downstairs in the Paul Bogle Ballroom. Daddy escorted me through the doors, and I was taken aback by the sheer size of the room. There was George Lewis and his Ragtime Jazz Band.

"Awww, daddy, is that?"

"Yes, baby, it's George Wallace himself," Daddy's face lit up at my excitement.

"Awww daddy, I love him," I squeal.

THE JOURNEY

"We all love George," daddy said, trying to contain his excitement. "Well, I hope that those pretty shoes can dance, as I plan to wear you out." He then showed me some of his dancing moves. My grandmama barged her way between us.

"Edwina, you are the prettiest woman here. I want you to have fun and commit to no one. You have the pick of the room, choose wisely dear," she stretched out her arm for two champagne flutes.

I blush and smile. I cannot believe she is being so nice to me. I must say that my grandmama seemed more relaxed with these people than she did at the plantation.

"I am not sure Champagne agrees with me," I confess.

"Nonsense. It's an acquired taste. You will get used to it." She jabs me back into position.

The evening was rapturous. There was an explosion of gorgeous women in luxurious beautiful dresses, handsome men, all looking important with their brandy glasses and shiny sleeked black hair, filled with brill cream and coconut oil. The banquet was fit for a king. I have never eaten so much at once, even my grandfather asked if I was ok. The conversation on our table was delightful, we were sat with Bradley Boullier, his excruciating annoying mother Jackie and his father Ken, otherwise known as Boxer, to his friends. The champagne made it all so bearable, and Bradley and I discussed plantations, politics, love affairs, marriage, and babies. In all accounts, anyone who was observing would be forgiven for mistaking us for a courting couple.

Jackie and my grandmother were deep in conversation,

yet observing our every reaction. The evening sailed past me and we were already at the coffee and mints.

"Edwina darling, let's go freshen up."

I look at my grandmother, undecided whether this was genuine, or an intentional ploy to prize me away from Bradley. My father and grandmother momentarily paused their conversation with Boxer and Jackie. Daddy raised his eyebrows, so I was pretty sure it was a strategy.

"Excuse me Bradley," I say politely. He looked disapprovingly at my grandmother.

"Of course ladies", with that, all the gentlemen stood up. I smiled, enjoying the etiquette shown to me.

"Come along dear," grandmother clucked with the broadest grin in her face.

We walked arm in arm to the powder room. We both used the cubicle, as if it were some sort of penance for leaving the table, in the absence of actually wanting to pee.

As we stood at the mirror, my grandmother fixed my fair. "Dear, apply more lipstick, you're starting to fade."

"Oh ok," I say with a smile. In all the years I lived with this witch, this was the first genuine attention she paid to my appearance. It just made me feel nice and wanted.

"Do you like him?" she asked, reasserting her sharp tone.

"Who?"

THE JOURNEY

"Bradley," she said exasperated and raising her eyes to the ceiling.

"He's nice," I giggle.

"Nice. Tsk…"

"Yes grandmama, nice."

"Hmmmm, well, he's not quite to our standard, but he will do."

"What? grandmama!" I exclaim.

"Yes dear," she turned and looked at me.

"I like him as a friend, I did not realise that you expected me to court and marry him."

"Oh, so you don't like him," she seemed confused.

"He is a nice man, but I would not call him a suitor. Why would you ask me that? We were just eating dinner. I was being polite."

"Well when you did not acknowledge Courtney?"

"What? When?" I am momentarily panicked that I slighted my honey in waiting.

When you were talking to Bradley, he walked past on at least four occasions, and you did not even look up once.

"Really, I did not see him," I say mortified.

"Oh ok. I just presumed that you had lost interest," she informed me.

"No, I must find him, he cannot think I am being rude."

Panicked, I was about to leave the bathroom.

My grandmother tugged my arm. "First apply your rouge. Now, if you do not listen to another word I say, please hear me now. Be cool. He loves it. He is boiling over for you and, whether it has been by design or a genuine mistake, your being embroiled in conversation with Bradley has him wanting." my grandmother said, with a spark in her eye. For a second she was reminded of memories in her prime. "Play it cool, if you chase him now, you will be chasing him forever."

"But" I try to protest, wanting to wear my heart in my sleeve.

"No buts. Be interested in Bradley, he needs to know that he is not the only bull in the steed." With that, she laughed mightily, clearly enjoying her own humour.

I smiled broadly and raised my eyebrows. "Grandmama," I say and smile. As instructed, I applied my rouge. I look at myself in the mirror. I momentarily see Harold's in my mind's eye. I shake him off. I lean to survey my face and hair, yep, perfect, now, time to have fun.

Back at the table, Bradley and I pick up from where we left off.

"Edwina, do you think that we could have dinner sometime? My cousin Evelyn can chaperone us it would be most proper," he asked.

"Umm, I am not sure. I may need to speak to my father," I smile politely.

"Arhhhh, yes, of course," he smiled. "So, you would consider it?"

THE JOURNEY

"I will ask him."

The band piped up, and I let out a sigh of relief. "I love this band," I shout over the southern dulcet tones of the percussion.

"Who are they," he shouted back.

"What are you serious? That" I point aggressively "is George Lewis." As I point, I spot Courtney at the corner of the room, he was talking to an older gentlemen, and they were both looking at me.

"Dance?" Bradley shouted.

"Pardon."

"Would you like to dance?" he shouted, not realising that the music was softening, and most people close by looked over and smiled at us both.

I try to think of something to say, desperate to save his embarrassment. "It's ok," I smile. I turn to my father, "Daddy, can I dance with Bradley?"

"You are your own woman. Don't ask me. Do you want to dance with him?"

I nod. He grins a little too wide for my father, with gratitude. We sway to the music, and Bradley cut loose. He was really quite good, we danced for what seemed a small age, but it was delightful, and one of the best evenings that I had ever.

An announcement was made that George Lewis Band were taking a break, so another band came on. They looked like one of the American Lindipop bands. The guitar started, and I immediately felt like I too had to cut loose.

The hairs on my body arose at his presence. Courtney slowly walked over towards me, grinning and locking my gaze. "Excuse me Bradley." He said without even looking at Bradley.

Bradley looked suspiciously at him, Courtney stretched out his hand to shake Bradley's, as soon as Bradley reciprocated he pulled him close and whispered something into his ear. Bradley looked at me apologetically and said "sure."

Courtney was absolutely edible in his tuxedo. His hair was slicked to one side, and his face had a glow to it, he stretched out his hand, which I immediately grabbed, he kissed the back of my palm, he looked at me, which made my nipples harden immediately. "Let's dance!" he shouted. The rock and roll beat took over, and we twisted and skanked, and he pirouetted around me like an old pro. He could tell that my gown was in part a restriction and also that most of the room was watching us. After the third rock and roll song, I mouthed, "I need a break."

"You ok," he asked.

"Hmmmm, I think so. I need air and lots of water. My mouth is dry."

Courtney grabbed my hand and led me out to the bar. It was outside, and the pool water shimmered aqua blue in the moons ray. The evening was warm, and there were many party goers outside sat down on the patio furniture.

"What does the pretty lady want to drink?" asked the barman.

"Madam," Courtney said sharply, "shall have a water with ice."

The barman nodded compliantly "Yes, sir," and continued with the task at hand. I walk away embarrassed and head towards the first vacant table I see and sit down, the arch of my right foot is aching.

"Here baby," he says, putting the drinks down and pulling out my chair.

I look up, grinning from ear to ear.

"What?" he smiles.

"I like the way you said that. A lot."

"Good, as I loved saying it." He sips his water, and I stare at his lips. "I better get you back inside, before Bradley comes and gives me an old fashion beating over his girl."

"What?" I giggle. "I am nobodies' girl," I laugh.

"Not even mine?" Courtney enquires, with a confident smile.

"Well, you have to earn me, I am a powerful, wealthy business woman. I am not just going to quiver at your feet, just because you call me baby."

Courtney looked at me, his face deadly serious, he pulled his chair close to mine, he positions his face a nose width from mine, I smell the brandy on his breath. I read the intensity in his expression. There is a connection between us. It feels needy. In his low gruff deep voice, he says, "When I have earned you, I will make your body crumble and quiver underneath me" with that, he leaned in and kissed me closed mouth hard and quick. I look at him, his head in the same position. I then bend, I wrap my arms around his broad muscular neck, and kissed him soft and slow.

This courtship was undeniably unexpected. It has only been three months, but I do love him. It's not infatuation, but love. I find him attractive in all ways, and I can't keep my hands of him.

THE JOURNEY

Courtney is everything that Harold isn't. He's really tall, at least six foot six. An athletic build, coupled with his perfectly sculpted upper body, each muscle is pronounced and cut to perfection, complimented with a high round stone-hard bottom, and strapping legs, that are so muscular that his thighs remind me of the well-honed muscles of my father's stallions.

I adore the fact that he loves me, and is open and gallant and unashamedly bold about it. This is the man that I need. Someone who is willing to show up for his woman. When he comes at the plantation, and he will get stuck in with any task that we are involved in. The other week, Bertha, my cow, was having a difficult birth. Courtney, my banking city trading boy, helped us hold her down, he even assisted Mackie in pulling out the calf, both men were elbows deep in Bertha.

"Mackie, we have to get it out, it's been too long," I wail desperately. The two men carefully tugged and pulled the calf out of her mother's womb, her life was hanging in the balance, and we all knew that each of us had to do all that we could to help her stay alive. Struck by the enormity of the moment, we all were desperate to set her free, and I with two plantation hands did our utmost to hold Bertha in place through the pain of calf birth.

I look at Courtney, I could not contain myself.

"Please, save her". He could feel my anguish. He pushed deeper into Bertha, she let out a huge wail and pushed her leg free, which caught me on the cheek. I saw a flash of yellow and orange in both eyes. I catapulted to the floor.

"Winnie!" Courtney screamed.

"I'm ok," I lied, the instant swelling rising like bread on the left side of my face. Dazed, I grabbed her leg and pushed it down through the stars and choir echoing in my ears.

My grandfather and father ran into the barn, "How long has it been?"

"Too long daddy. She can't die," Tears of grief, and the pain from my head stream down my face.

My father stood behind us. "Courtney, Mackie, on the count of four I need you to pull down." The two field hands hedged round to make space for daddy and grandfather. Both men were on their knees and their elbows were in the middle of Bertha's body. It was daddy who first pushed as hard as he could towards the top of the cow's stomach. She let out a wail and thrashed around. "Mooooooooooooooooooooooooooooooo."

"Keep her still boys," grandfather yelled to both field hands, then counted us in "one, two, three, four" and repeated the exercise.

Bertha screamed at the highest pitch. It was excruciating. Both Courtney and Mackie tugged hard and set the calf free, she slid out or Bertha with ease yet when she arrived she was limp and lifeless.

"She can't be dead," Courtney screamed at us angrily.

"Help me," my grandfather shouted. All the men lifted the calf and perched her limp body over the stable gate. The field hand grabbed a bucket of water and was washing away the mucus from her face, nose, and mouth. My father rubbed the calf's back vigorously, and Mackie pushed through the mucus glue as he blew into her mouth. The poor calf's airways were so blocked that when Mackie blew in its mouth, a mucus bubble popped out of its nose. Courtney took over the mouth to mouth when Mackie needed to catch his breath. Finally the bubble burst, he kept blowing, and a few seconds later, there was a splutter from the calf. She took her first breath.

They lay the new born next to her mother. She looked at her baby lovingly, licked her face, and closed her eyes for the last time. Her duty complete, her daughter saved, that is all that mattered. None of us had anything useful to say, all of us were drenched in sweat, blood and mucus. We were all terrified that she would not make it through the night, hastily we take this precious fragile new life to the house.

"How are they?" Rene ran off the porch to me with her lantern in hand, it was after 10 o'clock at night. She looked at me and knew that Bertha had died. In the distance she saw the men and the calf.

"I have a large dog bed under the stairs. Lucy made it for Daaaag." She pulled it out, ran upstairs, and came down with spare blankets.

Courtney was in the living room, the calf was shivering. Mackie took the blankets and wrapped her tight. Courtney still held her in his arms and stroked her head. "It's ok little bird," he said softly.

Unsure what to do, Courtney came in and took control of the situation. "I will sit with her. Rene, warm some milk for me. Winnie, go get a bath and get Barry to look at your cheek."

"No I'm fine baby," I protest. "I want so stay with her."

"Winnie," my grandfather put his hand on my shoulder, "go bathe and take Courtney with you. Let us help, you look exhausted. I will come up in a while and look at your face. Does it hurt to blink or talk?"

"No, it just hurts," I tried to smile, but the muscles in my face were in protest and refused to move.

I show Courtney to the main bathroom on the landing. Rene had been a dear and had the hot water running. The bath was filled with Epsom salts, and there was some imported lux soap on the side.

Courtney entered the bathroom and shut the door. He looked crestfallen by tonight events. As he shut the door, he weakly smiled at me.

"Come on," Rene beckoned me from my room door. "Your bath is ready." I undress and slowly enter the bath. All my muscles were aching and sore from the evening restraints. Rene takes a jug of bath water and wets my hair. She finds my shampoo and washes it, whilst humming. I scrub the evening off me mechanically. I had an overwhelming feeling of regret. I could have done more. I lie back, allow the water to absorb me, and dunk my head under the water.

As I surface, Rene is gone. I did not want to tell her to leave, but I am glad that I was alone. I get out, pick up my large fluffy towel and wrap my body twice. I find my short hair towel and wrap my hair. As I walk through to my room to find Courtney sat on my bed half naked, with a towel wrapped around his waist.

"Baby, I don't know about you but I need a hug," he tells

me. I run to him and push my face deep into his chest. He peels the towel off my head and strokes my wet hair. The more he stroked my hair, the harder it was for me to control my feelings. I fall into him and cry. He holds me firmly in his arms.

"Winnie, I am so proud of you. You are like no other woman I have encountered. Today, you were truly remarkable."

I look up, my face is swollen from Bertha's kick, my eyes are red, and there is snot falling out my nose. Is he serious? I pick up my towel and wipe my eyes and nose. He pulls me close and kisses me, my face hurts and I moan in pain.

"Oh baby, I'm sorry. How is your cheek?" he then turns me to inspect the damage. Courtney's eyes grow wide, and his face becomes very serious.

"What, what is it?"

"Honey, how you feeling?" he asks, with a hint of panic in his voice.

"I'm ok, my head is throbbing. Why?"

Courtney picked me up and put me on the bed carefully. "Don't move. I'm going to get your grandfather."

"What?" I sit up looking puzzled at the situation.

"Winnie, I said don't move," he shouted at me for the first time in our courtship. It really frightened me.

I lay back and feel water trickling down the side of my face. I realise that it has trickled to my collar bone. Hang on, something is not right, as my hair is only damp, not wet. I look at my crisp white pillows, it is covered in blood. I gasp, it's my blood. I begrudgingly inform my fingers to investigate. I look at my finger tips and do what I always do in any bloody situation. I pass out.

Chapter 17

THE JOURNEY

Mr. Lover Man

We run in the room, and she is very still. *Dear God, do not let this woman die on me. She is my everything.*

"Why is she naked, and why were you in here?" her father yells at me.

I look at him incredulous. "Sir, with the greatest respect, I think we need to concentrate on the blood that appears to be seeping out of her head," I say more assertively than I wanted to. He glares at me, I stare back. He does not frighten me. *I know this son of a bitch thinks he's in control, but he's not. Far from it. I see the way that he treats others around him, but I will not allow him to treat me this way. I plan to marry this woman, and when I do, I intend to leave this island with Winnie for good.*

"I'm serious!" he barks, as he walked around the bed.

"So am I." *Stand your ground, Courtney.* "I am neither intimidated nor bothered about you or this." I point to Winnie's exposed breast. "I just want to be sure that she is ok?"

"Winnie," her grandfather says gently rubbing her forearm. "Winnie honey, can you hear me?" he checked her pulse and swiftly grabbed his bag that he brought in the room and got a small light and checked her pupils. He shook her more vigorously, "Winnie?"

"Hmmmmm," she lay there dazed.

"Winnie, I need you to open your eyes." He shook her again more vigorously. "Winnie!" he started to shout at her.

Both her father and I look at my beautiful woman lying lifeless in the bed.

"Winnie," grandfather shouted.

"Dad, what's going on? What's wrong?" Barry enquires visibly worried.

"She's had a blow to the head, it could be a number of things." The old man looked concerned.

Winnie slowly opened her eyes. "My ear is bleeding."

"I know, my darling. I just need to examine you to determine why?"

"Ok," she whispered. "I think I fainted when I saw the blood."

"Hmmm, hmmmmm," her grandfather said smiling.

"What can I do to help?" I ask feeling completely useless.

"How about you put some fucking clothes on," her father snaps.

"They are dirty remember?" *This man is such an idiot. What does he think happened here? I heard about him, the women, his bullying nature, his unpredictable temper. I will not be toyed with. He does not control me.*

Right on que, Rene came in with a pair of work trousers and a short sleeved shirt. To provoke him, I slowly dress myself.

"What's the prognosis, doc?"

THE JOURNEY

"Not sure, but what I do know is that my granddaughter needs privacy. So, please, all of you leave the room."

We walk down the stairs in silence.

"Everything alright?" Mackie asks. He seemed genuinely concerned for her. I like him, he is like a caring father to my baby, and a much better role model than the one she actually has. He really loves her, and for that, I love him.

I shrug my shoulders, "The truth is we are not sure," I say feeling even worse than losing Bertha.

"Sit guys have some tea," Rene chimes in. Barry is a great doctor, he will find out what is wrong with her."

Barrington takes the hot tea. He looks visibly worried, which reassures me a little. I am not sure why. He looks old, tired, like life is wearing on him. As he sits down, he stares at me with peppered intensity.

"Why were you in my daughter's room without your clothes on boy?" he said in his most menacing voice.

Stand down old man. You have no idea who you're playing with. "Firstly, Barry, I am not your *boy*. To answer your question, I was pretty shaken up by Bertha so thought I check in on Edwina. I was consoling her, she was upset."

"Are you sure that's all you were doing." he asked.

"For God sake man, have some respect, that's your daughter we are talking about. May I remind you that she has a nasty bruise on her face? I just wanted to make sure she was ok," I look him square in the eyes.

He backs down. "Well, I just needed to hear it," Barrington snarled. "I don't want anyone taking advantage of my daughter".

"Barry, not all men likes their women battered and bloody." I say sarcastically.

Barrington leapt off his chair and grabbed me by the throat. I push him off. Rene jumps in between us.

"No. No. No. No." she shouts angrily at the both of us. "You are not here for this. Take this macho melodrama out of here. She is upstairs with God knows what injuries," Rene was fuming, realising she was shouting, she lowered her voice, "she loves you both. There is enough room in her life for you both, so stop this now."

I look at the old man, he was panting hard. I step away. I feel sorry for him. She is all that he has in his life.

"Sir, this evening's events have taken me by surprise. I apologize for any comments that may have caused you offence." I stretch out my hand.

Rene looked at Barrington as if to say "well?"

He steps back, stretched out his hand "I apologize, Courtney, this evening has stirred up unpleasant emotions, and I would like you to know that I regret my actions."

Rene smiles. "What you both need is a beer. She walked to the cooler and pulls out two red stripe beers. "Go on, go outside, walk and talk. You're practically family now, sort this out properly. She cannot choose, so don't make her."

THE JOURNEY

We look at each other. For appearance sakes we knew this has to be done. Rene would tell Winnie exactly how we behaved, and we both knew we have to end the story on a positive note.

Barrington strides ahead, he throws the beer to the ground. "She knows that I don't drink."

"Why not?" I ask, knowing the truth.

"I just can't. It's a long story," he shouts me down.

"I heard that you were a sorry drunk, but you have turned your life around." I look him squarely in the eye.

Barrington turned around and gazed at me. "Listen kid, for whatever reason, she loves *you*. I think she could do much better, but she has chosen you." he looked directly at me.

I soften my stance I can see that this is hard for him. "Like you, I do love her Barry. I know what it looked like, believe me Sir I would never disrespect her. She is too special to me for that. I want it to be special, you know."

"What your first time?" Barry said sarcastically.

I smile, "Yes, I wouldn't do that to her. Look, we have not had the best relationship, but we have to try for her sake."

"Why?" he snapped.

"Because we are going to be married. I love her. I would have asked her today, but Bertha died then her ear, now you" Barrington is just glaring at me. I nervously drink the beer.

"What makes you think she'll say yes?" he asks.

I shrug, "Just a feeling. Life..." I start to tear up. I clear my throat and push this feeling aside. "It's fragile, and I just want to be with her."

"Well," Barrington said cheerily, "welcome to the family." He opens his arms to me and walks towards me. He bear hugs me, which throws me off guard, then he cups his hands around my face. "If you hurt her in any way, I will kill you."

"Gentlemen," her grandfather shouts, suspiciously eyeing us up, trying to decipher whether this is friendly banter, or we have entered into enemy territory.

"She's going to be fine. The kick to her face ruptured her eardrum. She will need to rest and keep it covered for a week or so, as she will be prone to infection, but the sight of blood frightened her, so she will be a good patient."

"Can I go and see her please?" I ask politely.

"Of course son."

I run up the stairs. She was lying on her bed in a white night gown.

"My poor darling, Bertha brutalised you," I laugh. I lay next to her, Winnie looks me up and down and smiles. "Baby, what *are* you wearing?" she asked me trying not to smile.

"Rene clearly does not like me. Can you sit up for a bit?"

"Yes," she looked confused. I help her get up and prop

her pillows around her, so that her head and neck are covered.

"Baby, I need to ask you something very important." I kneel down next to her, the injury to her face is horrendous, and her complexion illustrates the iridescent spectrum of bruising in all its hues. The whole of her left jaw is inflated, her cheek bone was burgundy and black, her eye was swollen, and the rest of her jaw was purple. I smile.

"You look awful," I whisper, she wants to laugh, but can't. "I need you to know that you are the most extraordinary young woman I have met in my life. Today, has made me realise that if your heart tells you to jump, you should jump." She looked confused. I gently hold her hand, "I need you with me, baby, not just as my girl, but as my wife. Will you marry me?"

She smiles, then winces, then smiles. "Yes baby, now get in here and cuddle me to sleep. Grandfather gave me some morphine, and I am woozy as hell," tears trickle down her face.

"Are these tears of joy Winn?" I ask.

"Yes baby," she smiles through the pain.

"Then I am the luckiest man in the world."

Chapter 18

The Making of the Man

Our seven bedroom beach house in Negril is the family retreat from the city, and we all love it. This house has fond memories for me. It belonged to my grandfather, and once he had passed away, my mother gave it a much needed make over.

Stretched over three floors with decking on each level, there was no area of this house that did not represent a sun trap. My adorable fiancé loved it, and I for one loved her even more for that, as we will be spending so much time here. My bedroom is located downstairs, as I enjoy the sound and smell of the sea. As a teenager, I kicked up an almighty fuss to have my own way, and smile each time I sit in this room with the patio doors open. My landscape for as far as the eyes can span is cloudless clear blue skies and aqua blue water. Breathtaking!

Sitting on my beach wooden decking, looking at the unknown and sipping some mango juice, my intimate thoughts are interrupted.

"Court, I am so excited for you. You're going to be married in a month. Are you getting nervous?" Lynnette bounces in my room with her red bathing suit on.

My sister literally did cart wheels in our living room when I informed my family that Winnie and I were engaged. With immediate effect, my mother and Phyllis moved into action and between them have planned the biggest society wedding Jamaica will ever see. It's indulgent, extravagant, opulent, and over the top, hell, it will be a great shindig, and I for one am very excited.

"Hey there loved up boy, did you hear what I said?" she pestered me.

"I did Lynne?" I say with exasperation and roll my eyes at my sister, "and yes, I am excited about married life, but this wedding is all about mum and Phyllis. You *do* realise that right?"

"I know, I know", she said apologetically. "Courtney, *you* are the heir and only son to one of the wealthiest men in Jamaica. You are marrying the bastard heiress of one of the wealthiest families in Jamaica. This *has* to be celebrated," she giggled.

"Lynn, don't let me warn you again. That's not funny," I smile, even though my sister was offensive, she did not mean anything by it.

"What is so funny is how mum and dad have made such allowances for the Barnett Princess. If she was one of your local common round the way island girls, this would not be happening. Admit it."

"Lynne enough," I bellow. "She is my choice, and that is it."

"Bruv I know. She is a lovely choice, you will be enjoying her for years to come," she laughed.

"I sincerely hope so." I wink.

"So what's the plan for tomorrow tonight?"

"Barry, dad, and I are going to some old club in Morant Bay. This is the preamble to the stag party. It should be a hoot."

"Who else is going?"

"Ronnie and Jeff are flying in from Miami." My sister tried not to look too interested, but she was real sweet on my boy Ronnie.

"You going to spend time with Barrington the Barbarian are you?" Lynne said sarcastically and raised her eyebrows.

I laugh, "I am." I look at my sister and wipe my brow and laugh hard. "Now that's progress for you."

"Just you make sure that you don't get in a punch up with him, or this fairy tale wedding is over. You hear me?" We both laugh, and Lynn heads out to the beach for a swim. I lay back allowing the sun to warm my skin, and start to daydream of married life. Edwina Barnett loves me to the point she scares me with her intensity. I am genuinely mad over heels in love with her. No question, but I am fearful. I just don't want to hurt her. My father adores my mother, but he still has women all over town. Will I burn with desire for my wife in ten months, ten years? Suppose the sex is terrible, then I am trapped.

I immediately shrug off this feeling. No Court, you may be your father's son, but you are not your father. She is the one, and you felt that from your first kiss. The quality that I admire the most is that she is completely independent. If I acted like a fool, she would not be dependent on me or my family, she is her own woman. I am not sure why I find this so attractive, but I do, she is so young, yet so capable.

My wanting to be married is not just about sex, but I'd be a liar if I said that I was not looking forward to undressing my beautiful virginal bride. I know what pleasures await me. I have restrained myself many a night. The urge to rip her clothes off and have her mount me has been my fantasy for months. Now, in one month, she will be mine completely and I have a promise to deliver. I smile remembering that I told her that I plan to make her crumble and quiver. I remember the first night that we kissed, it was magical. Since that week, I have locked off all my lady friends. I am completely committed.

I have laid it all out to her. There is nothing that she does not know about me, and there is nothing I will not do for her. I have never been so devoted to one woman, and so honest. My parents have seen the change in me. For years, father has pressured me on a date when I will join the Bank. I gave him one, the day after I proposed. I know that I don't have to provide for her, but I want to.

I will finish my masters at George Town University. Then I will move my wife and I to the capital and learn to be the next CEO and owner of Jamaica's First National Bank. I have it all. The wealth, the family, the career, and now a very accomplished and beautiful wife. As the sun beats down on my naked body, I smile.

"Hello son, you look like you got the cream," my dad asks.

I laugh out loud. "You think?"

"So you're sure then?"

What is with everyone? "Of what dad?" I try not to sound too annoyed.

"Marriage?" he looks at me seriously.

"Yes sir, 100% pop. She is just adorable, and I don't mean the obvious. She is the whole package."

"If you're happy with her, then I am happy," he smiled. He looked pensive. "Courtney, I am not in the habit of delving into your business, but I have to ask. Have you ... well?

"What Dad?" *Is he serious? Do we need to do this now? I mean, he knows that I am his son in that area.*

"You know what I am trying to ask?"

"Dad, are you asking whether we have we slept together?" I ask him directly.

My dad nods apologetically.

"No dad. She is a lady and you know that." I reply annoyed.

"Even nice rich ladies like to chew sugar cane from time to time," he smiles broadly. "Also, she is a country girl and they are hot. Believe me." We both laugh out loud.

"Wait. Do you think she is knocked up?" I laugh and point at my father as if he is crazy. "Come on dad, wash you filthy mouth out with soap."

He slaps my back. "Well, now that I know that she is what I hoped her to be. I am satisfied."

"Why dad? What difference does it make? You know

that I am not a virgin." I am intrigued by this train of thought.

"You are the man. You need to feel that you conquered the mountain first. No man wants to walk on another man's beaten track." He looked at me when he said it. I am not sure that I am that bothered. I don't want the town tramp, but I would have preferred some experience. Although, I can teach her everything she needs to know.

"Listen, it's important to me too, so even though I should be just as virtuous, I am happy that she is a virgin," I say to placate him. We both laugh. "Now, what do they have in store for us tomorrow night?"

"No idea son, but if Barry has anything to do with it, it will be fun. He was the original wildcat in his day."

Ronald Whole and Jeffery Finch have been my best pals since elementary school. We met in the playground on our first day. This fat kid called Carl was picking on Jeff and pushed him to the ground, Ron and I stepped in, and that was the last day that Jeff got picked on. Since then, we have been inseparable, we went to the same boarding school and we all travelled to Miami to go to university together. These guys were not just my friends, they were my brothers. Both men ran into my room in their swimming trunks.

"Hey man, why so glum?" Jeffrey asked, concerned as he saw me lounging on the deck.

"I'm cool man. Just chilling and contemplating." I say.

"What? How you're going to make your wife scream." Ron crudely chimed in. We all laughed. I stood up and put on my trunks.

"Nah brother," I say seriously. They looked at each other and sat down next to me.

"What's going on?" Ron said. "Cold feet?"

"No. I am just conscious of the magnitude of what I am doing. This is for life, and I want to be sure in myself that I will not let her down in any way. She means that much to me."

"Man, you are one of the wealthiest men in Jamaica right now." Jeff retorted, amazed that I was thinking so deeply about such matters.

"Jeff, being a man is not about money."

"Tell that to most, if not all of the women I know." We all laughed. "I mean that, and start with my mother. I get what you are saying, but you will not have the same issues that face millions of married couples today. You will never have to worry that she is with you for your money, as she has money and lots of it. You do not have to scrimp and save to buy your house, as you have one already. It's not that bad for you guys. All you have to do is just love her. That's it. That's your job. Everything else, and I mean everything else, is already taken care of."

"I hear you, but"

"There are no buts," Jeff spat out the words angrily. "Can you love this woman? Simple. Yes or No?"

"Yes!" I say smiling head down.

"Then, that is all that we have to talk about. Let's go and get you married boy. But before that, can I take a swim in that gorgeous Jamaican water please? Come on, the last man to the water is buying drinks all night."

With that challenge ahead of us, we all sprinted to the sea. I, as always, was last. The following night was a treat. Barry and his father went all out. We had the private dining room, there were beautiful waitresses everywhere. Jeff and Ron were in their element and had spotted a few country girls that they would definitely get close with very soon.

The humidity in the air was stifling. We all wore loose fitting linen shirts and slacks. The Morant Bay hotel was nice, but lacked the finesse that we were used to. That said, there was everything we desired: booze, cards, roulette table and women.

"Thank you, Barry and Dr. Barnet, this is some shindig," I smiled.

Even my dad was delighted at the welcome, and I had to keep his roving eye under control. Barry and Dr. Barnett invited their friends, which included Mackie.

"Court can I get you a drink?" Mackie enquired.

"Sure, why not?" I had had enough, but wanted to be polite. He was the one man in the room that I wanted to spend time with.

Mackie returns with the drinks "So how are you my young brother?"

I laugh, he always made me feel part of the family, "I am cool, I am looking forward to married life."

Mackie smiled, he looked behind him, the barman, a tallish medium sized man was listening intently.

"You know Mackie, you don't need to worry. I will take care of her. I love her. You know, she is the best thing that happened to me."

"More soda sir?" the barman chimed in and interrupted our flow.

"Err.... No, thanks." Even though I had said no, the waiter took my glass and diluted my neat aged Wray and Nephew Rum.

He slammed the glass on the bar. I glared at him, *'What was his problem?'*

"Now that you have ruined my drink, make me another one, and don't take your time about it," I snap at him.

He eyeballs me like I know him. "Yes Sir!" he says sarcastically.

I hear him crashing around behind me. "Hey, do I know you?"

"Harold cut it out," Mackie warned. Mackie gave the young man a stare that I would never want to be on the receiving end off. All background noise calmed down. Harold gave me my drink, and Mackie suggested that we go outside.

"You know him?" I ask.

"Yeah, he's a mixed up kid, pay him no mind."

"Why is he upset with me? I have never met the jerk."

THE JOURNEY

"Look, he used to work at the plantation, and we fired him about six months ago."

"Really? Why?"

"It didn't work out," Mackie said quickly.

"Is that all?" I ask.

"It's complicated. You know what they say brother, you can't please all of the people all of the time. We dealt with it," Mackie said reassuringly, but now I am aggrieved. I look towards the bar.

"Let it go young brother, So tell me again, are you ready for this?"

"By 'this', you mean marriage?" I smile, remembering my gorgeous bride to be.

"Absolutely. Like I said before we were rudely interrupted, she is the one. There is nothing that I would not do for her."

"That's good to hear, she is a diamond. A rare treasure, and you must ensure that you treat her like that. Defend her always, take care of her, honour her and always ensure that she's safe."

"Jeez Mackie, you make it sound like she's in mortal danger," I laugh.

Mackie laughed nervously. "No man, I just want you to take care of her. I have been in her life since she was five years old. She is like a ... a... daughter. My wife and I loved that little girl."

"Your wife? I didn't know that you were married."

"She died some time ago," Mackie said quietly.

"I am so sorry to hear that man. What happened?" I asked. Mackie looked pained as he talked about this.

"I just don't know," he said, his voice gruff, he gazed to the stars and exhaled. "That's the worst of it, you know. I have no peace, she was on her way to her sister's and went missing, she never turned up, and I have not heard from her since. She's dead though."

"How can you be so sure?" I asked. An ache developed in my chest. I would not be able to function if that was me.

Mackie pounds his chest, with his fist. "I feel it in here, every day," his voice broke. I did what any human being could have done, I hugged this man and told him how sorry I was for his loss. It was real and raw. I so wanted him to have peace.

We both pulled away and drank our rums. "Another one?" Mackie asked wiping a tear from his eye. We both acknowledged that he needed something to do.

"Sure," I nod looking in my glass.

Jeff and Ron walked onto the patio "Hey you alright man?" Jeff asked concerned.

"I am just fine," I say quietly.

"Why so glum?"

"Nothing, just talking."

"You're not having cold feet again are you?" Ron asked, a little too loudly. We heard a crash of glasses in the

THE JOURNEY

distance. It was Harold, he just glared at me.

"You ok man?" Jeff asked.

Harold did not answer him, he just sucked his teeth and put the broken glass in the tray. Another waiter came to help him, they looked similar, he was just slightly younger and shorter.

I look at this Jackass, he too starred at me. What is his problem? Let it go Court.

Harold walks past and looks at me and sucks his teeth again.

"What?" I shout at him. I hear the other waiter tell him to keep moving.

"That's right man, listen to your friend," I shout again.

"What's with you," Ronald asked.

This guy has been a rarsehole all night, man," I say loudly.

Harold throws his tray on the floor and there is a ferocious crash. He storms back, the other waiter trying to pull him away. I immediately stand up, my adrenalin pumping angrily around me veins.

"What's your problem boy?" I spit out the words.

"You're my problem rich boy," Harold says, squaring up to me. Other waiters run behind Harold. Mackie comes rushing out and immediately gets in between us. He pushes Harold away and whispers something in his ear. Harold looks at me hard. I see my father, Barry, and Dr. Barnet walking swiftly towards the fracases.

"I heard you. Harold shouts at me.

"Heard what?" Ronald chimed in aggressively.

"I heard him say that he has got cold feet," he snidely bellows looking in Mackie's face. All eyes were on me. I immediately shoot Ron a look.

"No, what you heard was me asking him if he has cold feet," Ron chimes in like a good friend and foot soldier.

"That's right," Jeff said. It was like we were all five years old again, ready to fight and protect one another to the end.

Daddy stepped in, he looked behind him and could see some of the other men were crowding the scene. "Listen fellas, please go inside. This waiter is clearly thinking that he can join the party, rather forgetting that he should be working for the party," the guest smile and some chuckle, already half drunk. "Please go inside, we will sort this. Can someone get the Manager out here please?" Dr. Barnett helped Daddy and them in and shut the door.

Dr. Barnet walked towards us, "Harold go home", he ordered.

"Dr. Barnet, I heard him. He is not worthy of her. How can he have second thoughts? She is a wonderful person." Harold said.

"She is," I tell him.

"What?" Harold said.

I see Mackie giving him a look. I could not put my finger

on it. "Who are you?" I ask not wanting to know the answer, "And why do you give a shit whether I have cold feet or not?"

The younger man next to Harold looked at us all and laughed. "Let's just say that he knows your wife to be far more intimately than you do."

Barrington immediately stepped in and hit him hard with the tumbler in his hand.

"Good God man, was that necessary?" my father shouted.

"Barrington," Dr. Barnet screamed at his son. The poor chap was writing on the floor, two older waiters rushed to his aide.

The humidity in the air became suffocating. I felt that I had been hit in the face with the tumbler.

"Calvin" Harold screams. Calvin staggers back to his feet, blood seeping from his eye. One of the waiters ran across and immediately pressed a napkin on it to stem the bleeding.

"Shut your filthy mouth, or I will permanently shut it for you," Barrington screams. A single vein in his head was protruding and throbbing, as he was about to step in for the kill. Mackie grabbed him and whispered in his ear. He stopped and looked at us all.

"I do not know who he is, or why he is saying this to you, but I assure you that it's not true. My Winnie is not that kind of girl. And you know it."

Harold looked at Courtney and his family, "Are you sure

that you want him for a father in law? Hmmmm. Look at him, he is a murdering rapist. This man murdered Edwina's grandmother, he killed her grandfather, and although we have no proof, we all know that after he brutality raped her mother then killed her too."

Barrington lurched forward to grab after Harold. Mackie thwarted this attempt.

"She was my girl for three years. Just ask your father, Mackie, or Rene" we all look at Dr. Barnett. I stagger back as I read his expression. He's telling the truth. Ron and Jeff are on either side to me. Ron immediately props up my shoulder.

Dr. Barrington flushed, he looked at Mackie, "Get them out of here." The manager runs over. A short dark man, with round glasses, he was sweating and nervous. "Harold, Calvin, get inside and wait for me." He looked at us all standing there. "Gentlemen, I am sorry for this disturbance. I know that tonight is an important night for both families." He genuinely sounded apologetic.

"I think the actual word that you are looking for is honesty," my father said, looking at Mackie, Barry, and Dr. Barnett, who were all stood together.

"Courtney, Jackson," Dr. Barnett walked forward me and held my shoulders. "That man," he points towards the bar, "paints a dishonest picture of my granddaughter. She is virtuous. Yes, they had a friendship, but that is all it was. I swear to you, they were no more than friends. Close friends, we admit, but friends none the less. She would never have spoilt herself, not with him. That why she ended it, she could not give him what he wanted, and that was that."

THE JOURNEY

I ask Mackie, "Why did he leave the plantation?"

Mackie looked me dead in the eye, "She told him that there was no prospects for them. He wanted more, and she would not give him what he wanted, so he left, and as you can see, he is still wounded."

"Sounds like a relationship to me," my father chimed in.

"Gentlemen, we have heard enough, we bid you goodnight," Jeff said, trying to spare me the details.

"Yes Jeffery, you are right, we need to get back," daddy told them all.

"It's only 11 O'clock," Barrington said, "This can be explained I'm sure."

"Can it?" I say. "Really.... Some low life has just told me that he knows my Edwina in ways that only a husband should experience. Explain that!" I yell.

My father held my arm and squeezed it. He could sense that this could turn either way.

"I am a simple man Barry. I do not condone violence, but understand that I am not totally against it in the right circumstances. Tonight was not the right circumstances it was about Courtney. I would like to thank you all for your hospitality gentlemen. It would not be presumptuous of me to say that Courtney needs time to digest this evening. Also, I think we can agree that he needs to talk to his betrothed at once."

Barrington, Dr. Barnet, and Mackie all nodded, they respected my father, but feared him also. He was a powerful man, far more powerful than any of them. They had heard the stories about him. He was ruthless and not to be challenged or underestimated.

We headed towards our burgundy Rolls Royce , the driver was waiting for us outside the hotel and looked surprised that we arrived so early. He immediately threw his cigarette on the ground, jumped out of the car and opened the door. Once inside, I ordered my driver to take me to the plantation. The thirty minute journey took forever, all I could do to retain my anger was to look out of the window. On arrival, the lights were on.

"Son, I think you should have this conversation tomorrow, once you had time to reflect on the situation. Hmmm?"

"No dad, the time for talking is now. Besides, I will not be able to sleep. I need to look at her. I need to hear her explanation."

I walk onto the veranda and Lynne automatically opens the door, I can hear Rene and Winnie singing, but I could not tell you what that was.

"Hey party poopers," Lynn chimes. I push past my sister- "Winnie!" I scream.

She sobers up immediately. "Court, what's the matter?" she looks at me worried. My father pulls Lynn aside, with Jeff and Ron they talk in hushed tones. My bride to be comes out of her living room, she has had a few.

"Hello Courtney, I was just telling my friends how much I love you," she says, trying not to slur her words. I push her away hard, and she lands on her sofa.

"Hey!" Rene screams, and jumps in front of me.

THE JOURNEY

"Court, what's wrong with you? Baby," she stands up, confused. "What's going on? why are you so mad?"

"I have two questions." I look and there in the doorway is my father, sister and two best friends. I walk toward the door and close it. "Rene, please leave." Rene does what is instructed, as she could sense this was a serious moment. "Who is Harold?" The colour from her cheeks drain.

She inhales deeply.

I repeat the question, unable to quash my temper. "Who is Harold?" I scream at her.

My dad opened the door. "Court," my father chimed him. I gave him a warning glance, and he read the message. "Stay out of this!"

She glances to the door, "Can we discuss this somewhere more private," she pleads.

"No, when Harold informed me of your relationship, he chose to do it in front of everyone at the club."

Winnie looked horrified, "He did what?" she asked, tears rolling down her face. "Harold and I met when I was fifteen years of age. We talked for three years. He wanted more than I was prepared to give. I ended it the night that he proposed. He got ugly, and I asked him to leave."

I stand there relieved. I believe her, my heart softens. "How ugly?" I ask.

"It was nothing," she said defiantly.

"I asked you a question?" I snap.

"He pushed me around, but we kicked him out."

"We?"

"A friend of my grandmother's, her name is Saint, she was wielding a machete and was passing, she came to my aid and helped me."

"Harold informs me that he knows you intimately."

Winnie gasps, "That is not true, baby. I never. Not with him. If you need proof before the wedding, we can find a doctor to confirm it, but I never slept with him, or allowed him to do anything to me other than kiss me. That is all. I swear it."

Lynne opened the door "Court, this looks like a misunderstanding," Lynn ran towards me and hugs me. I stare at my beloved, who is weeping silently, shaking her head. She can see that this has hurt me.

"Maybe you need some privacy," Rene pipes up.

"No," I say, "I've heard more than enough for one night," and I walk out of the door, pushing past my father and friends, heading towards the car. I hear Edwina sobbing, then hurried footsteps up the stair. I sit in the car, followed imminently by my father and friends. We drive back to the hotel, I sit with my head in my hands, disappointment in my heart and doubt creeping through my consciousness. Why? I begin to feel angered by him, Harold, why would he do this if it was not true?

"Wait!" I shout. "Let me out," I say, "I need to stay, pick me up tomorrow."

THE JOURNEY

"Like hell," my father says.

"I'm ok, dad, I promise," I try to explain.

"It's not you that I am concerned about. If what that boy said was true about Barry, I am not leaving you here."

"Nor I," Ron chimed in.

"Nor me," Jeff said.

"And I don't plan on going anywhere," Lynne told us all.

I walked to the house, knock the door, Rene opened it wide and looked up the stairs. I walk to the bedroom.

"There is some food left over from our feast, anyone hungry?"

"Yes please Miss Rene," Ron pipes up.

They follow me, she smiled and walked them to Lucy's kitchen and fed them until their bellows stretched.

Chapter 19

Father and Daughter

The men walk out of the club, I start pacing the patio. I look at Mackie who looks to his feet. My father walks into the club house main room and inform all guests that the groom has fallen ill and has retired, and the activities will cease. All the men groan and moan, and slowly trickle out of the club house.

My father walks towards me, disapproval all over his face. "What in God's name was that about?" he asks angrily.

"I couldn't help it, you heard what he said," I explode at him.

"Yes, we all did, but no one else tried to gauge out his

eye?" daddy said standing over me.

"He cannot speak about my daughter like that," I yell at him.

"Why not Barry? People say things all the time about one another. We could have dealt with this. We could have shrugged this off, but no, now he has gone and exposed *you* to Courtney, and his family. Don't you see, this was her chance to be someone normal, with normal people. Why could you not have laughed this off? You have ruined this for her."

"No" I start to consider my actions.

"Yes, I know Jackson more than you do and he is ruthless, especially when it comes to his reputation, money, but most importantly his family. You could have managed this so many other ways. If this is unsalvageable, she will never forgive you. I mean never."

"It will serve her right for going behind my back."

"Shut up, you buffoon. You have no idea what you have done to her." dad told me angrily.

"What?"

"You have exposed your daughter to heart break."

"Well, if it's all rubbish, Courtney can get over it," I say.

"You are such a fool. If they withdraw the offer of marriage, it will not be about Winnie, it will be because of *you*," daddy said quietly.

"This is a union of families, your anger has time and time

again got you and *us* in hot water. Tonight, you showed them your ass. Why would they trust their only son with *you* in this family? With you? I wouldn't if the shoe was on the other foot. You are a loose cannon. Someone to be wary of."

"That's nonsense," I say. *Deep down, my heart starts to sink. He is telling me truth. God, what have I done. He's right. I have ruined her opportunity of happiness.*

"Is it, really? There is only one person who will be responsible for her broken heart, and that, as always, falls to you." My father said with disgust, "well done."

"I don't think"

"Yes, I do, where are they? They have gone to consider their position. Jackson is the owner and CEO of the First National Bank of Jamaica. He cannot and will not be linked to scandal. That much I know." With that, my father walked out.

"Where are you going?" I shout after him.

"As far away from *you* as possible," he responds.

"Get me a drink, someone, anyone. I would like a rum now," I shout. Within a minute, a waiter was walking towards me with a glass of neat rum. I know it's weak of me, but I can't help it. I am ashamed of myself, my father was right, but it's like a switch goes off in my head. I just can't help it, and here we are again in a pickle, and it's down to me. She will never forgive me.

"Bring me a bottle of rum," I shout, there's no point in fighting it, I just need to blow off steam.

THE JOURNEY

Mackie walks towards and slaps the drink out my hand. "Barry, look how far you have come, why do you want to self-destruct all over again."

"You don't understand. She is going to hate me," I whine.

"Grow a backbone man! She will hate you more if you come back drunk," Mackie was really shouting at me. "Do you know how lucky you are to have a daughter like Edwina? She loves you, even after everything."

I sit down my head in my hands, Mackie stands over me, he was now towering over me, I knew that if I took another sip, he would beat me where I sat. I poured the contents of the rum bottle on the floor.

"Thank you Mackie," I say, ashamed of myself.

"For what?" my friend smiles.

"For sticking with me and having the balls to tell me when I am being the biggest jerk around."

Mackie smiled, "Well, we are stuck with each other now, aren't we? Beside, you have an engagement to salvage. Don't let her down."

One question, I ask standing up. "Why didn't you tell me about that little field hand touching up my daughter." I ask.

"There was nothing to tell." Mackie said.

"Really? That's not what it sounded like today. It sounded like a three year love affair."

"It wasn't like that?" Mackie's eyes grew wide,

apprehensive of me.

"You was meant to be my eyes and ears." I snap.

"I was always". Mackie raised his voice at me which was unprecedented.

"Then what the hell happened?"

"Winn and Harold was on a need to know basis. She was feeling lonely, and you just didn't need to know." Mackie said indignantly.

I could sense the vein throbbing in my head. *"What? Is he serious?*

"Have you considered what that little girl has been through? She lost her mother, her grandmother, and my wife. If I had told you about them, she would have lost her only friend too. She did not grow up like any other neighborhood kid, happy, carefree, and playful. You knocked that out of her. She was insular, isolated and alone. I just wanted her to have a friend her own age. She needed him more than you realise.

"It wasn't your decision to make." I say through gritted teeth. "You had no right Mackie, no matter how well intentioned."

"Well, I did and it's done and we're here. He did not take advantage."

"How do you know." I ask quietly.

"Because I know your daughter and she is no fool. It was only ever temporary," Mackie said quietly, trying to control his own temper. "We all could see it. Why

THE JOURNEY

couldn't you?"

"Who the hell is we?"

"The Doc, Rene, and ..."

"Who?"

"No one. We just knew, that's all." He says quietly.

"Well, you took that from me, didn't you?"

"No more than you deserve, you selfish son of a bitch. Just think about what you have taken from her? This is not about you. It's about your child and her happiness," Mackie chastised me.

"You know what? Make your own way home. I gone. I don't even work for you," Mackie erupted.

"You only work for her because I allow you to. Remember that!"

Mackie spun around, "So what, you think you own me?" Mackie pushed his chest into me.

"I own you, I own everyone here." I tell him.

Mackie laughs at me. "You own nothing, all you do is just take, because you own nothing. You have no natural authority. Jackson, now he is a man who commands respect, you don't. People fear you. No one respects you, not even your child."

"I own you and everybody in this village. I can have any woman, anytime, whether she wants me or not. It does not matter what I do, or how many women I take, hell, I have taken them young and old. I do what I want, as I am the privileged one." I pound my chest at him.

Mackie looked at me with renewed eyes. It was as if he could really see me. "It was … you, wasn't it?"

"What?"

"Did you force yourself on my Maggie?

"No. Mackie, you've had too much to drink." *How does he know? I have said nothing to give myself away. It must have been. No, she said that she would keep my secret. After everything I have done for her, she does this to me. Traitor!*

"As far as I am aware, you only raped Angeline. She was young, so who is the old woman that you abused. Hmmmm. Who?" Mackie stood still, though every muscle was flexed, and his eyes were wide. "Don't tell me no lie. Did you hurt my Maggie?"

I tried to style it out and flatly deny it. This was my friend. He knew me better than anyone, even when I was lying. I attempt to laugh it off, "Come on, Mack. Let's get out of here."

"Your face says it all. It was you. I could not, for the life of me understand why Maggie would wake up and just leave me. But it was you. I suspected, *we all* suspected, but I did not want to believe that after everything *I* had done for you, that you could…. I suppose I always knew, but I wanted to deny it. You really believe that you are superior to the rest of us, don't you?" he asked me quietly, too quietly.

I can't lie anymore, "I'm sorry," I break down. "I was in a different place than I am now. You know that."

THE JOURNEY

"Did you *rape* my Maggie?"

I cannot answer. I will not lie, but I cannot say the words. I look at my friend, and he is standing over me, crying, hands on his head. *I am being a good friend. I have released him. He can move on now, finally.*

"So you killed her. Where is she?" he asks.

"I buried her under the water well by the stables," I tell him. My burden lightened my spirit almost immediately.

"Why?" Mackie asks, his face soaked in tears.

"I don't know I was drunk, I honestly cannot remember," I tell him truthfully. "Not a day goes by that I don't think about her, you, Winnie, all of them. Not a day."

"Bullshit, then how come you did this tonight. You cannot be thinking very hard." Mackie told me.

"I am sorry Mackie. I know it sounds pathetic but I am sorry."

Mackie ran up to me and kicked me as hard as his leg would allow in my shoulder. I topple over violently.

"Get up," he screams.

All the waiters, including Harold and Calvin were witnessing my attack. I stand up looking at my friend, he comes closer and punches me hard square in the face . I stagger back and stand again, he punches me even harder, I fall backwards onto the patio furniture, blood spurts from my left eye and sprays the immaculately clean, white patio furniture. Mackie runs in for the kill, but Harold tackles him to the floor.

"No Mr. Mack. He is not worth it," he shouts. "You will hang. Despite all of *his* crimes, it's you that will be punished. What would Mrs. Mack want?" Mackie stepped back and looked at Harold. He was right. Maggie would not want him doing this in her name, she was a kind, loving, and a good woman. Mackie walked to the bar, jumped over the counter, and picked up the first full bottle of liquor he could find, it was gin. He came back to me, opened it, knelt down, grabbed my cheeks and started pouring.

"Earlier, I stopped you from drinking, as I been under the illusion that you were my friend. Well, had I known that you were my enemy, I would never have stopped you. Now I know that you are my enemy, have this drink on me."

He opened the bottle and shoved the bottle neck deep into my mouth. I attempt to spit out some of the contents. Mackie tilts my head back, and I am forced to drink. The poison hits my senses quickly. *Oh, how I have missed thee, my naughty mistress. I need you, I've been a bad boy, make me forget these feelings of fear, take away my pain.*

I pass out, I have no idea what time it is. My intention is to wait across the street until the police arrive, and I will hand myself in. I see my car across the road. Some rodent has vandalised my wheel, my passenger side window is smashed to pieces. I immediately check the glove compartment, my revolver is still there. I put it in my jacket pocket for safe keeping. I triple check that the safety catch is on. The last thing I need tonight is to shoot off my nuts. I laugh quietly to myself. I drive to my daughters plantation. I stop the car at the main road. I don't want them to see me approach also I need time to

THE JOURNEY

sober up.

I have to ask her why did she tell him. She promised me. I am approaching Edwina's Plantation, memories of the past come back to me. I wipe my eyes every so often, wondering what's wrong with me, why I am like this. I blink hard. I know why. I have buried this secret so deep, that when it resurfaces it turns me into this animal. Now that Donna has gone I am finding it hard to keep the monster at bay. I will come clean and tell them all. Then I will look for help.

I close my eyes, the same film is playing in my head. I am back in Mississippi, and my uncle Mason is on top of me and inside of me. Ravaging me, raping me, the more I cry, the more violent the attack. Every summer, since I was nine years old, without fail, he would take me fishing, and it was there that he stole my soul. The real Barrington is dead, he killed him a long time ago.. He would tell me, "Shut up boy. You think because you are light skinned that makes you kin? It don't! In Mississippi, you are one hundred per cent pure nigger boy. That means I own you, you are nothing, and you are nobody, you're just black. It was my uncle that gave me my first drink at the age of ten. "Shut up and stop whining. It's going to feel sore. Drink this boy and sleep."

I have tried to forget, but I cannot. This inferno inside of me is not containable and I have never been able to. The only person who doused the flames was Donna. Until Donna every sexual experience that I had with a woman has been when I was drunk. I just did not know how else to be. It was uncle Mason, he killed me, he has made me into this type of person. I am stuck with this guilt, I walk every day with the shame, and in order to feel, as I find it hard to love and to be intimate, I inflict pain. An angry reaction is better than no reaction right? I will sort this. I will pay the boy some money for his eye; give Mackie the equivalent of a year's salary, then I will travel to the United States and spend some time with uncle Mason. I need to pay my debts, all of them. My first priority is to make things right with Courtney and his people.

I emerge from my thoughts when I hear a sugar cane snap not too far away from me. There is someone there. I stop, look around, and nothing. I stay rooted to the spot. I try and concentrate on my breathing and start to listen intently.

"Who goes there?"

My senses tell me there is more than two. I listen again. Nothing. I get a bad feeling about this and start to quicken my pace. The lane was pitch black. I start to jog, and I hear at least three or four canes snap, my jog turns into a run, I take the gun out of my right pocket, I have my lighter in my left hand, ready to provide me some vision.

I feel a swoosh of air around my head then feel the a hard blow on the back of my head. I am momentarily dazed, I fall to the floor and stagger to my feet. I am seeing stars, something or someone hit me in the head with a really hard object. Within a few seconds I feel another lash across my back, I am thrown on my knees. That blow knocks the air right out of my lungs and I am panting and gasping for air. Whoever they are, they mean business. I am really scared. This could be it for me. I calm myself and close my eyes. There is more than two of them I am sure I heard four or even five different steps. One is breathing heavy, I slip off the

THE JOURNEY

safety catch with my thumb and flick the lighter, it doesn't work, and I aim the gun straight ahead of me and shoot anyway. I discharge my firearm twice.

"Arrrrrrhhhhh," a young man screamed. I aim the gun towards the steps coming from the west of me. I fire indiscriminately in that direction. Something hard hits the dirt just yards away from me. My lighter finally worked, I see two or three men running through the cane fields. *Oh no, what had I done?* Calvin, the man I glassed, was bleeding from his chest, he had ceased breathing, another man, much older was dead, his eyes were open, with two wounds in his head. They look related. I want to vomit, but am too petrified to stop. I sprinted as fast as I could to my daughter's home, I did not stop running until I got to the last two hundred yards. My father, Jackson, Courtney and his friends are on the veranda looking into the darkness. Winnie has lit the lights in the house and is holding a fully loaded rifle, as is my Daddy, Rene, and Mackie by her side. All four guns are pointed at me.

"Who goes there?" Mackie screams his voice menacing.

"It's me, don't shoot!" I hold my hands up.

"Barrington, throw the gun on the floor, but first ensure the safety is on." Mackie command angrily. I see Jackson pull his children and their friends inside.

"Who were you shooting at daddy?" Winnie sounded frantic.

"Oh my God, those dirty little field urchins tried to kill me," I say, shaking. I walk around the room like a mad man, my head is bleeding. My breath and body is soaked in the aroma of gin. I am so absorbed in my own fear that I did not notice that all around me was still and silent just staring at me. I look at Jackson. "They tried to kill me?"

"More the pity they did not succeed," Jackson's tone was icy.

I ignore him. "Winn, you don't understand, they attacked me, and I had to defend myself." I run my hands through my hair and sit on the armchair by the window. I look out the window into darkness, as if to face them would have been worse. "I think I have just killed two people. Dad it was the man who I glassed with a tumbler and an older man, I didn't recognise him, but he looks like a field worker," I say so quietly its practically inaudible. I momentarily look at them all.

My father just dropped his head. I could not read his expression at first, I thought it was anger, but it wasn't. It was indifference, fore in *that* moment, I understood that there was nothing that I could do further to disappoint them. It had already been done. This was yet another scenario that I had caused someone pain. I saw it for the first time, this night. They no longer cared. Who could blame them? I was a poor excuse of a father, son, and human being.

"Winnie let me go out and look to see who it is. It sounds like Calvin, maybe Baxter George," My father said quietly.

"Ok I'll come with you." Winnie said, her voice shaking.

"The hell you are," Courtney screamed, "anyone could be out there."

THE JOURNEY

"The men that may be dead out there are Harold's brother and father," Winnie informs the room. "We need to see if they are still alive and, if so, we need to help them."

Grandpa got his doctor's bag, Mackie, Jackson, Ron, Jeff, Winnie and me all had lanterns. We see a light in the middle of the field. Saint, is already there. Her face is covered she has sheets under her right arm and has wrapped Calvin's blood soaked body into the first sheet.

Winnie looks at Baxter on the floor, she kneels down and closes his eyes gently. I hear her saying a prayer and helps the others to wrap him up. I notice that Courtney, Ron, and Jeff move towards the main road, they don't need to say it, they are sickened to their stomach. They see me, my people, who we really are. It's not for them, this is not their world, nor should it be.

We get to the house, Courtney is still in shock, he walks over to my daughter, he hugs her, but he's different. I can tell that he is withdrawn, I can see that my actions have altered his love.

"Edwina, it's time we left," Jackson said, this time none of them protested.

I silently cry, my hand still soaked in the blood of these men. I go to touch Court, all he can do is jump back. I see the distain in his glance. He looks at his father who is watching my every move with his child. No words appear. The look says it all.

They walk to the car, I cannot leave it like this. "Courtney," I shout, he turns around. I walk towards him. "I am so sorry for this." He walks past me to Edwina.

"It's not your fault," he reassures her.

"Here," she give him back the engagement ring. He looks at her grateful for her courage. "I release you baby." She tells him visibly emotional.

He smiles, "I love you. I am just not sure that you will be content with boring old me. What I do know is that I cannot live with all of this." He says looking at me. "He is a liability Edwina. This much death and destruction will not go unnoticed. People will rise up against your family, you are *his* child. I fear for you. He does not deserve you, any of you. He is unwell, there is something wrong with your father. To hold so much rage is not healthy and definitely not good for the soul". He stepped close to my daughter and kissed her on the mouth. "If you need me, call, I will always come running".

"Courtney," Jackson bellowed, "let's go son," he snapped curtly looking at me. He tipped his hat to me, Lynnette waved goodbye, Jeff and Ron said nothing, and within a flash, they were speeding down the dirt road. I watched my only child fall to the floor and cry like I have never seen her cry before. They were right. I broke her heart.

Chapter 20

Pressure Burst Pipes

THE JOURNEY

Rene tries to console me. What can she say? There is nothing to be said. I stand up, drenched in my own sick, I survey my surroundings, as if it's the first time I see this room. It's so lovely, the long white drapes, the soft sofa with large green flowers, the fresh scent of mango's and limes. In front of every window sits a lemon, lime or orange tree. This house, my home, was truly beautiful, and the three years that I lived here, I have loved it, and my freedom. Today, I have learnt that freedom was just an illusion. I was never going to be free of him, his name, or his past. My father could not let me go. He knew that I would leave him, and he has done everything he can to tarnish me, ruin my life, my choices, my happiness. I walk up the stairs slowly.

"Winnie, are you ok?" aunt Rene asked concerned.

"This will never be ok aunty. I need to rest. I am so tired."

I walk into my bathroom and turn on the shower. The putrid smell of vomit, blood, and death is pungent. I take a brush and scrub my skin to free myself of this shame. I wash my hair and body, over and over again. Praying that I would feel pure, hoping that I could redeem myself somehow with my cleanliness. I tell myself repeatedly, like a mantra, "*This was not down to me; it's not my fault.*" The harder I scrubbed, the more I realised the simple truth. My father, no matter how much I loved him or forgave him, was nothing more than a savage murderer. The revelation hit me like a sledge hammer, the remaining strength in my limbs evaporate. I felt withered, like a dying shriveled up flower that has had no light. My legs are no longer able to support me, I collapse in the shower, the water bouncing off me, looking for a way out.

It's been three days and I have stayed in bed. I have never felt so fatigued in my life.

"Baby," he says quietly.

I stir, my beautiful sleep interrupted.

"Baby, wake up sleepy head," he says softly. I feel a warm kiss on my head, I open my eyes. Startled by what awaits me, I jump up disorientated.

"Courtney," my voice is gruff and my breath strong like a toilet pit. I leap out of my bed and run to the bathroom, wash my face and scrub my teeth and tongue. I look up in the mirror, I look awful. My eyes are sunken, my hair was slumped across my face and head, likes clumps of clay in a mound. I close my eyes, and pull my hair back in a bun and rub some coconut oil on my face. I dampen the towel and wiped under my arms, and my lady parts, and change into my navy blue house dress.

"You look lovely Winnie," he said. He looked worried.

"I feel like rubbish Court," a stray tear leaves my eye.

He grits his teeth and nods. "How are you?"

"Not good."

"What happened?" he looks at me accusingly.

"Well, when you left, I asked daddy to leave. I told him that I am done with him, his antics. All I have wanted since my grandmother died was to be in a happy home, you know I know that I would have had that with you."

He smiled at me.

"It's my fault, all of this is down to me. I should never have gotten involved with Harold. You have to believe me," I wail. "Do you blame me?"

"Never," Courtney shouted at me exasperated by the topic. "You father is a mad man. One of two things will happen: either the Lord or a man will take care of him. What is clear is that you have nothing to do with this. Baby, you do not control him or his actions," he came over and pulled me into him hard. "I just want us to be married, so that I can take you away from this all," he said.

"Really. You mean after all this, you want to marry me?" I whisper.

"Yes, I want to marry you. Who else would I love, who else would I marry?" He pressed his lips into my temple.

"But my father"

"He is *your* father. That does not mean he is you."

He pulled me away. "Baby, I think my parents would have preferred that we never met. They know I love you, but they are concerned about your and my welfare. You father he's unpredictable." I look at my fiancé, he looked tired.

"We should leave here. You're not safe."

"My father would not hurt me."

"It's not your father I am worried about. This community is tight. Your father killed two local men. There are murmurings. I think you should come to Negril with me."

"I can't," I protest.

"Edwina!" Courtney shouted at me. "There is no discussion, you will pack your things and come with me tonight. It's not safe. I will not, cannot leave my wife here. Now pack!" *I smile. Your 'wife'? He still loves me.*

I stare blankly at Court, he was not taking no for an answer. A timid knock at the door broke our thoughts.

"Come in," Courtney demands. My grandmother, grandfather and Rene, entered the room. My grandmother's appearance startled me. She looked drawn, her hair was not up in her perfectly manicured bun, her long, grey, wavy hair was freely scooped to one side of her neck. The rims of her eyes were red, her skin was blotchy, and she had no powder or make up on.

"Are you ok?" she asked me.

"Me. I am fine. It's you that looks like you have been through the wars."

My grandmother starred at me with a steeliness that I have not seen in a while. "Edwina, I want you to leave with Courtney."

My grandfather stepped forward and thrust a white folder in my hand.

"What this?" I ask. I open the folder, there is my passport, at least three thousand pounds, keys, and a UK bank account in my name.

"Here is keys to a town house in Islington London. It was going to be my wedding present to you both. When I was last there, I set up a bank account for you. The rest is all the sterling I could get my hands on. Your father has proven unpredictable, which has led the behaviors of others to be unpredictable. I have booked for you to fly to Miami, then, in a few days, you will fly to England. Your travel begins the day after tomorrow." Tears sprang to his eyes. "I can protect you from your father, but I cannot protect you from rogues in the village."

"But...."

"It's for the best," my grandmother says. She walked over to Courtney and held his hand, "Thank you. Please, take care of her. Promise me."

"I promise, ma'am."

"What about the wedding?"

"We can come back and marry later," Courtney reassures me.

"Baby, get ready. Pack. Do what you need to do. We will be downstairs. I promise you, we will marry, just not here. I was thinking that we could get married in the UK." He smiles weakly as he and my grandfather left the room.

Once the door was closed, Rene and my grandmother started to go through my drawers. "Phyllis, what will she need? I have not been to England?" Rene asked.

My grandmother picked out all my matching skirts and pullovers and jackets. *Hang on. When did you two become bosom buddies?*

"It's summer over there, so this should work for now. As the season changes, she can buy whatever collection she chooses," she said. She was emotional. I look at her and notice that her dress was new.

"New dress?" I ask.

Both women stop and look at me, "Yes, dear. I had it a while and thought that I should try something new." In unison, they both continued.

"Get showered, my darling. You need to get on the road soon," my aunt Rene says gently.

As instructed, I entered the bathroom and closed the door.

This is all happening so fast. England was never in our plan. There is so much that I do not understand. I need to talk to them all. They are treating me like a child. Why is that? And why is Rene and grandma such best friends all of a sudden. They hate each other. Something has happened, and they need to start being straight with me.

"Winnie there you are," my grandfather said, his voice still strained.

"What's wrong with your voice?"

"Nothing, my throat is sore," he replied.

"I am going to be in England in a couple of weeks, so I will pop in," he informs me.

"Since when?" I ask shocked by this news.

"Since my only grandchild will be living there." He smiled, which, in turn, made me smile. I walk up to him and give him a tight squeeze and a big kiss on the cheek.

THE JOURNEY

"Look, I don't want to be rude, but you need to travel before dusk," Grandpa instructed Courtney quite sternly. They all looked at him and nodded. Both Rene and my aunt started to move quickly.

"Why?" I ask them, and they all ignore me.

"Edwina, it's a long journey, and I am thinking of the driver," Grandpa finally responded. Again there was the knowing glances.

"What is going on?" I snap.

"Nothing." Courtney could see that I was not buying it. He sighed heavily. "Actually, there is a lot that has happened. I will explain it all to you on the way." Courtney looked at them, "Is that ok?"

They nodded silently at him, avoiding my gaze. Courtney held my hand, "We have to go, baby, please trust me."

I embrace my grandfather, he was shaking, "Are you ok?" I whisper.

"I am fine," he tries to reassure me.

My grandmother and Phyllis hug me hard, they both kiss me on each cheek. "Good luck. Be safe. I love you," is all I could hear.

Fear has gripped me. "What about me? Suppose I don't want to go." I hear myself and sound like a whining child.

My grandmother stood forward and held me by my shoulders. She looked deep in my eyes and said, "You are a woman now, you have to act like one. We all have to do things that we don't want to do. It's called life. Your life is with Courtney. You will be a wife soon, with responsibilities. You have to be brave."

Courtney tugged my hand, we walked to the car, and I noticed there were two cars either side of our vehicle, with men that I did not recognise.

"Who are these people?"

"They are my father's private security from the bank. They will get us to Negril safely"

"What's going on, Courtney," I ask, a queasy feeling in my stomach made me feel unstable.

He opened the door, "Get in darling, I'll explain everything."

The cars drove off into the orange sunset. I looked behind me at the plantation. Rene was hugging my grandmother, and my grandfather was sat on the porch. I roll down the windows and exhaled deeply and close my eyes. The sweet smell of the sugar cane filled my nostrils. I cry silently as we approached the main gates to my property.

"You alright?" Courtney asked.

"No I can feel it," I say so quietly it was hardly audible.

"What?"

"The fact that I will not be back here for a long time."

We sit in silence, my head is pounding. All I could do was shut my eyes. A few miles later, the aroma all around us changed. The air smelt smoky, I close the windows, as it started to tickle my throat. The closer we

THE JOURNEY

got to my old home, the stronger the aroma and thicker the air. My throat started to get real dry.

"Here," Courtney handed me a bottle of water. "This will make it better. He then took a handkerchief out of his pocket and gave it to me. You'll need this," he said. He puts his handkerchief over his nose and mouth.

I stare out of the window, the visibility was compromised. I know what this means but don't want to connect the dots in my head. As we turn the corner, with the orange sun setting over my grandparent's plantation, my magnificent stately planation house is nothing more than a burnt out old ruin. There is nothing left the hot ash is smoldering uncontrollably in the light evening breeze. The whole frame of the house appears to be leaning to one side. I view the sugar cane fields, they have been withered by the heat. The crop is ruined. I flash back to my grandmother earlier this day. She has lost everything. Her son, her granddaughter, and now her home. All the pieces are slotting into place. This is why Courtney and his father's security are escorting us to Negril.

"Am I in danger," I ask.

"Yes." My beautiful fiancé kisses the back of my hand, thinking that his lips would pacify me.

"Who did this?" I asked shocked and angry.

"It was your field workers, people who loved Mrs. Mack, Harold's family, who knows. The list is as long as your arm darling."

"My poor grandmother, she must be devastated. Why didn't you tell me?"

"It was agreed that we would not say a word to you. We all knew that you would not leave, so we made a pact." Courtney could not look at me and was left with no other option but to lower his eyes.

"Driver, turn around, please," I command. The driver looked at his rear view mirror and continued on his journey.

"Excuse me, please, can you turn the car around now?"

Nothing. I look at Courtney, his face was pained and desperate. "Courtney, I need to go back." I plead.

"No Winnie," he said quietly. He shook his head and held my hand. My lip started to quiver.

"You don't own me. I am my own person. Stop this car now!" I shout at the driver. I look at Courtney and try to get to the door, he is too quick for me, he grabs my arms and pushes me to the floor."

"Noooooo, please, they are not safe. I need to be with them."

"Winnie please, I can't let you go back there."

"Geeeeettttttt ooooooffffffff me! I want to go back. That's my family," I cry through my screams.

I struggle and punch Courtney in the face, it catches him off guard, he grabs both my hands. "Stop it, Edwina!" I kick him in the stomach, he flies back on the door. He seizes my shoulders and shakes me hard. He grabs my hands, throws them above my head and immobilizes me. To ensure that I don't attack him further, he lays on me. "Please Winn, darling, stop."

THE JOURNEY

"Why," I ask panting like a crazed, locked up animal.

"They have threatened to kill you, the plantation was a warning. It is you that is not safe," he says.

I stare at him blankly, he should have punched me, it would have been kinder.

"What?" I stare at him wide eyed.

"They want *you* dead," he shouted. All the strength in my body drained away. I felt weak, suddenly the heat was unbearable, and the weight of my fiancé started to crush my lungs.

"Courtney, I can't breathe," I whisper.

He jumps off me cautiously and looks at the driver. "She's ok," he nods. Perspiration runs freely through my pores.

"Winnie sit up. Here, let me help you," Courtney pulls me off the floor and seats me next to him. I stare at him blankly.

"We are going to be alright?" he whispers. "I am here, and I will get you out of here, I promise."

"Who wants me dead?"

"We think it's the family and friends of people your father killed."

"You're not sure?"

"They didn't leave a name, but it's pretty certain that the two events may be connected." I hold his hand and gently lay my head on his chest. His heart beat is strong and quick. He is anxious. Courtney rubs my arm, strokes my face, and kisses me. I drift off into a deep sleep.

A few moments later, the car comes to a screeching halt.

"What is it?" Courtney yells panicked.

"Trouble ahead Sir," his driver yells back. I bolt upright, it's pitch black outside, there is debris in the road blocking our path. The cars behind us and in front of us are forced to stop as well. Three men step out of each vehicle, all carrying shot guns. They watch each other as they remove the debris, I am looking deep into the night for signs of foul play. In the distance, I see a group of men with machetes and clubs making their way to the car.

"Look to the east," there are too many of them. I close my eyes.

"Hurry up," Courtney screams.

A rock is lobbed at us, and it hits one of the security guards hard in the head, they all panic and cock their guns, *no more bloodshed, please.* I start to feel sick. I hear Dexter galloping, I swing round and see her, it's Saint, she is riding Dexter like an old pro, wearing all white, the security detail take aim to shoot her.

"Noooooo," I scream and run out of the car. "She is one of us"

She rides up to them, "Don't shoot!" I scream. A stray rock flies past her, she dodges it. Mackie is behind her on daddy's jet black colt, she jumps off the horse and addresses the people. They stop and they listen. She holds up her hand, Mackie cocks his gun at the crowd.

THE JOURNEY

She speaks again. I glimpse the security men moving the rubbish from the road. It takes a few minutes, they are still holding off the angry mob. I want to get close, but Courtney is pulling me back to the car.

"Thank you," I say loudly, Mackie turns and nods at me. We drive off into the night.

"Who was that?" Courtney asks, I hold his hand and feel that he is shaking.

"Saint, she is the woman that saved me from Harold."

"Hmmm, Saint by name, Saint by nature," he smiled gratefully, "I will be sure to ask the Lord to bless her."

I hug him tightly, and we are both exhausted, but are far too anxious to sleep.

"Baby, baby," Courtney gently shakes my shoulders. "We are here?" I look around.

"What time is it?"

"It's around 10:30pm" he says.

"This is not Negril," I step out of the car. We were in Kingston, at the Pegasus Hotel.

"I'll explain later," he says. "We're tired."

Two concierge walk towards us. "Mr. Du Pille, we have been expecting you. Your father's suite has been prepared." We walk towards the elevator, Courtney did not look at me once. Once the door was opened, a long marble hallway awaited us. At the end of the corridor was a light, airy living room and dining area, towards the far end of the room, the patio doors led out to the balcony. The concierge put our luggage in the closet, Courtney paid him and went straight for the mini bar.

"Drink baby?"

"Yes whatever," I look for the bathroom and shut the door, the bathroom was huge. The shower could fit at least four people in it. I slowly take my clothes off, my limbs feel tired. I look at myself in the mirror.

"Tomorrow will be a better day." I reassure myself.

My clothes, hair and body reek of smoke. I strip without even giving it a second thought and step into the shower. The warm water flowing from the shower was inviting, I walk into the cubicle and let the water work its way over me. I masterly lather the bar of soap on my wash rag and gently scrub my body. The scent of the soap tingles my nostrils. I turn up the temperature, and stand under the water. It felt good on my breasts and back. The shower door opened. Courtney stood in front of me naked. I stepped back, he smiled and walked in. He starred directly into my eyes, my nipples hardened.

"Court..."

Her turned me around, lathered my wash rag and started to rub me with it. His hands were large, thick with broad fingers. He rubbed my neck in his right hand, and gently touched my breast with his left. His arms expertly explored my torso, buttocks and the back of my legs. He turned me around and used the soap with his bare hands to lather me. His fingers and the soap circled my body, moving towards my thighs. He abruptly pulled me into the water, smiling at himself, knowing that he had aroused me. I then watch him use my wash cloth on

THE JOURNEY

himself. I laugh.

"What?" he grins.

I snatch the wash cloth. "Why should you be the only person to have all the fun?" I rub his groin, moving towards his penis, which was rigid, I look down at this unsavorily looking piece of equipment. I drop the rag and take the soap bar and lather my hands, I gently hold my fiancé with both hands and stroke and explore him, he smiles at me.

"Having fun?" he asks.

"You're the first… I have never seen one of these before, you know, on a grown man, that is," I continue to fondle him. I feel the blood pulsing in his man friend, Courtney presses me hard against the wall and kisses me passionately, plunging his tongue into my mouth. I let go of his friend, he pushes him on me, and holds my head. I can't take it anymore. I push him off "I need air." Courtney smiles at me and continues to shower. I grab my towel and leave the bathroom. I gaze at myself in the mirror, I am flushed. I sparingly pour coconut oil in my hands, and rub through my hair and body, I find some white panties and a white night dress. I laugh to myself as the last thing on my mind is being pure.

Oh, he is a delightful man, his chest is high and proud, his neck thick, his abdominal muscles chiseled and defined. I blink, my man is naked in my mind's eye. I shrug off the feeling, the sensation inside my lady garden, she is ready. My nipples harden under my shirt. I squeeze my thighs tight and think of my new life with my soon to be husband.

Courtney enters the living room, his body is glistening as the waters slides down his smooth, dark chocolate skin. *This man is here to tease me.* I squeeze my thighs shut again and scrunch my eyes.

"Would you like a drink?" I leap off the chair. I feel his gaze and I know, I just know this is going to be too much for me to bear.

"Thank you, baby. Fix me a scotch and soda."

I look at him, *gosh, he is beautiful.* I stare a little too long, he catches me. I walk to the white bureau and slowly lift the bottles to identify the scotch. I feel him behind me, the heat from his body pierces my skin. *Hold off, Edwina, the deal is not yet done. Do not let him touch you, you cannot trust yourself to behave. I look at Court, and he has an expression in his eyes that I have not seen before. He pulls me close, my heart is exploding out of my chest.*

"Court," before I could finish my sentence, he pulls me close. He strategically puts his left hand around my waist and loops his right arm behind my neck. I'm trapped, and I love it. My fiancé's lips touch mine softly at first, then more wanton and needy. His hand starts to explore my body, he runs them down my back and cups my buttocks and squeezes hard. I pull away, he continues to kiss me, I wrap my arms around his neck, he feels strong. Courtney pulls me off the floor and leans back, my feet are off the ground, he then lifts me by my hips and rests my legs on his hips, kissing me tenderly throughout. *This is it, as hard as I try, I cannot stop my body responding to him. My man excites me. I want him.* As we lay on the bed, his hand explore me and I let him, he pulls my nightgown over my head. The reality of the moment sets in. I must have looked scared, he holds me and kisses me some more. "It's ok baby. I promise it will be ok. I will not hurt you," he whispers.

"No Court, I can't, please stop. This is not right, we're not married."

He kisses my neck, "Why not, you're going to be my wife within a week or two," we both giggle. "Do you want me to stop?" he asked. He ceases kissing me and looks at me seriously.

I pull him close. My small hands work their way to his towel, which was still wrapped around his waist, I tug at it and the once secure knot unfolds, he is exposed to me. I look at his beast and nervously smile.

"No Court, don't stop," I kiss his neck, he rolls me on my back and pulls down my knickers and throws them over his head. We both smile. I feel my heart in my ears. "Relax baby," he tells me.

I stare at his male muscle and feel queasy, it is erect, and it is too big for my girlie parts. Courtney parts my legs with his thighs and lays on top of me. He is heavy, and I push him off, "I can't breathe," I pant.

He alters his weight, kissed me neck, and moves his lips down to my breast, he licks, sucks one breast and cups the other. There is an explosion deep in my lady garden, all I can do is moan out loud, he looks up, pleased at his accomplishment. I arch my back, and he caresses my other breast. He raises his hand to my mouth and shoves two finger in it, I suck them obediently, he races them back to my nipple that is exposed and fondles her. "Ooohhhh…"

He resurfaces and kisses me again and again, "Baby, are you ok? I can stop whenever you want me to." My mind is elsewhere, it's with body parts in heaven. Courtney leans down further and kisses my stomach, my thighs, he then separates my legs.

"No Court, waiiiiiittttttttt," it's too late, his lips and mine meet, his tongue becomes his beast. He does things that I did not know are possible, I moan and pant, the feeling intensifies, and I try and wriggle from his grasp. He clamps down on my thighs with his hands, and my body reacts to him, the pleasure is unbelievable, man, I had no idea the tongue had more than one use. The volcano within me is unable to control itself and erupts with an intense explosion, and that sets off other eruptions within me.

"I told you I would make you quiver beneath me," he smiles and kisses me deeply, plunging his tongue deep into my mouth. I taste and smell myself for the first time. Not bad. I smile. Courtney kisses me again, not giving me time to recover, I groan in the back of my throat, and I feel his manhood twitch on top of me. He part my legs once more, and gently positions himself at the gate of my lady garden, he looks at me.

"Trust me," he commands. I nod, his tongue dances around my mouth once more, more intensely than before, he curls his hips and pulls my left leg out of the way in order to open the gate further, he starts to push, I shudder and tense my thighs, he stops, "It's ok, baby, breath and don't tense."

I look at him, smiling nervously. He kisses me more intensely than the last, he pushes deeper, I gasp, he rests his forehead on mine, intently staring at me, "Push

THE JOURNEY

your hips up," he instructs. I obey and he hurls the rest of his penis deep inside me. I close my eyes, my seal is broken. I yelp. Courtney ignores me and expertly and slowly maneuvers himself around. This is pleasurable and painful at the same time. He raises both my knees and thrusts deeper, he is locked in, he groans, and I feel the sweat on his back, boy, he's working hard. Something is happening to me. My toes are curling, the sensation in my garden hardens my nipples, I clench my gate to try and stop the beast, "Arrgghhh, baby, you feel so gooood," Court responds breathlessly. His pace quickens, my heart is ready to beat right out of my chest. I feel the heat mounting, "Court," I cry, he moves faster and deeper, I can't control the eruption. It's larger than before, Courtney stops suddenly, his chest raised, his arms straight, his eyes closed shut. His explosion is deep inside of me. I am his, he has released me.

Oh, this ache of mine feels sweet and tender, beloved. I look at my husband to be, he is beautiful whilst he sleeps. He's strong, kind, loving and he loves me for me, and not for who he thinks I can be. He loves me not for what I bring to him, but for what I can enhance in him. He loves the good, the bad, and the downright sad. *Fore he is my king.*

Courtney opens his eyes, "Good morning, my precious."

I smile and stretch, "Hello."

"Hungry baby? You worked up an appetite on me."

"I could eat a feast fit for a king," I smile.

"Then a feast you shall have." Before he jumps out of our love nest, he kisses my head. I too jump up from the bed, but my body ached with vengeance, my lady parts are battered and sore, and are in need of an ice bath.

"Ok?" he asked concerned, I look back and saw the red blood stain in the bed.

"Oh, Court, is that normal?"

He is genuinely shocked and laughs, "You'll live," embarrassed, I ran to the shower, the water was warm and lovely. I gingerly washed myself. As I turned the water off, I heard voices. "It must be the maid," I dry myself off and put on the bathrobe.

"Edwina, so nice to see you," I stop in my tracks, it was Courtney's father Jackson.

"Morning," I say and scurry to get my clothes and run back in the bathroom. Whilst I put on my underwear, I hear Mr. Du Pille shouting at his son.

"How can you be so irresponsible? She is not one of you gals, she's a Barnet!"

"I could not help myself, dad, she ... it was ..."

"Spare me the details," he snapped. I smile to myself, his father is just old school, we are going to be married in a couple of weeks. I put my dress on and walk back into the room. That was when I heard him.

"I mean it, you are on your own. I forbid it, put an end to this now."

I look at Courtney, who is sat on the bed with his head lowered, his white towel loosely draped around his waist. My lady garden twitches at the sight of him, I look at

THE JOURNEY

Courtney's face.

"End what? What do you forbid, Sir?"

They were both startled to see me so soon. Mr. Du Pille walks towards me and kisses me on the head, "Goodbye, dear."

"No sir, please tell me what is happening here? I will be your daughter in law in a few weeks. Sir, please tell me."

"This was not supposed to happen. The agreement was that he would bring you back to Negril, we would watch over you, he ..." and he looks at his son with distain, "he was supposed to let you down gently, and you would travel to Miami tomorrow. That was the agreement."

I stare at Courtney puzzled, he looks like he needs to be sick.

"What is your father talking about? Agreement?" I start to get angry, "With whom?"

"Darling, come and sit down," he motions to the bed. "My parents have forbid me moving to London with you."

"So you will come later then. Will I travel on my own?"

"Yes, we're connected now. You are my wife, and nothing and nobody is going to get in the way of that," he says looking at his father.

"I have made my decision. It's nothing personal Edwina, it's just that your father, it's all too complicated and quite frankly its beneath us," he tried to sound definite. "In the beginning you seemed so suited, but it's clear that we are all such different people."

"My parents want me to call off the engagement," he tells me, looking at the floor. He looked up, "Dad, I think you should leave now," Jackson looked at his son pained, he nodded and walked out on cue.

I stand up, "Why?"

"Winnie, you know the reason why," Courtney tells me calmly. "It's him, your father, what he represents. My father does not want to be connected in any way to a scandal. People entrust their life savings with him, his image, and ability to make sound and credible judgments is everything. Its everything," he said, defending his stance.

"What do you think?"

"Well, I told him that I would marry you come what may, and this morning he turned up to tell me that if I go ahead with it, he will cut me off."

"Cut you off?"

"Financially. I will not have a penny to my name."

"I have money," I scream. "We're fine, you don't need his money."

"What kind of man lives off his woman?" he says.

"The same man that can live off his father," I snap.

"I am not giving you up," he says seriously. "We leave tomorrow as planned." *I smile but feel a queasy feeling in the pit of my stomach. I feel it. My happiness will be short lived.*

"Courtney. I do love you."

"Me too, the soon to be Mrs. Du Pille." He smiles weakly.

Chapter 21

January 14th 2005 8.36pm

Farewell

It was evening, I could tell. My bright winter sun has disappeared and in its place is the most beautiful well-lit full moon I think I have ever seen. It's a cold night, as the skies are clear. My body feels oppressed with this unmanageable cancer. I look at Alice, she reads to me. I am uncomfortable. Without asking, she props up my pillows and adds another behind me. She can see that I am having difficulty breathing. Lying here, watching my family, I feel sorrow for them. I know that I need to leave this body here, I am withered, old, and diseased. Most of all, I am damaged, and, at 69 years of age, I am still ashamed of him, my father and all that he represents. I suddenly feel sorrow, as I can feel his pain, he was not all bad, he loved me in his own way, but was a relentless tyrant.

The lights in my room are dimmed, the TV is on in the background, it's my favorite TV soap, Coronation Street. Harold looks awful, he has strategically positioned himself to the right of me. I am not sure if he sees me anymore, or whether he is consumed with this disease. My sweet, pathetic Harold, how he needs to cope and keep the children together. He must. I am relying in him. He needs to be strong.

Dr. York takes my vital signs again. He scrutinises my face for signs of something, I am not sure what. Now, I just don't care, I will take what comes. We are all fearful regarding what is ahead of us. Me. I am petrified of the unknown. I pray that it is as I believe it to be, and, on the other side, that I am happy and pain free, and with people who love me. No matter what, death has to be better than this suffering.

Mr. York speaks quietly with Alice. She shakes her head and they look at me. *Oops, there it is. The pity stare.*

He walks over, "Edwina," Mr. York says softly. "Alice tells me that you don't want any stronger pain relief, is that true?"

I nod and close my eyes.

"Things may get rough later, so I will see how you are in in twenty minutes or so." I motion for him to come closer.

"I need to be here," a tear leaps from my eye.

Dr. York clenched his jaw and nods his head. "Whatever you think is best," he holds my hand with a firm but gentle grip and looks me deep into my eyes. We connect, and we both know it's for the last time.

"I just want *you* to be as comfortable as possible," he forces himself to say. I blink slowly and give him a half smile.

"Hmmmmmmm," is all I could muster.

I look at Jonathan, my first born, my heart and soul, and best friend. I smile to him, he comes over and strokes my face. Harold holds my hand and kisses it, I feel his

THE JOURNEY

damp tears on my hot skin. He is his father's son, tall, broad, and strong, he even had his head for numbers. There were so many times I wanted to tell him. Courtney wanted to see him long before now, but when I told him that he was gay, those requests stopped overnight. I have left Jonathan a letter explaining everything. His father, well, he will soon be aware. I emailed him for the last time two weeks ago with Alice's help. All my secrets will soon be free. I just hope Jonathan forgives me, and his biological father accepts him.

"How you feeling baby?" Harold mutters.

"Not good," I whisper. "Water." I take a sip of the cold liquid, which instantly refreshes my mouth. "It's up to you." Harold looks at me, something has happened to me, it's as if a switch has been turned off. I don't have the energy to speak to him. *"Take care of my flock my darling, and for the record, I love you. Tell Ange to come quickly, I need to see her."*

Harold nods, "I go and get Ange, she is next door, she needs to say goodbye," he says. I look at him astounded. He heard my thoughts. *This is just crazy. Typical! I am dying, and this is the first time in my life that he understand my thoughts. I smile. If I had the energy, I would laugh.*

I stretch out my hand to Phoebe, I cough slowly and deeply, my lungs explode. Alice is all over me, she sits me up and injects something into my drip. This is to take the pressure off, and it will help with your breathing. She puts on my mask. I pull in as much air as possible for the next few seconds. I hear my heart beat in my ears and it's slowing down. My eyes start to twitch, and my vision is starting to become hazy, like sun rays zig zagging across the room. The back wall is no longer there, instead of the wall is a garden. It's my front garden and porch at the plantation. How I missed that place. It is absolutely beautiful, the sun is shining and there are people there. I can't see them clearly, I just see their shadows and outlines. Whatever is going on, it looks like a party. Maybe it's a welcome home party. I smell Mima's cooking, the jerk chicken and rice and peas tantalizes my nostrils. This is going to be a real homecoming.

"Mum," Phoebe sits next to me. I look at my child, confused, angry, and bitter. *"Enough of this. Those that know better, do better, and you was raised,"* I say crossly in my mind's eye.

She nods. Tears roll down her cheeks, she is trying to be strong. I feel her fear. I want to tell her that it's ok, but I have lost my voice. I feel so light headed.

"No, God damn you. I need time. Give me more time," I scream in my head. Finally, she is listening to me. There is so much more that needs to be said.

The lights in the room start to dim, and the colors in my garden are more vibrant and iridescent.

My spirit is starting to descend, I look up and she is there. I feel better knowing that she is here. She is beautiful, just as I remembered her all those years ago. She is not old, she is my mother, and I see her youthful face. I cannot help but acknowledge her, all eyes in the room are watching us. They feel that something magical is happening. I close my eyes and start to feel well again. She has to hear me say it. I breathe in hard, "Muuuuummmmmmm." She falls back into Niall and my

THE JOURNEY

brother Phillip. We look at one another and both cry, she leaps towards me and holds me.

"Don't try and speak Edwina, concentrate on breathing," Alice tells me.

Harold is sobbing uncontrollably by the bed. Maddie and Jon are supporting him. I look at him, *he knew, didn't he? All these years, he's known. Unbelievable, if I wasn't dying, I would rip him a new one. Now I know why God sent me back, it's so I can remember you. It's so I don't die alone. You were right, you are my Saint. Thank you, Saint Mum. Thank you.*

"Help me, I need to hold her," Mum says.

Alice turns to say something, and I hear those words I have longed for my whole life.

"I am her mother please help me raise my child. I need to hold my daughter now." Her sobs are uncontrollable, but she pulls it back. She does not want her last moments to be consumed with this, she can cry when it's over. *No, Nooooooooo, I need more time, this is my mum, there is so much that I need to tell her.*

My children are rooted to their spots, confused to the point of disbelief. Somehow, my beautiful 84 year old mother slides behind me and holds me. All of my memories of her flash before me, playing with me at the plantation, rocking me to sleep as a child, shadowing me at the Morant Bay Market, protecting me from Harold when I broke off our engagement, making sure that I got out of Jamaica alive, being my friend, neighbor and protector for the last 50 years. My half-brother Phillip and step father Niall walk over to the bed. They both kiss me on the head. I always loved them both. My brother looks at me with renewed eyes. He has travelled from New Zealand, Niall insisted that Ange came clean, and he is glad that she did.

"Forgive me. I am so sorry, my darling," she sobs, "I had to protect you and this was the only way I knew how. Forgive me. I had failed you. You still ended up with him. I tried to get you back, they were too strong. Forgive me, my darling."

I turn and look at my mother. I hold her little finger and gently squeeze. It means the world to her, she knows that I have no malice. She squeezes me and kisses my face. I look at her for the last time, my ears start to buzz, she hums the same song she sang to me as a baby and toddler. I remember it. I look around the room, my family is with me. I feel love and acceptance. I feel my mother's embrace, and deep inside me of me for the first time in my life I feel complete. All my life I have yearned for my mother to hug and kiss me, to hold me and tell me that she loves me, and today, she is here, and I feel her love running through me, and see her love in my children.

"Wiiiiiinnnnnnnnnnnie," I hear her. I would recognize her voice on a room filled with a thousand voices. My heart skipped a beat.

"Yes, Mima."

"Come on baby, it's time to go. I have your dinner waiting," she tells me. "I have baked your favorite, coconut cake."

"Mima, I need more time," I say. "Just five more minutes."

THE JOURNEY

"Winnie, you have had a lifetime. It's time to say your goodbyes and be sure to make it count. I feel sad, but grateful for my journey so far. I see the other side, and I like it. I am no longer scared but excited.

My breathing slows, she sees that she is losing me.

"Love you," I say to her. She smiles through her pain. My mother strokes my hair, the only way that a mother can.

"I got you baby girl," she whispers. "Mummy is here. Don't be scared honey. The Lord is going to protect you, and I know that Mima is waiting for you."

The pain is gone and I am free. My body transforms, I am young again, beautiful, energized and healthy. I laugh out loud, no one can hear me.

"Noooooooo," Mum cries out. Niall immediately runs to his wife and holds her.

"Mum, oh God, she's gone," Maddie cries.

I hear them crying, but its muffled now, the room is getting darker, I hit the ceiling with a thud, I roll over and look down, they look so sad. Dr. York stands close by and strokes Alice's arm. This is so hard for everyone. My mother looks in shock. They have noticed I have left them. Mummy holds me tightly and kisses me repeatedly. *"I am here,"* I want to scream. *"I am still with you. Please don't be sad, it's fine. I'm fine, and so will you be, just fine."*

My mother starts to pray. "Yeah thought I walk through the valley of the shadow of death, I shall fear no evil. For you are with me, your rod and your staff shall comfort me."

Harold bends over in his chair, his head in his hands, he is rocking. Jon and Maddie cry on each other. Phillip holds Phoebe's hand. But my mother is still talking to me.

"I know you're here, baby girl. I still feel you. Mima is going to take care of you," she tells me. "Don't be afraid, she will not leave you. You need to get there and make it comfy for me."

Dr. York looks at Ange, "She is gone, Madam."

"Young man, I have waited 65 years to hold my daughter. You will not rush me. I am her mother," she said and stroked my hair. He immediately backed off.

"Winnie," Mima shouts.

I look at the plantation and see them, I am shocked. It's Mima, grandma Phyllis, aunt Rene, Mrs. Mack, Mr. Mack, grandpa Barrington, and daddy, they are all there. I see a beautiful man, he is dark and tall in the distance, he is sanding down that beautiful wooden chair on the veranda. It was grandpa Vincent. He looks up and smiles at me. I turn to my family and smile.

Grandpa Vincent walks over to me, "Mima has told me a great deal about you young lady. I have waited a long time to meet you?" he smiles.

"As I," I laugh. I love him already.

I look at them now and shout to them all, "I will be with you all each and every day. I have to go now. I don't want to leave, but I have to. It will be well. Always remember that I love you."

THE JOURNEY

THE RETURN

Sequel to 'The Journey'

The truth will set you free, or does it? **With Edwina gone, her children soon realize that the mother who raised them is unrecognizable to the woman they learn about. Their legacy and heritage is strong. They are not nobodies from London, they belong to a strong wealthy and powerful Jamaican dynasty.**

Their grandmother Angeline insists that they go back to Jamaica and reclaim what rightfully belongs to them. This means taking control of their successful plantation and global businesses. On their return back to their mothers land unspeakable secrets are unlocked. They find their great grandmothers Lucy's diary and finally put together the missing elements to their mothers and grandmothers story.

Edwina's children who are dysfunctional and

fractured, have to find a way to come together. This is no longer about sibling rivalry and petty jealousy, their bond and cohesiveness will be tested in their brave new world. This is about their survival and honoring the memory and legacy of Lucy and Vincent George.

THE AUTHOR

This manuscript has taken me ten years to write. Having experienced extreme grief and loss of losing my mother to cancer in 2005, and the sudden death of my sister in 2007, grief encapsulated every aspect of her life. My only outlet through this depressing time was writing. The reason why writing this book took so long, was that I was slowly going through the process of dealing with my loss. The last chapter was the hardest to write. It has taken me three years to get here, however, once completed, it was as if a large weight had been lifted from me and the burden of grief was gone. This has been a cathartic and healing process on so many levels.

Only since embracing my forties have I gained the confidence to share with the world a collection of poetry "Laid Bare." Also, this novel which is a trilogy. The sequel 'The Return' will be available in the summer of 2018. Thank you for your time and

THE JOURNEY

energy in committing to read this story, I hope and pray that I have taken you on a journey and that you continue to want to learn more about my characters.

Made in the USA
Lexington, KY
13 May 2018